W9-CNL-142

The *Methodical Memory*

Invention in Current-Traditional Rhetoric

Sharon Crowley

Southern Illinois University Press
Carbondale and Edwardsville

Edited by Carol A. Burns
Designed by Shannon M. McIntyre
Production supervised by Natalia Nadraga
93 92 91 90 4 3 2 1

Library of Congress Cataloging-in-Publication Data

Crowley, Sharon, 1943–
    The methodical memory: invention in current-traditional rhetoric
/ Sharon Crowley.
        p. cm.
    Includes bibliographical references.
    1. Invention (Rhetoric) I. Title.
    PN221.C77 1990
    808—dc20   89-37101
    ISBN 0-8093-1615-3   CIP

The paper used in this publication meets the minimum requirements of
American National Standard for Information Sciences—Permanence of
Paper for Printed Library Materials, ANSI Z39.48-1984. ∞

For Edward P. J. Corbett

Contents

Preface

This book is a study of the theory of invention entailed in two modern rhetorical theories: British "new rhetoric" and the American school rhetoric now called "current-traditional." I undertook this study because the status of current-traditional rhetoric as a historical artifact is not evident to the many people who think of it as a natural, self-evident, and universal system for the invention of discourse written in school.

Since the late nineteenth century, teachers of writing have occasionally complained about the aridity of current-traditional rhetoric. But it began to come under sustained and serious fire from composition theorists almost thirty years ago, chiefly because it lacked a viable theory of invention. Nevertheless, current-traditional attitudes toward composing are still entrenched in much college writing instruction. I point to E. D. Hirsch's *Dictionary of Cultural Literacy* (1989) as a very popular example of the comfortable lodging of current-traditional thought within contemporary folklore about school writing. Hirsch, a professor of English at a distinguished American university, includes some prominent current-traditional features—the thesis, the topic sentence—in his discussion of writing conventions. He justifies his use of these terms on the grounds that they are the standard ones associated with school writing, part of its common parlance.

Hirsch is not alone in this. Thousands of university professors outside of English departments assume that any decent student theme will begin by stating an obvious thesis and that each of its paragraphs will likewise begin with some sort of controlling generalization. And within English departments, professors who regularly write sophisticated critical analyses of literature still believe that the discursive paradigm described in composition textbooks like the *Harbrace Handbook* is the one which should be taught to novice writers. The *Harbrace,* originally published in 1939 and now in its tenth edition, sells hundreds of thousands of copies every year. Its editors tamper with its allegiance to current-traditional thought at the risk of losing sales.

I find this state of affairs extremely provocative. The epistemological underpinnings of current-traditional rhetoric were assembled in the eighteenth century. Despite the fact that its theoretical backwardness and its pedagogical limitations have been apparent for some time, current-traditional thought still exerts a potent influence on writing instruction in American colleges and universities. *The Methodical Memory* is an attempt to figure out why.

I wrote this book with teachers of writing primarily in mind. Current-traditional rhetoric has prospered partly because college composition teachers generally do not devise the curricula they are asked to teach. Most teachers of composition are graduate students, part-time instructors, or teachers of literature. Since composition teachers work at the very bottom of the academic pecking order, they are not often entrusted with the tasks of devising programs or syllabi or selecting textbooks. And, because of their professional circumstances—which often include the combination of teaching with graduate course work, or four or five or six sections of composition and as many as 150 students at two or three or more institutions—few such teachers have time to read about the scholarly and pedagogical developments that are taking place in rhetoric and composition theory. It is difficult to question a practice so thoroughly institutionalized as current-traditional pedagogy when its teachers do not have access to the scholarly conversations that question its soundness. When teachers are not allowed access to alternative theoretical and pedagogical models, it is difficult even to know that alternatives exist.

The Methodical Memory tries to undermine the ordinarily unspoken institutional assumption that current-traditional prescriptions and college writing instruction are somehow synonymous. One of my book's central points is that current-traditional rhetoric is a historical hangover. Its epistemology, and the pedagogy associated with it, need rethinking. But this rethinking is difficult to do when an array of powerful institutional forces presents current-traditionality as the natural way to do things in a writing classroom.

I hope that scholars in rhetoric and composition theory will also want to read this book, since it makes a few contributions to their fields. No sustained critique of current-traditional rhetoric has ever been made, even though it is the most pervasive discursive practice ever used in writing instruction (aside from classical rhetoric, of course). Thus my study of its theory of invention has unearthed some modifications to current scholarly opinion about it. For example, *The Methodical Memory* establishes that a viable theory of invention was implicit in the new rhetoric and in current-traditional rhetoric and that this inventional theory was intimately tied to modern privileging of the authorial voice. It also establishes the importance of method to the theory of invention and to the discrimination of the genre theory that characterized the new rhetoric as well as current-traditional thought; it argues, for example, that method is the source of Alexander Bain's theory of the paragraph.

However, this book is not a historical survey either of the new rhetoric or current-traditional rhetoric. Historical surveys of these two schools of rhetorical thought are readily available. For a history of the new rhetoric, see Wilbur Samuel Howell's *Eighteenth-Century British Logic and Rhetoric;* for current-traditional rhetoric, see Albert Kitzhaber's dissertation, "Rhetoric in American Colleges, 1850–1900," and James A. Berlin's *Writing Instruction in Nineteenth-Century American Colleges;* for recent developments, see Berlin's *Rhetoric and Reality: Writing Instruction in American Colleges, 1900–1985*. Robert J. Connors' essays, many of which are listed in the bibliography, constitute a fine introduction to the history of composition studies. *The Methodical Memory* is very much indebted to the pioneering work of all of these historians.

Strictly speaking, *The Methodical Memory* is not a history. It does chronicle the development of the modern theory of invention that I call "introspective." In this sense, chapters 2 and 3 are historical in that they deal with invention in the new rhetoric, while later chapters deal with nineteenth- and twentieth-century developments in current-traditional thought. I also found it useful to invent terms to designate developments in the tradition, so I somewhat arbitrarily divided it up into "early" manifestations (1800–1870); "mature" works (1870–1900); "late" works (1900–1975); and "very-current-traditional" textbooks. I felt no need to remain faithful to chronology, however, since each chapter of the book undertakes synchronic analyses of given features of introspective invention.

The Methodical Memory contains no new historical discoveries. For the most part the textbooks read here are known to historians of rhetoric and composition studies. However, I read these books from a postmodern perspective. This perspective assumes that the intellectual trappings of modernism—such as the sovereign authoring subject—are no longer useful as theoretical resources for the teaching of composition. To put this another way, *The Methodical Memory* is a deconstruction, rather than a history. It tries to unravel some of the strands that make up the fabric of modern rhetoric to see where they intersect and where there are holes in the fabric. A deconstruction of a discursive practice allows it to be critiqued. Of course, deconstruction is a way of reading invented by Jacques Derrida, to whose work I am indebted throughout this book.

In the early sections of my discussion I play with a number of manifestations of the internal-external dichotomy that Derrida identifies as central to Western thought. He argues that Western culture is built on a series of hierarchical dichotomies in which a term is paired with, and privileged over, an opposing term. Such dichotomies authorize the creation of entire discursive practices. A series of hierarchical dichotomies pervades the discursive practice I analyze here: aside from inside-outside, current-traditional practice relies on distinctions between nature and artifice, body and soul, invention and style, content and form, subject and expression.

I exploit some of these dichotomous distinctions to make polemical points. In the first chapter, for instance, I treat the topical theory of invention developed by classical rhetoricians as though its impetus were always communal, while I define modern notions of invention in terms of its focus on the private authoring mind. Of course these generalizations do not hold for all classical rhetoricians or for the whole of modern rhetorical practice. In the second chapter I treat eighteenth-century psychology as a theory of the inside that had to account for the mind's contact with an outside—nature, or whatever it is that is perceived by the senses. In the third chapter, I apply the inside-outside dichotomy to the two faces of method—investigation and communication. This chapter also introduces another dichotomy—natural-artificial, which was operative in seventeenth- and eighteenth-century discussions of method. In chapter four, I write as though the inside-outside dichotomy posed an intellectual problem for nineteenth-century rhetoricians. But the presence of this dichotomy in my study supplements its absence in the texts of the writers I study.

I make no claim that the discursive practice described here is the only one that has ever informed modern writing instruction. Nor do I wish to makes heroes (or anti-heroes) of the authors mentioned in this text. Still less do I claim that the discursive practice I study here was the only one available during the modern period. These caveats underscore my uneasiness about the fact that I have pulled the texts under study here out of history, so to speak. I treat them as a description of a certain discursive practice, as a set of rules for what could be said about the production of school writing during a certain era. Hence I ignore the historical detail that surrounded their composition—the biographies of their authors, the social and political circumstances surrounding the teaching of writing in the nineteenth and early twentieth centuries, and the like. I am acutely aware of the fact that my account is susceptible to the same charge I level against the textbook authors I study—that in eliding difference, I have reiterated the hegemony of the same.

If this book is, finally, a discourse on method, I can only offer the defense that it was not written in the general spirit of essays on method. Such essays are ordinarily intended to abstract the human components out of intellectual endeavor in an effort to universalize and therefore to naturalize whatever method they explicate. In contrast, I want to de-nature method. Perhaps the only satisfactory way to do this is to fore-ground it momentarily.

The table of contents is nearly as detailed as those that grace eighteenth-century essays on rhetorical theory. It was designed so that readers could decide what to read and what to skip. Of course I hope that teachers and scholars will find the entire work worthwhile. Throughout it, I made a concerted effort to commit the most egregious grammatical or stylistic errors castigated by current-traditional rhetoricians. The text contains one-sentence paragraphs, split infinitives, and even worse, a few sentences and paragraphs that begin with the words *and, or,* or *but.* I alternate the use of male and female pronouns where possible.

Acknowledgments

Many persons have been complicit, like it or not, in the genesis of this book. From the beginning its presiding spirit has been Ed Corbett, whose work as scholar and teacher has provided me with an exemplary but finally inimitable model.

I thank everyone who took the time to read drafts at various stages of the book's composition. These persons include E. P. J. Corbett, Win Horner, Don Stewart, Ross Winterowd, and other persons who are unknown to me. Several of my colleagues were more than generous with their time. Joe Boles, Greg Larkin, Nancy Paxton, and Victor Villanueva read early drafts. Jim Bartell and Bill Grabe made especially extensive and useful suggestions for revision. Linda Robertson straightened me out on the supposedly elementary stuff: audience, voice, and scope. Mike Malone, philosopher and crap detector *extraordinaire,* helped me to clarify my thinking about the philosophical issues raised in the text. Of course none of these people is responsible for my mistakes.

The reference librarians at Northern Arizona University equably tolerated my recurring requests for old textbooks, found them and wheedled other libraries into loaning them to us with remarkable economy. I also received assistance from librarians at Ohio State University and the University of Texas at Austin. All the librarians who helped me to locate old textbooks were unfailingly resourceful and cheerful.

For conversation and collegiality, I thank my friends and colleagues in Ed Corbett's 1981 NEH seminar in the history of rhetoric. Thanks as well to the students in my modern rhetorical theory classes, who kept me honest. Thanks also to Tilly Warnock and the good people who gather in Wyoming in the summertime.

Thanks, Coley, for being a fast friend. My other river-running buddies deserve mention for help that was not directly tied to the composition of this book but that was nevertheless crucial to its completion. Lady and Gatzo helped, too, in their way.

The *Methodical Memory*

1 Public Knowledge and Private Inspiration: On Invention, Classical and Modern

In Western rhetorical systems, invention is the first of five canons, or divisions, of rhetoric. It is accompanied by arrangement (the appropriate ordering of arguments within a discourse), style (the clear and felicitous composition of sentences), memory (the memorization of a completed argument or a series of prompts), and delivery (the appropriate management of the voice, gestures, and appearance). In classical rhetoric, the canons were supposed to represent the process followed by rhetors as they composed any piece of discourse.

A given rhetorical system may concentrate on one or more of the canons and virtually ignore the others. During the Middle Ages, for example, rhetoricians were interested primarily in style. And since literacy is now relatively widespread in the West, contemporary rhetorical theorists are not so concerned with memory as classical rhetoricians were. But the canon of invention has proven particularly vulnerable to shifts in the relative importance of the various canons. Classical rhetoricians placed primary emphasis on invention; it was the first subject studied by novice rhetoricians, and it enjoyed first place in their preparation for speaking as well. In modern rhetoric, however, attention to invention has been overshadowed by interest in arrangement and style.

Rhetorical invention goes in and out of fashion because it is intimately tied to current developments in ethics, politics, and the epistemology of whatever culture it serves. It has ties to ethics and politics because rhetoric is always situated within human affairs. As Aristotle pointed out in his *Rhetoric,* many rhetorical premises have to do with questions that are specifically political or ethical (1.4.1359b). Rhetors must invent

1

good answers to such questions as, What is the best course of action in these circumstances?, How do we keep the peace?, What is honorable?, and What is expedient?

From a practical point of view, then, invention can be defined as the division of rhetoric that supplies speakers and writers with instructions for finding the specific arguments that are appropriate to a given rhetorical situation. Cicero's *On Invention* contains a list of potential arguments that might be used in any circumstances in which rhetoric is required. Rhetors could select from this list the arguments that were appropriate to the occasion that confronted them and could refine those arguments to fit the specific details of the case at hand.

But invention also has a theoretical aspect. From this point of view, invention becomes the study of all the possible means by which arguments or proofs can be discovered and developed. Rhetoricians develop theories of invention when they focus on questions about how people may be persuaded to accept something as worthy of belief. Aristotle's *Rhetoric* contains a theory of invention that is explicitly intended to discover all the means of proof that are available in rhetoric.

And so theories of rhetorical invention must also be articulated with current thinking about how people change their minds or make discoveries—that is, with some currently accepted theory of knowledge. For example, in *On Christian Doctrine* St. Augustine named Scripture as the proper locus of invention for Christian rhetoric, since he believed that text to be the primary source of human knowledge about the will of God. Some modern rhetoricians, on the other hand, located the wellspring of invention in the sovereign reasoning processes of the individual mind. This happened because the epistemology to which they subscribed privileged human reason as a very important, if not the sole, source of human knowledge.

Invention in Classical Rhetoric

Quite different epistemologies prevailed in classical times, however. Some classical rhetoricians and logicians assumed that knowledge was contained in the collected wisdom of the community.[1] In other words, whatever was worth knowing was known by most persons who spoke the common language and who engaged in discourse about pressing community issues. Teaching and learning began with what people already knew and proceeded toward new discoveries by testing them against the collective wisdom. This is why classical rhetoricians developed a series of inventional devices that depended upon readily acceptable statements. It also explains the necessity for the successful classical orator to be acquainted with ethics, politics, law, history, poetry, popular culture, folklore, and myth—valuable and persuasive knowledge could always be mined from proverb, precedent, or premise.

In a fundamental sense, knowledge did not exist outside of language for classical rhetoricians. The ancient rhetor's task was to compare statements about what was known or agreed upon with statements about which there was disagreement. He made this comparison in such a way as to move an audience toward acceptance of the disputed point. Successful invention and arrangement depended on his ability to discern whether his language would affect listeners in the desired fashion. Thus classical rhetoricians treated language as a powerful means of moving people to action.

One classical inventional scheme involved topics or commonplaces to which rhetors could resort as a means of asking a systematic set of questions about any rhetorical situation. In his *Institutes of Oratory* Quintilian defined the topics as "the secret places where arguments reside, and from which they must be drawn forth" (5.10.21). He likened the places to the haunts or localities frequented by certain species of birds and fish; experienced hunters knew where to look for these animals and didn't waste time beating the bushes for them. The topics, then, were a set of argumentative strategies that were available to any trained rhetor. Since the topics represented common strategies for acquiring knowledge, the rhetor who employed them could be confident that an audience would immediately understand his procedure. (Whether they agreed with the particular conclusion he drew from his application of the topics was another matter, of course.) Cicero's list of topics included definition, similarity, difference, contraries, antecedents, consequents, contradictions, cause, effect, and comparison (*Topics* 2–4).

Classical systems of rhetorical invention also included discussions of two other sorts of proofs: ethos and pathos. According to Aristotle's *Rhetoric,* a rhetor's character, whether it was improvised for the occasion or derived from his reputation in the community, was almost the most impressive mode of persuasion he possessed, since "we feel confidence in a greater degree and more readily in persons of worth in regard to everything in general, but where there is no certainty and there is room for doubt, our confidence is absolute." But persuasion could also be effected by appealing to the emotions of an audience; Aristotle's sensible estimate of human response caused him to observe that "the judgements we deliver are not the same when we are influenced by joy or sorrow, love or hate" (1.2.1356a). Thus he and other classical rhetoricians gave a good deal of attention to emotional states and to the ways in which these could be roused or quelled.

Relying as it did on notions about knowledge as possessed in common by all members of a community, ancient inventional theory was viable as long as rhetoric was defined as the art that studied the generation and reception of effective public discourse. Thus the topics were studied in Western schools and universities until the eighteenth century. But the instructional dominance of classical rhetoric began to diminish with the emergence of modern thought. Modern rhetorical theorists realized that if a viable new rhetoric were to be developed, classical invention had to be altered or rejected altogether, because it was utterly unsuited to the modern belief that knowledge resulted from the actions of individual minds on the things of the world.

Modern Epistemology, Authority, and Representation

In 1953, rhetorician Richard Weaver posited that a list of "ultimate terms" could be worked out for every era of history. Any such list of terms would identify the "rhetorical absolutes" of a given historical period—"the terms to which the very highest respect is paid" ("Ultimate Terms" 212). Weaver argued that in every age "conscious life" has to revolve around some value or set of values that provides human beings with a sense of their place in the ideological cosmos. In ages past, the terms that named those values were drawn from religion, but in the modern period these terms have clustered around our relationship with the natural world, where humans "pass increasingly into the role of master" ("Ultimate Terms" 213). Accordingly, many of the terms Weaver identified as the ultimate terms of his own age were associated with scientific thought. Among these were *progress, fact, science, modern,* and *efficient.*

When Weaver drew up his list of terms, the intellectual set I call modernism was fully developed, and I would argue that his ultimate terms are precisely those of modernism, at least in its later manifestations.[2] As I use it here, the word *modern* designates a worldview that has dominated Western thought for nearly three hundred years and that is just now being revealed as a mind-set from which we might want to extract ourselves. The most important entailments of the modern worldview, as far as modern rhetorical theory is concerned, are its privileging of human reason as the source and foundation of knowledge, its concomitant reduction of the functioning of human nature to principles of similarity, and its isolation of the primary function of language as a representation of thought.

An intellectual revolution of immense proportions took place in the seventeenth century, a revolution stimulated by the newly glimpsed possibility that the workings of mind might constitute an ultimate source of knowledge. This discovery was a crucial component of an important new discursive practice.[3] For seventeenth-century thought, the discovery of knowledge was an internal procedure; it resulted from the thinker's perception of ideas and from his manipulation of the relationships between ideas. In his *Discourse on Method* (1637), René Descartes demonstrated that a person could use a rational methodology to doubt everything, finally, except his own existence as a thinking being and that of the God who had created him. (Much of what Descartes doubted was the classical book learning taught in universities, including the inventional devices inherited from classical rhetoric and logic.) And in *An Essay Concerning Human Understanding* (1690), John Locke argued, in essence, that knowledge amounted to a thinker's perception of the various relations between the ideas that populate his mind (4.1.2). This possibility was revolutionary in that it located the production of knowledge within individual minds.

Medieval scholars had assumed that whatever could be known was enshrined in authoritative books and commentaries or in God's law made manifest in the nature of things.[4] In contrast, modern epistemology internalized the process of knowledge production. An individual mind, working at its best, could analyze its experience of the world in unique and original ways in order to produce new or heretofore unthought knowledge. This metaphoric individualization and internalizing of the process of acquiring knowledge mandated a number of important changes in thinking about thinking; that is, new descriptions of the nature of reasoning had to be written, while older descriptions, such as scholastic lore about syllogizing, had to be modified or rejected.

The parameters of a modern theory of knowledge were worked out by Francis Bacon, Descartes, the Port-Royal logicians, and Locke, among others, during the seventeenth century. For these thinkers, the source of knowledge was human intuition, "a singular act of pure and attentive intelligence," as Michel Foucault puts it (*Order of Things* 52). This move constitutes the decisive mark of modern epistemology, which defines knowledge as the conceptual ordering made possible by the thinking mind. Descartes' "cogito ergo sum" was the "exemplary formal statement" of modernism, according to Timothy Reiss; that is, Descartes' slogan presumed an equation between reason, a mediating system of signs, and the world. Reiss argues that the inaugural premise of modern thought was "that the 'syntactic' order of semiotic systems (particularly language) is coincident both with the logical ordering or 'reason' and with the structural organisation of a world given as exterior to both these orders" (31). Both language and logic accurately reflected the organization of the material world.

One of the germinal documents of modern thought is, of course, John Locke's *Essay Concerning Human Understanding*. In this work Locke firmly tied the production of knowledge to the workings of the human mind, arguing in essence that knowledge amounts to a thinker's perception of the various relations that exist between the ideas that populate the mind (4.1.2). Locke further divided the actions of the mind into two broad categories: the power of thinking and the power of volition (1.6.2). Seventeenth-century philosophers were fond of distinguishing between contemplation and deliberation, and Locke's twofold division of the mind into the faculties of the reason and the will specified and reinforced the commonplace assumption that two opposing kinds of operations took place there.

The burgeoning of scientific knowledge created a sort of faith that the human will to know, as this was manifested in scientific investigation, could finally succeed in solving most earthly difficulties. Jurgen Habermas observes that the modern age has been dominated by the "belief, inspired by science, in the infinite progress of knowledge and in the infinite advance towards social and moral betterment" (4). In the modern worldview, "progress" toward some better state was supposed to come about through the application of reason to physical and social problems. Reason was always hampered, though, by the barriers thrown up to it by human desire—that is, by the part of human being that was not rational. If progress were to continue, the nonrational or irrational functions of human thought would have to be curbed or stilled by reason.

By the nineteenth century, most thinkers were comfortable in assuming that, in an ideal world, the workings of the reason could be made to overcome the urgings of nonrational mental functions. Thus G. W. F. Hegel, in his lectures on the philosophy of history, said: "Two elements therefore, enter into the object of our investigation; the first the Idea, the second the complex of human passions; the one the warp, the other the woof of the vast arras-web of Universal History" (23). Hegel identified the "Idea" with objectivity, while the will and the passions were tied to subjectivity. And though it was the will of individuals— their interest in self-interest—that caused history to develop, nevertheless human history had always aimed toward the achievement of "the realization of the Idea of Spirit. . . . Reason governs the world, and has consequently governed its history" (25). Indeed, the privilege awarded to reason in the modern period was such that its claims to epistemological superiority far outweighed those of any other aspect of human capacity. This confidence in the ultimate ability of reason to solve human problems was responsible for the peculiarly modern notion of history as a record of ever-increasing human achievement. The modern sense of historical development is so strong that few moderns can tolerate the notion that their culture might be intellectually less rich than that of their medieval forebears (not to mention that of "primitive" or "savage" peoples). The modern sensibility freezes history and distances us from our past as well as from non-Western cultures. Habermas suggests that the term *modern* has been in long use, ordinarily as a means of making a radical distinction between some present moment and some historical past. In the early Middle Ages, for example, *modern* was used to distinguish a distinctly Christian era from an ancient, classical, and pagan age. But it is only in our own time that the term *modern* has lost its relationship to any historical past, according to Habermas. Rather, anything that is "authentically modern" is so by virtue of its novelty, its distinction from whatever preceded it. The assumption always is that "the new" will "be overcome and made obsolete through the novelty of the next style." Thus, for Habermas, "our sense of modernity creates its own self-enclosed canons of being classic," a situation which permits us to dismiss the work of previous ages as merely a prelude to our own (4).

Weaver noticed the rhetorical force of this curious modern use of the term *modern* when he pointed out that its connection with the notion of progress implied that anything labeled as modern had to be superior to whatever preceded it: "Where progress is real, there is a natural presumption that the latest will be the best" ("Ultimate Terms" 217). This attitude toward the modern associates value with novelty, with what is presently the case. Such an association is, as Weaver notes, at least inappropriate. On this account the modern mind can be thought of as "something superior to previous minds," and "modern living" can be "urged upon us as an ideal" simply because modernity encapsulates and improves upon all that has gone before ("Ultimate Terms" 217). It is as though modern consciousness had overcome, overpowered, history.

Such a stance toward history is idealist, in the sense that it permits stability and permanence to be ascribed to human motivation. In his lectures on history, Hegel argued that "occurrences [historical events] are, indeed, various; but the idea which pervades them—their deeper import and connection—is *one*. This takes the occurrence out of the category of the Past and makes it virtually present" (6). A static view of history tends to elide differences and emphasize identities. Thus, for example, a modern thinker can quote Plato as a source for this or that point of view, as though he spoke with perfect articulation to the modern age, as though he inhabited an intellectual milieu so similar to the present one that any differences existing between our age and his own are so small as to be negligible. In short, the modern worldview, in order to privilege reason, must hypostasize human consciousness and, in doing so, collapse history into an eternal present.

The modern worldview was not without its difficulties, however. For one thing, the location of a speaker or writer's invention within the individual mind problematized the authority of any thinker's discourse, insofar as the only authority he could cite for the validity of his analysis was the process of his private ruminations. Medieval thinkers had secured authority for their discourses by connecting them to the "book of nature" or to the authoritative works of classical writers or to the word of God itself. Thus their words carried with them the weight of history as well as that of divine authority. But the modern writer had no such recourse, having cut himself off from all of these sources of authority (with the important exception of the voice of nature, which he assumed he could faithfully represent).

Seventeenth-century thinkers solved this problem by occulting the individual locus of knowledge and by transferring authority for their discourse to the texts they produced. The existence of an orderly completed text, which reproduced the history of the thinker's investigation, was assumed to constitute sufficient testimony to the authenticity of its findings. In Reiss' words, Bacon and Descartes made it possible for modern writers to engage "in a discursive practice asserting discourse to be at once a mechanism transparent to the truths it transports and an ordering system whose coherence alone is responsible for the 'value' of those truths"; that is, the orderly presentation of knowledge embodied in the discourse itself became the self-validating source of its authority (223).[5]

The modern problem of who (or what) authorizes philosophical and scientific discourse persists into the twentieth century, and the same self-validating answer is still being given. In his review of modern French thought, for example, Vincent Descombes poses the central question that faces modern philosophy (and that is left unanswered by it) as follows: "How should we prove that the subject who enunciates a philosophical proposition is not specifically the philosopher's person but the world itself, to which the philosopher merely affords the occasions for speaking out?" On Descombes' reading, one answer would have it that the "circularity of discourse" is itself the proof that "the subject (author) of the enunciation is identical with the subject (matter) of the statement" (42). The seventeenth-century assumption—that minds, as well as the discourses they produce, reflect the world—still operates in modern thought.[6] The mind's reflective capacity lends authority to the speaking subject and to its discourse.

The modern program could not have been launched unless some adequate medium of translation were found for the translation of internalized orderings of concepts into available knowledge. Modern philosophers nominated language for this role.[7] Locke, for example, posited that the sounds of language are "*signs of internal conceptions*"; for each man, such sounds "stand as marks for the *ideas* within his own mind, whereby they might be made known to others, and the thought of men's minds be conveyed from one to another" (3.1.2). But language not only represented one person's ideas to another; it also represented the things of the world. The modern model required a double assurance—that human understanding could be brought into direct contact with the things of the world and that the syntactic order of language corresponded in some essential fashion with the ordering of things in nature. Locke grounded this double set of representative relationships in the primacy of sensation: the senses handed over accurate information about the world, which the operations of the mind translated into ideas. With care, the names given to these ideas could assume a degree of accuracy that insured, in turn, that they represented the things of the world.

Other modern thinkers simply preferred to take these relationships as given, as Bacon did when he asserted that language and reason were one, since they were copied "from a very ancient model, even the world itself and the nature of things and of the mind" (1:123, trans. Reiss). In the modern worldview, then, according to Reiss, "language reveals thought, and inasmuch as that thought can be taken as referring directly to objects (in perception) language can operate as a perfect stand-in for both. To be sure, it is not the object itself, but it is a sufficiently accurate representation for the purposes of discourse, into whose analytical process it can be inserted" (36). In other words, for modern thinkers the grammar of language represented not only the grammar of thought but the grammar of the world as well.

Invention in Modern Rhetorical Theory

The modern faith in scientific knowledge as the resource that would ultimately improve the quality of human life, along with the modern reduction of language to a medium of representation, had disastrous effects for a number of classical disciplines. Among these, rhetoric was a primary casualty. Rhetoric is notoriously unscientific—which is to say that it attaches as much importance to human passion as it does to reason. Rhetorical force derives from its appropriateness to particular circumstances, and so it is difficult (but not impossible) to make predictions about the potential effectiveness of this or that piece of rhetorical discourse. Further, rhetoricians tend to depict language as generative of persuasion, rather than as a servant of reason. Thus modern epistemology, with its insistence on the superiority of reason, its interest in systems, and its assumption that language is a docile, reflective medium, was inimical to rhetoric.

This is not to say that rhetorical theories ceased to be constructed after the demise of classical rhetoric. On the contrary, the eighteenth century witnessed a remarkably widespread and profound interest in rhetorical theory. Modern rhetorical theory announced itself rather decisively with the publication of George Campbell's *Philosophy of Rhetoric* in 1776, although, to be sure, glimmerings of modernism appear in Adam Smith's lectures on rhetoric, which he initiated at Edinburgh in 1748, and in Joseph Priestley's *Course of Lectures on Oratory and Criticism* (1762). It was apparent to these rhetoricians that the classical theory of invention was simply not consonant with new ways of thinking about the generation of discourse.[8] Among influential modern rhetoricians, Joseph Priestley alone favored the use of the classical topics, but he put them to a distinctly modern use by firmly locating them within the rhetor's mind.

Priestley argued that invention in general amounted to the recollection of experience or ideas. He labeled the classical topics as "artificial recollection," as opposed to the natural process of recalling experience or ideas. He apparently thought of the topics as a feature of written discourse, rather than as a process of inquiry; he referred to them as the "general heads" that marked off major sections of a composition. He further relegated them to the status of an aide-mémoire, since their sole use during invention was to assist the writer who wanted to recall a chain of associated ideas: "It is impossible to endeavour to *recollect* (or, as we generally say, *invent*) materials for a discourse, without running over in our minds such general heads of discourse as we have found by experience to assist us in that operation" (22). A writer's mental sortie through closely associated topics could also assist him in planning a discourse, though. "If a person have any *regular method* in his compositions, he must, moreover, have arranged those topics in his mind in some kind of order; the several particulars of which, being attended to successively, furnishes him with *a plan for composition*" (23). In other words, the topics applied after the fact of "natural" investigation, either as a stimulus to memory or as an aid to arrangement.

Priestley thought that the topics could be put to fruitful use in the composition of argumentative discourse, which was the genre that modern rhetoricians most regularly associated with classical rhetoric. He did concede, however, that the topics might be of more use in the composition of school exercises by young people than they are in "the communication of original matter, and to persons much used to composition. Original thoughts cannot but suggest themselves, so that all the assistance any person can want in this case, is a proper manner of arranging them. And a person much used to composition will have acquired a habit of recollection, without any express attention to topics" (24). Priestley's attitude toward the topics, then, was that they were altogether less natural than the process of recollection. Interestingly enough, however, the topics could be used by children. Perhaps he assumed that young people required some sort of artificial stimulation of their natural inventive process, since they had not lived long enough to think "original thoughts."

Another influential eighteenth-century discourse theorist ousted invention from rhetoric altogether, on the ground that appropriate arguments on any subject would be found by investigation of that subject, rather than by rhetorical means. In the *Lectures on Rhetoric and Belles Lettres* (1783), Hugh Blair rejected classical topical invention on the ground that the "study of common places . . . could never produce useful discourses on real business" (2:401). What was persuasive, Blair thought, "must be drawn . . . from a thorough knowledge of the subject, and profound meditation on it." Consequently, he advised writers "to lay aside their common places, and to think closely of their subject" (2:402). In a single stroke, Blair placed the entire process of invention beyond the province of rhetorical study, arguing that the art of rhetoric can only teach people how to manage the arguments they have discovered by other means.[9]

The Argument of This Book

Not all eighteenth-century discourse theorists were content to make an easy gesture of dismissal toward invention, however. While they did reject the epistemological arenas to which classical rhetorical theory had been most closely allied—law, history, poetry, politics, and ethics— they devised an inventional theory explicitly designed to conform to current developments in philosophy, psychology, and logic. George

Campbell developed a theory of invention based on association psychology; Richard Whately founded his inventional scheme on a conflation of the new empiricism with Aristotelian logic; and Adam Smith and Joseph Priestley took advantage of the twofold aspect of method to establish new approaches to both invention and arrangement. I discuss Campbell's and Whately's uses of association psychology and logic in chapter 2; I turn to Smith's and Priestley's uses of method in chapter 3.

The theory of invention developed by the new rhetoricians relied on three unspoken assumptions about the human mind: first, that it could reliably investigate its own workings; second, that when a mind was engaged with a specific problem, it worked in an organized linear sequence, moving from specific to general or from general to specific; and third, that the mind's sequential workings were accurately inscribed in memory and could be accurately reproduced upon demand (hence my title). New rhetoricians assumed that invention occurred by means of introspective or retrospective investigation of the workings of the rhetor's own mind. This examination would suffice as a means of discovering the workings of the minds of those persons in their audience, since all minds worked alike. Thus, introspective analysis could supply a model for moving the minds of others. The allegiance of eighteenth-century discourse theory to psychology and logic permitted two relatively new features to emerge within rhetorical theory: the privileging of a single authorial mind, rather than community wisdom, as the source of invention and the concomitant privileging of texts as reflections of the workings of this sovereign authorial mind.

British new rhetoric influenced the development of the American rhetorical tradition now called current-traditional rhetoric. Important nineteenth-century American rhetoricians regularly cited their indebtedness to Campbell, Blair, or Whately. Many early American texts are simply redactions of the work of one or another of the British rhetoricians. The new rhetoric was not the only rhetorical tradition available to American teachers of course. Most knew classical rhetoric well, having studied it in the Latin texts of Cicero and Quintilian. A Romantic rhetorical tradition was also available to those who were acquainted with the work of certain British and German rhetorical theorists.[10] No doubt other traditions were available as well—for example, a vigorous homegrown rhetorical practice, marked by its preference for Biblical quotation and imitation, flourished throughout the nineteenth century.[11] But the rhetorical tradition that eventually came to dominate school composition instruction was that fostered by Lockean discursive practice and enshrined in rhetorical theory by the new rhetoricians.

By the middle years of the nineteenth century, the new rhetoric had given way to its American variant in the most popular textbooks, and by the last decades of the century, this variant—now called current-traditional rhetoric by historians—had taken on the outlines in which it was to be presented to students throughout most of the twentieth century.[12] In an essay published in 1978, Richard Young listed its overt features as follows:

> The emphasis on the composed product rather than the composing process; the analysis of discourse into words, sentences, and paragraphs; the classification of discourse into description, narration, exposition and argument; the strong concern with usage (syntax, spelling, punctuation) and with style (economy, clarity, emphasis); the preoccupation with the informal essay and the research paper; and so on. (31)

With regard to invention, I elaborate Young's "and so on" as follows: current-traditional rhetoric occults the mentalism that underlies its introspective theory of invention; it subscribes to the notion that "subjects"—the "matter" of discourses—are mental configurations whose existence is ontologically prior to their embodiment in discourse; it prefers the discursive movement from generalization to specification; it concentrates on expository discourse; it recommends that the inventional scheme devised for exposition be used in any discursive situation; and it translates invention out of the originating mind and onto the page. In other words, this rhetoric assumes that the process of invention can be graphically displayed in discourse.

In the chapters on the current-traditional theory of invention (4–7), I argue that this theory has a decidedly mentalistic bent because of its association with psychology and logic. Thus the pedagogy based on it was centrally, if quietly, concerned about the quality of authorial minds. But since it was beyond the province of pedagogues to contribute to the quality of minds—aside from recommending certain habits and practices that might strengthen them—writers in the later tradition transferred its concern with minds to concern with the shape of texts. The hope was that a well-formed text would reflect a well-oiled mind at work.

In chapter 8, I begin to mount some arguments against the current-traditional theory of invention. I argue that it suffers from intellectual poverty; that it stands in for writing; and that it shifts discursive authority away from students and onto the academy. Once current-traditional rhetoric was thoroughly inscribed within college composition instruction, its description of the ideal text was identified with the way things ought universally to be done in academic writing. The pseudoscientific bias of the five-paragraph theme, which substitutes the voice of the institution for those of writers, was congenial not only to the composition of scientific and technical discourse, but to the increasing institutional need to standardize and thus regulate instruction in composition.

In the final chapter, I address the pedagogical and ethical difficulties entailed in generalizing the invention process and in universalizing rhetoric. I argue that modern rhetoricians' allegiance to psychology and logic opened the possibility that first principles could be established for rhetoric, principles that would always govern the generation and presentation of discourse no matter what constraints were entailed in a given rhetorical situation. Eighteenth-century inventional theory was oriented toward the establishment of first principles insofar as its progenitors developed it out of what they took to be universal truths about human nature. Such truths were "universal" in the sense that they were thought to describe the way in which every human being functioned, now, in the past, and in the future. Because of this, these universal principles could be used to predict future human behavior. On this model, rhetoric could be defined as the art of predicting which psychological appeals would stimulate the desired reaction in members of an audience.

Any theory of discourse that tries to establish first principles can fairly be called metaphysical. I conclude by arguing that metaphysics is an inappropriate starting point for writing instruction. Rather, such instruction must draw its inspiration from rhetoric, which always prefers the celebration of difference to the repetition of the same.

2 How the Outside Gets Inside: The Psychology of the Methodical Memory

On the very first page of *The Philosophy of Rhetoric* (originally published in 1776), George Campbell defined eloquence as "that art or talent by which the discourse is adapted to its end." He then discriminated four such ends: "to enlighten the understanding, to please the imagination, to move the passions, or to influence the will." For Campbell, the art of rhetoric was aim-centered, the rhetor's aim being to touch and move the mental faculties of an audience in some desired fashion.

Campbell's "aims" seem to have included at least two sorts of intention: first, a rhetor must intend to transfer her thoughts as clearly as possible to listeners or readers during the rhetorical act; second, she must also intend to arouse some sort of response in the minds of her audience, such as conviction, persuasion, delight, or action. He simply assumed that rhetors' intentions were always clear and available to them on reflection. Their intentions guided them as they conducted an investigation, and this process was then stored in memory. Subsequently, the memory of the investigation could be transferred to a text.

Campbell's location of the starting point of invention in the aims of an individual author was a momentous innovation in inventional theory.[1] Contemporary writing teachers may have difficulty accepting that the "aims of discourse" have a specific historical locus in the eighteenth century, given our ubiquitous assumption that writers have "a purpose" and that when they write they install that purpose in a discourse. Nevertheless, the first page of the *Philosophy of Rhetoric* represents a real departure from classical thought about rhetorical invention, which as-

15

sumed that rhetors began their investigations with what other people thought, rather than with an introspective review of their own thought processes.

The assumption that minds could conduct accurate introspective tours of their own workings was crucial to the modern worldview, of course. In his *Essay Concerning Human Understanding,* for example, Locke had defined consciousness as "the perception of what passes in a man's own mind" (2.1.19). Locke was confident that people could reflect on the workings of their own minds, that they could be conscious, in an accurate way, of their own mental states at any given time. Campbell shared this belief, arguing that persons can not only reflect on their experience but that they can also contemplate propositions and make judgments about the relationships between their ideas (1).

Unlike classical or medieval rhetoricians, then, modern discourse theorists assumed the existence of an individual ordering consciousness that was always in touch both with nature and with its own operations and that was not necessarily constrained by community expectations. This originating consciousness manipulated its "ideas," which represented either the things of the world, related ideas, or propositions. The stuff of invention—subjects, ideas, knowledge, discoveries, and thoughts, as well as aims or intentions—preceded discourse; it existed in some coherent and knowable way prior to and outside of discourse.

In this chapter, I explain how Campbell justified the introspective character of minds and how he certified the authority of memory. I also show why he placed much more importance on logical proofs than he did on other kinds of appeals. Eighteenth-century discourse theorists also placed much more faith in the information given to minds by the senses—that is, in empirical evidence—than had classical rhetoricians. In another section of this chapter, then, I show how Campbell, along with Richard Whately, altered the character of rhetorical proofs so that the evidence given to minds by nature could assume a respectable place in rhetorical invention.

Faculty Psychology and Associationism

Campbell's theory of rhetorical invention was indebted to two psychological traditions: faculty psychology and associationism. Since both traditions have long been out of vogue, I make a small detour from my central argument in order to explain their relevance to Campbell's introspective theory of invention. Faculty psychology is the source of his notion that minds are divided into compartments. Association psychology is the source of his assumption that minds contemplate separate, specific "ideas" that they connect to each other by means of a few invariant operations.

Throughout the Middle Ages minds were described as collections of divided cells or compartments, each of which housed a separate mental faculty. Authorities on mental geography usually named six such faculties: understanding, reason, imagination, memory, appetite, and will. Each division of the mind had its typical sort of work to do. For instance, the understanding or intellect housed innate ideas or first principles that were not available through experience, reason made comparisons and classified data, and the imagination made pictures based on its responses to the world. Francis Bacon used the faculties as means of discriminating among kinds of knowledge: history flowed from memory, poetry from imagination, and philosophy from reason, while rhetoric applied "the dictates of reason to imagination, in order to excite the appetite and will" (4:455).[2] Campbell's division of the "aims" of rhetoric into appeals to the understanding, imagination, the passions, and the will, then, is perfectly consonant with faculty psychology.

The publication of Locke's *Essay Concerning Human Understanding* in 1690 caused something of a furor because he dismissed the medieval assumption that human beings came into the world equipped with innate ideas that enabled them to function in it (1.1.3).[3] His innovation was to aver that the mind at birth was equipped, not with ideas, but rather with certain powers that allowed it to make connections among the welter of sensory data given it by experience. He replaced medieval faculty psychology with the notion that minds consisted of a set of discrete mental operations. According to Locke, human minds operated on the knowledge garnered through experience in two ways. First, the senses perceived simple ideas offered to them by objects in the world "and thus we come by those ideas we have of yellow, white, heat, cold, soft, hard, bitter, sweet, and all those which we call sensible qualities" (1.1.3). Second, the mind conceived complex ideas about the world through reflecting on its own operations, "and such are perception, thinking, doubting, believing, reasoning, knowing, willing, and all the different actings of our own minds" (1.1.4).

Locke thought of the mental operations as working according to the principle of relation. Minds habitually made comparisons between their ideas.

> The understanding, in the consideration of anything is not confined to that precise object: it can carry any idea, as it were,

beyond itself, or at least look beyond it to see how it stands in conformity to any other. When the mind so considers one thing, that it does, as it were, bring it to and set it by another, and carries its view from one to the other . . . this is . . . relation. (1.25.1)

Minds connected sensory perceptions according to habitual patterns of relation, such as cause and effect, or identity and diversity. Locke defined knowledge itself as "the perception of the connection of and agreement, or disagreement and repugnancy, of any of our ideas" (4.1.2).

While later thinkers were not ready to adopt Locke's theory of knowledge in its entirety, his location of the epistemological process within the human mind was nearly universally subscribed to, as was his theory of the association of ideas. According to Vincent Bevilacqua,

> after repeated examination of man's faculties by British writers following Bacon and Locke the principle of association was a commonly accepted element of human nature whose influence in philosophy and *belles lettres* was fully developed in the works of [David] Hartley and [Joseph] Priestley, as well as in [David] Hume, [Alexander] Gerard, and [Henry Home, Lord] Kames. ("Philosophical Influences" 206)

Hartley and Hume were philosophers of mind, while Gerard and Kames were aestheticians and critics. Priestley was an eclectic thinker who wrote treatises on chemistry, grammar, history, and rhetoric.

These proponents of associationism postulated, as Locke had done, that minds worked according to innate principles of association—"the sequences that occur in trains of memory or imagination or thought . . . one such experience follows another through certain definite relationships. Thus, one idea may serve to recall another which resembles it or which was contiguous to it in former experience" (Warren 12). These trains of thought were most often supposed to work by means of the principles of resemblance and contiguity in space or time. However, as eighteenth-century philosophers soon realized, one could postulate an endless series of principles of association, adding to the list succession, repetition, enumeration, cause and effect, and so on. In his influential *Elements of Criticism* (1762), Lord Kames observed that the "relations by which things are linked together . . . are not more remarkable, than the various relations that connect them together: cause and effect, contiguity in time or in place, high and low, prior and posterior, resemblance, contrast, and a thousand other relations, connect things together without end" (1:18).[4]

Here, then, is the picture of mind drawn by Lockean associationism. Persons receive information about the world through their senses. The information so garnered is stored in the mind in the form of particular "ideas." The mind continually processes its ideas, comparing them to similar, contiguous, or related ideas. The products of this process are complex ideas, which are usually in a constant process of revision by means of comparison with other simple or complex ideas. Since the quality of ideas depends upon the quality of sense experience, persons' different experiences in the world account for their different ideas of it, although seeming differences can sometimes be accounted for by the mistake of using different names for the same idea. While individual ideas of the world may differ, due to different experiences of it, all normal minds function along the same lines.

This is essentially the model of the mind with which Campbell worked while he composed the *Philosophy of Rhetoric*. Like Locke, he was confident that minds could procure evidence about the world because they were in direct sensory contact with it. For Campbell, "logical truth" consisted "in the conformity of our conceptions to their archetypes in the nature of things." This conformity of the mind with nature could be either simple or complex. In the former case, conformity was achieved "immediately on a bare attention to the ideas under review." In the latter case, the conformity of the mind with nature was mediated by the mind's associative actions, which compared its simple ideas "with other related ideas" (35).

Logical proof thus procured consisted of two kinds, intuitive and deductive. The distinction depended on whether ideas arose from the mind's immediate contact with nature (the source of intuitive evidence) or on whether ideas had been mediated by the making of connections between related ideas (deduction) (see fig. 1). There were, in turn, two categories of deduction: demonstration and moral reasoning. Demonstration involved pure intellection—the mind's pure association of ideas. Moral reasoning, on the other hand, resulted from the mind's operations on its knowledge of things, knowledge handed it by its sensory contact with the world. This second category was "the proper province of rhetoric . . . for to the second belong all decisions concerning fact, and things without us" (43). For Campbell, then, the available logical proofs were a product of the operation of the mind, either on materials given

Kinds of Evidence Discriminated by Campbell

Intuitive Evidence
   Intelligence
   Consciousness
   Common sense

Deductive Evidence
   Demonstrative
   Moral
      experience
      analogy
      testimony
      probability

Kinds of Evidence Discriminated by Whately

A Priori

Non–A Priori
   Arguments from Sign
      testimony
      fact/opinion

   Progressive Argument
   Example
      experience
      analogy
      contraries
      real/invented examples

Fig. 1.   A Comparison of Campbell's and Whately's Theories of Evidence

it by its intuitive contact with nature or of its deductive reflection on its own operations. The latter process could involve the manipulation either of pure ideas or of ideas of things.

   This theory of invention struck a nice balance between two dissonant eighteenth-century philosophies of mind. Empiricists argued that human minds were empty at birth and that their contents were solely the result of experience. Rationalists, on the other hand, argued that people were born with a limited stock of innate ideas. If this were not the case, they pointed out, infants would have no way of making sense of the world into which they were born. Campbell's religious convictions made it difficult for him wholly to accept the empiricism advanced by David Hume, whose work he nonetheless admired. So he retained a rationalist basis for his category of intuitive evidence, which was appropriate for use in such fields as mathematics and theology. Most important, however, he designated empirical evidence as the kind of proof that was most appropriate to rhetoric: moral reasoning was based on information gathered by the senses as this was mediated by the associative powers of the mind. In any field, however, logical proof was crucial in attaining either conviction or persuasion: "The speaker must always assume the character of the close candid reasoner: for though he may be an acute logician who is no orator, he will never be a consummate orator who is no logician" (61).

The Role of Memory

Memory is a crucial (though often unacknowledged) component of any introspective theory of invention.[5] The rhetorician's memory of her mental procedures must be accurate; if it is not, the outcome of the entire process is thrown into doubt. Alone among modern rhetoricians, Campbell addressed this problem head on.

In his analysis, the sources of experience were two: the senses and memory. As sensory impressions came into the mind, the memory recorded or imprinted them for later reference. The faith in memory was a product of common sense, which Campbell defined as "an original source of knowledge" (38–39). Common sense said that our conviction that "I am certain that things happened heretofore at such a time, in the precise manner in which I now remember that they then happened" was a conviction that could not be questioned (41). Thus our faith in the accounts given us by our memories was a first principle for Campbell.

Further, the acquisition of experience was intimately bound up with the operation of memory: "Remembrance instantly succeeds sensation, insomuch that the memory becomes the sole repository of the knowledge received from sense; knowledge which, without this repository, would be as instantaneously lost as it is gotten, and could be of no service to the mind" (47). Repeated observations of a given natural fact produced repeated memories. This in turn fed our capacity to make generalizations about natural laws. But repeated experiences could also correct a faulty or indistinct memory: "Experience is of use in assisting us to judge concerning the more languid and confused suggestions of memory; or, to speak more properly, concerning the reality of those things, of which we ourselves are doubtful whether we remember them or not" (41). Extremely vivid impressions were also easier to remember, as were those reasoning processes in which thinkers engaged with a high degree of consciousness (49).

The potential fallibility of memory did not worry Campbell overmuch until he realized that memory was also crucial in the assembly of demonstrative, or scientific, evidence.

> It was observed of memory, that as it instantly succeeds sensation, it is the repository of all the stores from which our experience is collected, and that without an implicit faith in the clear representations of that faculty, we could not advance a step in the acquisition of experimental knowledge. Yet we know that memory is not infallible: nor can we pretend that in any case there is not a physical possibility of her making a false report. Here, it may be said, is an irremediable imbecility in the very foundation of moral reasoning. But is it less so in demonstrative reasoning? (58)

The potential fallibility of memory posed a hazard to scientific demonstration because scientists must keep an accurate mental record of successive axioms as they build their chains of reasoning. In practice, however, the thinker could, with the aid of an occasional diagram, repeat the reasoning process a number of times to see if each trial obtained the same result. Nevertheless, Campbell acknowledged, such repetition amounted to little more than "reiterated testimonies of his memory, in support of the truth of its former testimony" (59). However, he immediately turned the potentially tautological feature of this necessary repetition into a virtue. He noted that "the repetition, when no error is discovered, enlivens the remembrance, and so strengthens the conviction" (60).

In these passages Campbell came very close to acknowledging the implicit difficulty that faces an introspective theory of invention. The final authority for the quality of the results of introspection (or retrospection) is the thinker's faith in the quality of the mental processes that gave birth to the investigation in the first place. In the case of empirical reasoning (which, we recall, is the reasoning appropriate to rhetoric), the thinker cannot assume that she has learned anything about the world unless she trusts that the skill or originality with which she made connections between ideas is accurately reflected by her memory; more fundamentally, she must trust that she faithfully remembers her sensory impressions, as well as the sequence of the connections she made between them and other ideas. The thinker must trust further that any discourse that results is itself an accurate representation of all of these processes.

Of course she can await repetition of her work by other thinkers. But, finally, there is no real assurance that the testimony given by others is any different in quality from the repeated testimonies given up by the thinker's memory of the original process.

Campbell is the only eighteenth-century discourse theorist who noticed that introspective invention fundamentally depends on the assumption that the mind's memory of an investigation is an accurate record of its manipulation of ideas. Other rhetorical theorists took for granted the mind's ability to record and faithfully repeat a process of investigation.

Moral Reasoning and Experience

As I noted previously, Campbell designated moral reasoning as the mode of proof that was most appropriate to the questions investigated by rhetoricians. This was consonant with classical thought, in which one important role of rhetoric was to debate moral questions. But he further associated moral reasoning with empirical evidence. On the face of it, this was a remarkable move, since it located rhetoric (as well as ethics) solidly within the sphere of sensory experience; that is, he removed moral reasoning from the sphere of public discourse, placing responsibility for ethical decisions squarely in the minds of individual actors, who would derive their solutions to ethical problems from private experience. Rhetors would now have to convince audiences that their individual assessments of ethical dilemmas were the correct ones. As though he were aware of its revolutionary quality, Campbell provided an elaborate rationale for this move: evidence from experience was rhetorically effective because it reminded people of the way in which they garner knowledge every day of their lives.

In Campbell's model of the mind, the senses perceived data singly, but these single facts or events were stored up in the memory until one of the higher faculties made a generalization concerning them. He illustrated this notion by pointing out that the senses may once notice a stone falling to the ground: "This single fact produces little or no effect upon the mind beyond a bare remembrance." But, having later observed a tile, or an apple, falling to the ground, the mind would be able to generalize about all falling bodies, "for, with regard to the similar circumstances of different facts, as by the repetitions such circumstances are more deeply imprinted, the mind acquires a habit of retaining them, omitting those circumstances peculiar to each wherein their differences consist" (47). Thus, the piling up of relevant pieces of experiential data could readily convince an audience of the truth of a general proposition, since the reasoning process employed would imitate the movement of minds when they process sensory perceptions in order to formulate abstractions. In other words, the construction of rhetorical proofs now amounted to imitating the experiential process by which people acquire knowledge.

Campbell subdivided moral evidence into four categories: experience, analogy, testimony, and chance. Experience could be either uniform or various. In the first case, if all experiences of a given thing or event were alike, any conclusion drawn from them could be held with moral certainty: iron sinks in water, while wood always floats. In the case of variable experiences, conclusions were only probable: since experience has shown that it usually snows during the last week of December, we can probably expect snow during that time. Analogy represented a sort of shortcut through the experiential process. For example, if experience had demonstrated that blood circulates in animal bodies, a rhetor could argue from analogy that sap circulates in vegetables. Evidence based on chance, or on what we now call mathematical probability, worked in the same way. The chance fall of thrown dice was analogous to the movement of the mind when it compared its experiences: "When five instances favour one side to one that favours the contrary" the mind "determines the greater credibility of the former" (57).

Campbell likewise justified his inclusion of testimony in this list of empirical evidence on the ground of its similarity to the experiential process. Testimony was "a serious intimation from another, of any fact of observation, as being what he remembers to have seen or heard or experienced." There was no reason to doubt such evidence, he wrote, since "an original principle of our nature (analogous to that which compels our faith in memory)" leads reasonable people to give their assent. Testimony was effective when the status of a particular instance was in dispute: "When experience is applied to the discovery of the truth in a particular incident, we call the evidence presumptive; ample testimony is accounted a positive proof of the fact" (55). In other words, testimony given by several witnesses has more weight than that given by a single person, on the analogy of the mind's moving toward certainty as it adduces more and more similar instances.

Clarence W. Edney points out that Campbell's distinction between demonstrative evidence and moral evidence was similar to Locke's distinction between "knowledge" and "opinion"; that is, "whereas the truth arrived at by demonstration has a high degree of certainty, the belief arrived at by means of moral evidence has only some degree of probability and must be considered merely as opinion" (25). However, "opinion" and "probability" were not "mere" forms of proof during the seventeenth and eighteenth centuries, when they enjoyed higher status than they currently do.[6] Since classical times, a rhetorical probability had denoted something like "what people are likely to do," while an opinion meant "what reasonable people are likely to think." In other words, one could entertain an opinion about the moral nature of human beings that was widely accepted as truth, simply because most thinking people believed it to be the case. So Campbell apparently felt no uneasiness in awarding equal persuasive status to moral evidence, even though it was based on "the actual, though perhaps variable, connexions subsisting among things" and even though demonstrative and deductive evidence produced higher degrees of certainty (43).

Because of his enormous influence on later rhetorical theory, Campbell's connection of rhetorical inquiry with empirical evidence was to have long-lasting effects. Ironically enough, he apparently made the connection in order to rehabilitate rhetoric for modern use. Instead, his association of rhetorical proof with empirical investigation eventually limited the pertinence of rhetorical inquiry to issues for which an appeal to experience supplied the most certain proof, that is, to scientific (or pseudoscientific) investigations of the physical world. This happened despite Campbell's assertion that moral evidence was appropriate not only for the investigation of nature but for arriving at an understanding of human nature as well: "Reality or fact comprehends the laws and the works of nature, as well as the arts and the institutions of men; in brief, all the beings which fall under the cognizance of the human mind, with all their modifications, operations, and effects" (46). According to Edney, since moral evidence proceeded "on the assumption that the course of nature in the future will be similar to what it has been in the past," rhetoricians could use it to mount arguments about what people generally do. But Campbell's inclusive definition of "facts" was narrowed by his imitators so that it encompassed only those pieces of evidence that were gathered from observation of the natural world. Despite Campbell's attention to moral evidence, his progeny tended to concentrate on empirical questions and to exclude moral issues from the province of rhetoric.

Ironically enough, this narrowing of the field appropriate to rhetorical inquiry may have had something to do with the popularity among nineteenth-century rhetoricians of Richard Whately's *Elements of Rhetoric* (originally published in 1828), which offered up a tidy system for classifying the sorts of evidence that could be derived from sensory impressions.[7] Bishop Whately divided evidence into two great classes, just as Campbell had done. However, he preferred a logical classification to the psychological distinctions that had given rise to Campbell's categories. Whately, an Aristotelian logician, was pretty much opposed to newfangled modern notions about empiricism. He engaged in a running battle for many years with his colleague, John Stuart Mill, over the nature and function of inductive evidence.[8] He was altogether skeptical about whether such a thing existed or, if it did, about whether it had any uses in either logic or rhetoric. Nevertheless, his reluctant comments on the category of evidence that I call "non–a priori" by default (Whately didn't even bother to give it a name) found their way into nineteenth-century discussions of evidence, sometimes almost verbatim. No doubt, Bishop Whately would have been disgruntled, if not horrified, by the uses to which later rhetoricians put his analysis of this second category of evidence.

According to Whately, arguments were composed of two great classes. A priori arguments were employed "to *account for* the fact or principle maintained, supposing its truth granted"; such arguments always moved from cause to effect, since "to *account* for any thing, signifies, to assign the Cause of it" (46). Campbell had been able to assert the certainty of such arguments since they rested with the universal psychology inherent in human nature. But Whately never acceded that rhetorical conclusions derived from cause-effect arguments were certain; rather, insofar as their premises were probable and their conclusions plausible, they tended to produce a "general belief." Since Whately insistently mounted his discussions of a priori evidence from the perspective of logic rather than from a set of postulated universal principles of human nature, he argued that certainty could only be had if certain formal relationships were rigorously observed. However, formal rigor was ordinarily not possible in rhetorical discourse because the premises used there involved probabilities rather than certainties. In his denial of logical certainty to rhetorical deduction, Whately followed Aristotle, who distinguished between demonstrative and rhetorical syllogisms on the grounds of the relative certainty of their premises.

Whately's attitude toward his second category of evidence was on the whole more positive than was Aristotle's toward similar procedures; yet on the whole his treatment was more conservative than Campbell's. Nevertheless, non–a priori evidence interested Whately a good deal, if the length of his treatment is any indication. But his interest in nondeductive modes of argument had a very different inspiration than Campbell's. As Ray McKerrow observes, Whately desired to "separate logic's role of testing relations among premises from induction's role of investigating nature" (11). In other words, he made a firm distinction between the sort of inductive proofs that could be produced by logical means and those that could be adduced through empirical investigation. As McKerrow demonstrates, Whately was not opposed to empirical evidence as a means of proof; he simply did not want it confused with logical induction (as he implied Campbell had done).

Throughout the *Elements of Rhetoric*, Whately demonstrated a conservative skepticism regarding the modern reliance upon empirical evidence. In his introduction, he remarked that "a prevailing fault of the present day" was the tendency "to trust to accumulation of facts as a *substitute* for accuracy in the logical processes." The Bishop was perfectly aware that this tendency to valorize factual evidence resulted from widespread subscription to the new philosophy, and he called on the authority of Bacon himself to correct the impression that a list of facts sufficed as argumentative proof: "It was not that men were taught to think correctly by having new phaenomena brought to light; but on the contrary, they discovered new phaenomena in *consequence* of a new system of philosophizing" (15). Whately never succumbed to the fallacy (from his point of view) that effective rhetorical proof could be mounted by a mere appeal to the facts of the matter. Nevertheless, his categorical mind, as well as his respect for theoretical precedent, committed him to an examination and classification of the sorts of proofs that could be generated by means of empirical investigation.

Non–a priori evidence accrued from two sources: sign, which included testimony and progressive argument; and example, which included experience, analogy, and contraries. Whately's extensive treatment of testimony as a kind of argument from sign represented a marked departure from the classical habit of doubting the worth of any evidence provided by witnesses. Testimony was an argument from sign insofar as the condition of its having been given argued for its truth. Whately included a long and careful discussion of the considerations that might qualify the force of testimony, dealing in turn with the character, possible motives, and numbers of witnesses. Like Campbell, he gave great weight to concurrent testimony, on the grounds that "each testimony, though given to an individual case, has a tendency towards the general conclusion in which all concur; viz. the *possibility* of such an event; and this being once admitted, the antecedent objection against each individual case is removed" (75). And, again like Campbell, Whately argued that the weight given to evidence collected from testimony increased with each new instance of it.

Whately introduced a sophisticated discussion of the difference between fact and opinion into his comments on testimony. A "fact" was "something which might, *conceivably*, be submitted to the *senses;* and about which it is supposed there could be no disagreement among persons who should be *present*"; an opinion, on the other hand, was "anything respecting which an exercise of *judgment* would be called for on the part of those who should have certain objects before them, and who might conceivably disagree in their judgment thereupon" (58–59). Fact was never superior to opinion as a kind of evidence, either in degree of certainty conferred or in number of persons agreeing to it. While all sane persons would agree, for example, that the poisoning of Alexander the Great by a friend was a question of fact, the perpetrator's identity would forever be shrouded in doubt. On the other hand, most persons readily shared an opinion about the immoral nature of the act. However, Whately's insistence on the importance and value of opinion as a mode of proof was forgotten by his many imitators, who borrowed his categories of non–a priori proof almost without emendation, but who missed his subtle distinction between empirical and more strictly rational or logical processes of reasoning.

Whately concluded his discussion of arguments from sign with the procedure he called progressive argument. This sort of argument involved the assembly of a series of testimonies in order of increasing probability. He observed that each of the signs or testimonies taken separately would not carry much weight, but taken together and assembled in their proper order, progressive arguments exhibited high degrees of probability. This sort of argument was apparently best adapted to science and philosophy.

Because of his reliance on classical sources, in which examples, analogies, and contraries were held in high regard as persuasive strategies, Whately gave a good deal of attention to the argument from example. Given his bias against empirical means of proof, however, he considered that exemplary experiences could constitute a rhetorical argument only insofar as rhetors could construct minor premises out of past experience.

> Strictly speaking, we know *by* Experience only the *past,* and what has passed under our own observation; thus, we know by *Experience* that the tides *have* daily ebbed and flowed, during such a time; and from the Testimony of others as to their own Experience, that the tides have formerly done so: and *from* this Experience, we conclude, *by* Induction, that the same Phenomenon will continue. (88)

Thus Whately reiterated his disdain for empirical evidence. The force of any conclusion based on experience derived from the power of the inductive inference. Inductive inference was a process whose validity was guaranteed by the operations of logic rather than by any necessary operations decreed by human psychology. Again, however, this distinction was missed by the nineteenth-century rhetoricians who borrowed from Whately's discussion to found their own accounts of evidence.

The Primacy of Logical Proof

Thus modern discourse theory presented its readers with two quite sophisticated accounts of evidence, one firmly based in current epistemological speculation, the other grounded in logic. The notion of evidence—especially inductive evidence in its empirical guise as the proofs drawn from the experience of particulars—usurped the place of topical invention in modern discourse theory. The new process of invention depended primarily on a rhetorician's private and internal mental experiences; proof consisted in his imitating this process in as exact a manner as possible, so that the experience could be recreated in the minds of an audience. Proof could also depend on the reports of others about their experiences. The assembly of a number of testimonials made for stronger and more convincing proof; that is, testimony from others increased the chances that an internalized account of an experience had some external verification in the minds of others.

Campbell shared the modern faith in the uniformity of human nature. Because of this uniformity, the contingencies presented by rhetorical situations were more similar than various. Rhetors had only to grasp the workings of "certain principles in our nature" in order to "promote belief" in any reasonable person. Campbell devoted only two chapters of the *Philosophy of Rhetoric* to consideration of probable audience response. In the first of these, "Hearers, as men in general," he reviewed the rhetorical strategies that appealed to each of the faculties possessed in common by all persons (71). Since the operations of the faculties were similar in every human being, rhetors were not compelled to analyze specific audiences to determine their probable response. Indeed, the uniformity of human nature certified that a rhetor's introspective review of her own probable response sufficed as a prediction of the response of other "thinking beings endowed with understanding, imagination, memory, and passions, such as we are conscious of in ourselves, and learn from the experience of their effects to be in others" (94).

In the second chapter devoted to audiences, "Hearers, as men in particular," Campbell briefly surveyed the potential stumbling blocks posed to rhetors by the political and social diversities that might obtain among members of an audience, such as their adherence to party spirit or their differences with regard to "education and moral culture," habits, or occupations (95). He noted that even though "the characters of audiences may be infinitely diversified," any "person of discernment" should be able to ascertain the influence of this diversity on her relationship to them; that is, he assumed that any rhetor, by virtue of her very humanity, could find a link between her aim and those of her audience (96).

Campbell also shared modern faith in the superiority of reason. Rhetors appealed to the nonrational faculties only as reinforcement for the "conclusive arguments" generated by reason, since "these are not the supplanters of reason, or even rivals in her sway; they are her handmaids, by whose ministry she is enabled to usher truth into the heart, and procure it there a favorable reception" (72). Campbell also assumed that human sympathy was so strong that its force could be dampened only when audiences held a low opinion either of a rhetor's intellectual ability or of her moral standards.[9] He elided the possibilities that listeners or readers could be apathetic, inept, perhaps even hostile. In fact, the *Philosophy of Rhetoric* painted a picture of the rhetorical scene that was curiously serene and univocal: communication takes place in an ideal discursive world where rhetors always know exactly what they intend, and where, with the proper care, their thoughts and intentions always and inevitably make their way into the receptive minds of capable listeners and readers.

Nor did Campbell's contemporaries paint a very different picture. Whately's remarks on persuasive strategies did offer traditional advice about pathetic and ethical appeals. But he centered the force of these sorts of appeals on the matter of the discourse itself, rather than on the character of the rhetor or the emotional disposition brought by an audience to the rhetorical situation. He argued that people would be moved to action when "the proposed Object should appear desirable" and when "the Means suggested should be proved to be conducive to the attainment of that object" (175). In the last resort, for Whately, the will was moved by appeals to the reason, rather than to the passions.

Like his more conventional fellows, Joseph Priestley was also content to observe that the principle of sympathy usually disposed people "to conform to the feelings, the sentiments, and every thing belonging to the situation of those we converse with." As a consequence, his ethical advice amounted to the recommendation that orators and writers give the impression of being thoroughly convinced of the soundness of the propositions they advanced.

> Prior to hearing any arguments, we are naturally inclined to suppose, that a strong conviction and persuasion in other persons could not be produced without a *sufficient cause;* from being sensible that a like strong persuasion is founded upon sufficient reasons in ourselves. The ideas of *strong persuasion* and of *truth* being, on this account intimately associated together, the one will introduce the other. (109)

The uniformity of human nature, in essence, obviated the need for persuasive appeals. In modern rhetoric, telling the truth about one's experience was tantamount to persuading others to accept it. Ethos and pathos, so important to classical rhetoric, took a back seat to logos in modern rhetorical theory.

An Introspective Theory of Invention

Associationism springs from a tradition that was hoary with age even in Locke's day. In an interesting compromise with the general tendency of modern thought, Locke's introduction of associationism into his philosophy was authorized partly by its presence within a scholarly or bookish tradition that extends back at least to Aristotle. In fact, associationism seems to have been part of the mental baggage of an era, part of its common sense, so deeply engrained that its efficacy was seldom questioned. So when Campbell worked out his innovative theory of invention, it was fully consonant with contemporary notions about how minds function.

The accuracy of associationism as a description of mind was brought into question by empirical psychology during the nineteenth century. Nevertheless, considerations about its accuracy did not keep it from becoming a crucial focal point of the theory of rhetorical invention that was to develop out of eighteenth-century discourse theory. Here we have the first of a series of instances that will recur again and again in this account: the theory of invention whose genesis I trace here—while originally based in intellectual currents that had wide circulation—continued to invest in these long after they had gone out of fashion within the fields from which they were borrowed. I think that associationism hung on in rhetoric long after it had become obsolete in psychology simply because it provided rhetoricians and composition theorists with an authoritative picture, not only of how minds get information, but of how they process it (to use an anachronistic term).

However, the linkage of invention with psychology had far-reaching theoretical and pedagogical implications. For the first time in the history of rhetoric, the inventional process was focused solely on the individual creative mind of a rhetor working in relative isolation. Furthermore, the quality of her discourse now depended to some extent on the quality of her experiences. She would be able to tell or write only what she knew from her examination of, and meditation on, the world around her. Thus it was incumbent on her to be observant, to gather sensations and produce ideas, to study, to think. Add to this the assumption that her discourse would depend for its persuasive force on how faithfully it represented her introspective analysis of her own mind's workings, and you have a rhetorical theory that can only be described as author-centered. This theory of invention created all sorts of pedagogical difficulties, especially when it was taught to young people. In essence, it demanded that rhetors bring one crucial asset to the act of composing: a full and self-reflective mind.

3 How Insides Get Outside Again: The Logic of the Methodical Memory

Since eighteenth-century discourse theorists accepted the notion that the process of inquiry was constituted by a review of the mind's contents and operations, they next had to find some way to insure that when the results of inquiry "went public" these results exactly represented the primary, internal mental process that had produced them. The problem was this: How could a speaker or writer's memory of her investigative process be accurately translated into discourse that would be intelligible and coherent to outsiders? Discourse theorists found a solution to this problem in a logical tradition called method. Method had the handy properties of being suited to the arts of discovery as well as those of communication. In other words, method could function in the interior world of individual minds when they were engaged in investigation, as well as in the external world as a means of establishing connections between minds through discourse.

The term *method* has been used since classical times to designate any orderly or systematic procedure, and it continues to be used in this loose sense. However, an important technical use of the term *method* began to emerge among the generation of scholars who immediately preceded Descartes. Walter Ong defines this historical use of method to mean "a series of ordered steps gone through to produce with certain efficacy a desired effect—a routine of *efficiency*" (225).[1] During the late Renaissance, method was a process of inquiry; thinkers who were rebelling against scholasticism turned to it as a non-Aristotelian means of finding new knowledge and of organizing received knowledge.

The description of method that follows will probably cause contemporary readers to wonder how any serious thinker could ever have relied upon it as a procedural guarantee for the truth of an inquiry process. But post-Renaissance logicians and philosophers took method very seriously indeed. It seemed to them to offer a guarantee that the operations of the human mind were consonant with those of nature. As I have tried to establish, modern thought relies at its core on the assumption of a representative consonance between minds and nature. So, as we shall see, the philosophers who expounded the virtues of method were anxious to ground its authority in the natural order. Method also offered the twin promises of efficiency and comprehensiveness to the new philosophers who launched the project of studying the physical world by means of empirical investigation. Its use lent a kind of security to the intellectual adventurers who had rejected classical texts as an ultimate source of knowledge, who were setting out, in fact, to rewrite what could be defined as knowledge. Of course, faith in method still lingers in the contemporary notion of the scientific method, which is widely accepted, even today, as a procedural guarantee for certain kinds of truth.

Early in the history of method (1637), René Descartes averred that

> method consists entirely in the ordering and arranging of the objects on which we must concentrate our minds's eye if we are to discover some truth. We shall be following this method exactly if we first reduce complicated and obscure propositions step by step to simpler ones, and then, starting with the intuition of the simplest ones of all, try to ascend through the same steps to a knowledge of all the rest. (20)

In other words, the methodical movement from the complex to the simple induced a native, elemental understanding—an intuition—that could not be questioned, apparently because of its irreducibility to anything else. Once the investigator had discovered this irreducible, elemental minimum, she had a basis from which to begin a systematic inquiry into the more complex features of any field. The orderly nature of this process reassured the investigator, in essence, that she had left no stone unturned in her pursuit of knowledge.

But method had yet another use, and that was to explicate the results of mental investigations to others. From its beginnings method was associated with teaching. For example, in 1599 the British logician Thomas Blundeville defined method as "a compendious way of learning or teaching any thing" in his *Logike* (qtd. in Howell, *Logic and Rhetoric* 289). Contemporary commentators, like Hans Aarsleff, have noted that the attractiveness of method as a means of learning anything was its efficiency:

"Method is . . . a problem in learning theory and practice, designed to shorten the job of learning" (105).[2] Method was touted throughout the seventeenth century as an efficient way to learn almost any subject, since it relieved the burden placed on memory by calling on the assistance of reason. In the methodical literature, school subjects would ideally be organized according to method. For example, students would begin their study of grammar with the smallest constituent component of a language—letters—and move successively through the study of larger and more complex components such as syllables, words, parts of speech, and so on.

Sixteenth- and seventeenth-century logicians generally divided method into a series of binary distinctions, the most basic of which was that between natural and artificial method, that is, between nature's disposition or arrangement of things and that imposed on it by human agents. Natural method, in turn, was divided into two kinds: analysis and synthesis.[3] Analysis described the mental process of investigation, while synthesis described the discursive process of communication. Analysis and synthesis were generally thought to move in opposing directions; most often, theorists of method argued that analysis moved from the specific to the general, while synthesis began with general observations and moved to more specific details. Both analysis and synthesis were "natural" methods because they were thought to recreate the principles of order found in nature.

In sum, during the seventeenth century, method was regarded as a means of charting the course of a mind's movement, and it could represent that course for others to follow as well. In its guise as analysis, natural method provided an orderly model of the mind's workings; in its guise as synthesis, natural method provided thinkers with a way to make this model of the mind apparent in discourse.

Eighteenth-century discourse theorists adapted method to their own uses. Specifically, they employed it in their rhetorical systems primarily as a means for arranging arguments in such a way that they reflected the progress of the investigation that had given rise to them. In this way method became a theory of composing. In order to explain how all of this came about, I must detour into some popular seventeenth- and eighteenth-century logic texts.

A Brief but Compendious History of Method

Method was apparently first endowed with a separate, technically defined existence by a sixteenth-century rhetorician, logician, and intellectual maverick named Peter Ramus. In his treatise on dialectics, Ramus argued the usefulness of method by means of a metaphor drawn from gaming (Ong 245). He envisioned an imaginary lottery wherein the parts of all the arts were discovered and inscribed on bits of paper and placed into a jar. By what logic, Ramus asked, could an uninitiated student rearrange the pieces in their proper order? Ramus then proposed method as a means of laying out all the arts in their proper relations and sequence. Versions of Ramus' analogy recurred throughout the literature on method whenever writers wanted to argue the superiority of method to "mere orderliness." For example, in a series of essays on method composed for *The Friend* (1818) almost three centuries later, Samuel Taylor Coleridge rationalized the importance of method by imagining a "savage" who tried to sort the letters of the alphabet into groups. Lacking an understanding of the principle which controlled the system, the savage was helpless until given instruction in its method by a helpful missionary (4.1.455). In both of these illustrations, method is a systematic means of classifying the relations of a whole to its parts; it somehow picks out and represents the principles of ordered arrangement that supposedly underlie any seemingly random collection of items. Ramus and Coleridge stubbornly identified these principles as natural even though the arts and sciences, as well as the alphabet, represent human attempts to make sense of the natural world.

For Ramus, natural method was the method appropriate for teaching, since by means of the movement from the general to the particular "the whole matter can be more easily taught and apprehended" (Ong 245). Apparently, Ramus thought that the world, or at least the universe of discourse about it, was naturally organized by the movement from general to specific, since he associated natural method with this movement. Prudential or artificial method, on the other hand, could have "no training or art in it," since it depended "merely on man's natural judgement." Prudential method was to be employed when teachers needed to avail themselves of all the resources of the communicative art. In cases where "the audience is sluggish, the matter to be explained disagreeable, the time not suitable, the place strange," or where "one has to teach persons who do not want to be taught," one should "disguise" the method in use, according to Ramus (Ong 246). Perhaps because of its "unnatural" connotations, artificial method commanded far less attention from logicians than did its companion.

Ramus confined both kinds of method to the presentation of knowledge rather than to its generation. It was only in the seventeenth century that a method suited to investigation was developed by the new philosophers. Again, natural method was of more interest to them than was artificial method, which was consistently relegated to use in the composition of nonscientific discourse such as oratory and poetry.

Francis Bacon saw that the kind of knowledge appropriate to experimental science would require not only new means of communication or presentation, but new rules of investigation as well. Thus in *The Advancement of Learning* (1605) he made method an important part of his "Art of Transmission," noting that it corresponded to the canon of *dispositio* (arrangement) in rhetoric. Method was of two kinds, magistral and initiative. The function of magistral method corresponded closely to that of arrangement in rhetoric, since it was used to transmit knowledge to "the crowd of learners" who were obligated to believe what they were told. Its end was to teach people how to use all the arts and sciences as they currently existed. Initiative method, on the other hand, was the way of the "sons of science" who wished to examine the frontiers of knowledge; its end was the continuation and further progression of knowledge (4.449). Thus, while he opened the door for an association of method with rhetorical theory, Bacon did not confine its usefulness to the mere arrangement of arguments. Rather, magistral and initiative methods formed two sides of the same coin: "Knowledge that is delivered as a thread to be spun on, ought to be delivered and intimated, if it were possible, in the same method wherein it was invented" (289). This was as true for knowledge that was already revealed as it was for "knowledge induced."

A group of seventeenth-century French philosophers and logicians gave method its authoritative formulation as a means of inquiry: René Descartes in two works entitled *Rules for the Direction of Mind* and the *Discourse on Method* (1637) and the Port-Royal logicians Pierre Nicole and Antoine Arnauld, whose *Art of Thinking* (1662) was enormously popular in Britain throughout the eighteenth century (Howell, *Logic and Rhetoric* 351).

In the treatise on method, Descartes isolated his four famous rules of inquiry: accept no judgments except those that present themselves to the mind clearly and distinctly; divide difficulties into as many parts as necessary; think in an orderly manner, beginning with knowledge of the simplest objects and proceeding to knowledge of those that are more complex; and enumerate completely, so that nothing is left out (120). Thanks to Descartes' influence, *clarity* and *distinction* became hallmark terms in methodical literature. A subject of investigation would be clear when it was reduced to its absolute elemental minimum; it would be distinct when all the parts into which it could be divided were clearly enumerated and separated off from one another.

Thinkers needed a method of this sort, Descartes thought, to prevent them from directing their "minds down untrodden paths in the groundless hope that they will chance upon what they are seeking, rather like someone who is consumed with such a senseless desire to discover treasure that he continually roams the streets to see if he can find any that a passer-by might have dropped." Consequently, he defined method as "reliable rules which are easy to apply, and such that if one follows them exactly, one will never take what is false to be true or fruitlessly expend one's mental efforts, but will gradually and constantly increase one's knowledge till one arrives at a true understanding of everything within one's capacity" (16). Descartes' rationale for employing method was clear: fixed and simple rules of procedure insured that inquiry could not be led astray nor fall into error.

Antoine Arnauld provided a discussion of method which worked out its progress a bit more thoroughly. Arnauld employed the terms *analysis* or *resolution* to designate the mental movement—from the known to the unknown—that thinkers used to discover truth. Like Bacon's "initiative" method, analytic method was appropriate in inquiries about specific empirical questions rather than in those that concerned whole arts or sciences. The essential analytic skill lay in an investigator's ability to isolate "from the conditions of the question those assumptions sufficient to lead us to the unknown we seek" (309).

Arnauld adopted the terms *synthesis* or *composition* to designate two other movements: from the general to the specific and from the simple to the complex. Since synthetic method was appropriate for teaching what had already been found out, it began either from a broad generalization about the subject under discussion or from its simplest postulate. Since general propositions are also abstract, Arnauld apparently assumed that they were both simpler and more widely accessible to uninformed audiences than were the minutiae of a detailed investigation. As such, general propositions could serve as handy common ground from which to begin discourse aimed at learners. Thus synthetic method, like Bacon's magistral method, was the appropriate approach to understanding the outlines of whole sciences.

Hugh Davidson observes that for Arnauld the power of proof that was inherent in method stemmed from "linearity of thought, from strict observance of the order in which principles and consequences occur. In analysis, one searches for the antecedent or consequence upon which a given affirmation depends for its cogency. In synthesis one reverses the direction: both antecedents and consequents being known, one simply displays their interrelation to the person being taught" (89).

Indeed, Arnauld sometimes regarded analysis and synthesis as simple obverses; he wrote that they differ from one another only as roads ascending from valley to mountain differ from roads descending from mountain to valley (307–8). Analysis was particularly suited to the discovery of knowledge that had previously been unsuspected, while synthesis could be used as a method of organizing what was already known so that it could be taught to the uninitiated.

According to Perry Miller, Ramean thought was rampant at seventeenth-century Harvard, where teachers based a pedagogy of composition on method (134). Like Ramus, they treated analysis and synthesis as opposing movements. Thinkers could analyze a proposition into its constituent elements by division, or they could construct a proposition by collecting all its elements under a single head, that is, by defining it. In their Ramean framework, analysis and synthesis were identified with the much older inventional techniques of division and definition. For purposes of presentation, analysis governed the process of carving discourse into its constituent axia or premises, while synthesis involved the collection and ordering of relevant axia. In either process, arguments could be invented to support every crucial axiom. Axiom was then added to axiom in order to compose a complete discourse.

In its initial seventeenth-century manifestations, then, method was a procedural device whose aim was to get at the whole of some small problem or some large area of study in systematic fashion. Not the least of its attractions lay in its users' assurance that they had covered all relevant intellectual bases when they employed it. But more important to this discussion is the fact that method could also serve as a theory of composition. Discussions of analysis and synthesis continued in philosophical and logical treatises written throughout the eighteenth century, by which time method was generally discussed in company with more traditional means of reasoning. And it was generally incorporated into logic because of its usefulness as a composing process.

In *Eighteenth-Century British Logic and Rhetoric,* Wilbur Samuel Howell notes that modern philosophers of mind divided the reasoning process into four "degrees" or steps.[4] He describes these four steps as follows: "that of discovering proofs, that of arranging them in the order in which they have to be put in finding truth, that of perceiving more or less clearly the connection between ideas in each part of the deduction, and that of making a right judgment and of drawing a just conclusion from what has gone before" (301). The four steps involved discovering ideas through perception and association, developing propositions based on those ideas, subjecting the proposition to one or a number of established reasoning processes, and casting the result into argumentative form. Apparently all of these steps, with the possible exception of the last, could be carried on mentally, without the aid of discourse. This inquiry process was an agglutination of Lockean empiricism, associationism, propositional logic, and method.

Howell's discrimination of these four steps harmonizes with the parts into which popular eighteenth-century texts on logic and the philosophy of mind were divided. This indicates that eighteenth-century logicians recognized the four steps as distinct stages in the logical inquiry process. For example, Dugald Stewart's *Elements of the Philosophy of the Human Mind* (originally published in 1792 and 1814) represented the four steps in the two major parts of the work: the first part dealt with the powers of perception—attention, conception, and abstraction—the means by which truth is discovered; the second part treated the movement of reason and the understanding—the means by which truth is evaluated. In this second section of his massive work Stewart considered traditional logical instruments such as axia, deduction, and syllogisms, but he assigned method—which he clearly associated with empirical science—equal weight with these older means of reasoning.

Isaac Watts' popular *Logick; or, the Use of Right Reason in the Inquiry after Truth* (originally published 1724) preserved the four-part procedure even more clearly.[5] He dealt with the relations of objects, ideas, and words in the opening section of the *Logick,* entitled "Perception of Ideas," while its second section dealt with making judgments and forming propositions. The third section presented an Aristotlean discussion of reasoning and syllogizing. However, Watts devoted the entire fourth section of the *Logick* to method. For Watts, then, method was associated primarily with the formation of arguments—the step in the logical reasoning process where proofs were cast into discourse.

Watts conducted his discussion of analysis and synthesis under the head of natural method, since in nature the "knowledge of things which follow depends in great Measure on the things which go before" (340–41). In other words, since the two varieties of natural method rely for their ordering principles on the relation of things in nature, they should be used whenever the object of discourse is discovery or instruction. Like many other logicians of the period, Watts was at a loss to expatiate at length on artificial method, which could not easily be submitted to a systematic exposition of its functioning. He recommended arbitrary method for works that appealed to the memory or that were aimed at producing persuasion or delight; thus it was suited to the composition of history and its associated forms, as well as to oratory and poetry. For these last genres, he advocated the use of the "cryptic" method, where the writer "hides" the method being used by means of a variety of artistic techniques (346–48).

Watts' treatment of analysis and synthesis differed from those of earlier writers in that he identified analysis as the movement from whole to part whether that whole is a species or an individual, while synthesis was the logical movement from part to whole and simple to general. But, he wrote, it was difficult to keep the two movements distinct in practice. Watts' list of rules for method as communication was similar to those found in earlier discussions of synthetic method, and he exemplified the movement of synthetic method with the traditional allusion to the study of grammar, which proceeded from part to whole by moving from letters to syllables to words to sentences to whole discourses (342).

Since Watts' discussion of his seven rules of presentation appears to have influenced nineteenth-century rhetoricians, I review them in some detail. According to the *Logick,* writers' method should first of all be "safe," that is, free from error. Four rules obtain here: care must be taken in laying down the proposition to be established; the relation of its terms must be carefully examined; the links of the chain of reasoning between propositions must be sound; and the writer should anticipate objections to the argument. Second, the method employed should be "plain and easy." Skill in this aspect of method had partly to do with the writer's habits; Watts encouraged care, caution, and the study of excellent models. To insure that their method of expression was plain and easy, writers should begin with the best known parts of the argument, include only a few heads, or subtopics, and be sure not to crowd too much into a sentence or paragraph. Observance of these two rules would insure that the writer had accurately represented the first two steps of her reasoning process—making judgments and forming propositions.

The next three rules covered the division or partition of the proposition, so that its parts would be both distinct from one another and fully covered. The rule of distinctiveness required that the subject of the investigation be unified rather than heterogeneous. Writers could secure distinctiveness by dividing complex ideas into more simple ones; by putting things in their proper places, that is, in the classes to which they belonged; and by observing the principle that different levels of generality ought to be kept separate from one another. Once the proposition was divided into its constituent parts, rules four and five mandated that care be taken to insure that these were fully enumerated but that the list of parts not be drawn to excess.

Watts' sixth and seventh rules of method were designed to assist writers in laying out the arguments that were to support each part of the proposition and to show their internal connections. Rule six insisted that writers choose a method appropriate to their subject, its design, and the occasion for which the discourse was composed. Rule seven posited that all parts of the discourse be connected. Writers could establish coherence by keeping their aim in view, by insuring that the mutual relations between arguments were apparent, and by acquainting themselves with the grammatical and logical means of transition available to them (349–65).

Watts' discussion of method combined rules drawn from several logical traditions—Aristotelian logic, propositional logic, and method—with a dash of rhetorical advice thrown in for good measure. The point to notice, however, is that method as presentation amounted to a theory of composition.[6]

Method continued to be an object of intellectual discussion well into the nineteenth century. Samuel Taylor Coleridge went so far as to establish a metaphysical ground for method in a series of essays written for *The Friend* published in 1818. Coleridge described method as a happy combination of unity and progression (4.1.476). Method always involved "a union of several things to a common end, either by disposition, as in the works of man; or by convergence, as in the operations and products of nature" (4.1.497). "Disposition" and "convergence" were Coleridge's terms for artistic and natural method, respectively. Unity was imposed on any methodical project by the establishment of an initiative, a term Coleridge apparently borrowed from Bacon. The "initiative" represented some leading thought or intention that brought "the most remote and diverse things into mental contiguity and succession" (4.1.455). Unity of intention insured and determined the results of method: "In all aggregates of construction, therefore, which we contemplate as whole, whether as integral parts or as a system, we assume an intention, as the initiative, of which the end is the correlative" (4.1.498). Thus method was purposive; its purpose was achieved by adhering to some plan or system that the thinker imposed on whatever material method was to act upon.

Coleridge advanced beyond the empiricism of Locke and Hume, however, in bestowing both natural and divine sanctions on method. He thought that the operations of the mind reflected those of nature and through it, divine law. The "creative IDEA" of the divine mind "not only appoints to each thing its position, but in that position, and in consequence of that position, gives it its qualities, yea, it gives its very existence, as *that particular* thing." When the human mind contemplates the world of things and their relations, "the whole is determined by a truth originated in the mind, and not abstracted or generalized from observation of parts" (4.1.459). In other words, minds could create generalizations from whole mental cloth; they were not fettered by experience, as empiricists supposed. When minds worked in this creative but methodical fashion, their procedure repeated the procedure of nature, and through this, that of the mind of God. Thus Coleridge reinforced the authority of method by observing that when thinkers followed its path, they were operating according to their natural inclinations, as God and nature intended them to do. Method had a metaphysical, even a theological, rightness; its use lent any investigation the sanction of natural—if not divine—authority.

In sum, the methodical mind first defined a single element for study in order to insure that the investigation had what Coleridge called "unity"; it then examined this unity to determine the number of its parts. Natural method then offered two ways of arranging the discussion of the parts of this elemental proposition: analytic or synthetic—from part to whole or from general to specific. The arrangement of discourse should be a reflective or retrospective recording of the inventive act, unless, of course, the writer or speaker were interested in engaging in one of two derivative processes: teaching an uninformed audience or displaying his discursive artistry. Advocates of method usually characterized synthetic method as less valuable than and secondary to analytic method, since the former was less original. The work of synthesis, gathering up and distributing what had previously been thought, was parasitic on some more primary work. (This set of notions secondarizes the act of teaching at the same time as it awards primacy to original research.)

Method offered its users the advantage of efficiency. As Gerald Bruns points out, Descartes' insight was that method could protect the mind from its own unpredictability: "Method rescues the mind from the contingency of invention by turning its history into a program (investing it, literally, with the power of writing itself down beforehand)" (88). Method gave the investigator control over both the progress of the investigation and the display of its results because of its linearity and its regular disposition of parts within space and time.[7] And, since method rendered all the dispersed parts of a whole accessible to the uninterrupted gaze of an interested observer, it lent her a certain control over nature as well. Method made the hidden visible.

Eighteenth-century rhetoricians certainly exploited the predictive aspect of method, using it to channel the flow of thought and discourse into a prescribed set of foreordained paths. They agreed with logicians that there were two kinds of method: either it followed the order of nature or was subjected to the artistic impulses of human beings. Natural method had two aspects, analysis and synthesis. Eighteenth-century rhetoricians never confused analysis and synthesis with two similar processes that had been delineated in Aristotle's logical and rhetorical systems—induction and deduction. Analysis and synthesis described the movements of minds as they conducted investigations and reported on them. Induction and deduction took place entirely in language and involved the appropriate placement of premises in relation to one another.

The new rhetoricians did disagree about which method was most appropriate to the composition of rhetorical discourse. Given his association of rhetorical reasoning with empirical evidence, George Campbell preferred analysis as a means both of inventing and arranging rhetorical discourse. Adam Smith and Joseph Priestley, on the other hand, preferred to confine analytic reasoning to the production of a new genre they called narrative or didactic discourse. Smith and Priestley associated more traditional means of reasoning, such as induction and deduction, with argumentative discourse.

Method as a Theory of Composition

George Campbell defined rhetorically effective proofs as those that repeated the process of acquiring knowledge. An accurate memory was crucial to the inquiry process, and as Campbell observed, "all the world knows . . . the utility of method for aiding the memory." Method could render such assistance to the memory because it connected "the parts [of a discourse] in such a manner as to give vicinity to things in the discourse which have an affinity; that is, resemblance, causality, or other relations in nature; and thus making their customary associations and resemblances, as in the former case, cooperate with their contiguity in duration or immediate succession in delivery" (77). In other words, the arrangement of a discourse should directly reflect the kinds and sequence of the processes that had created it: resemblance, contiguity, causation, and order in space or time. Such an arrangement would jog the memories of both rhetor and audience, since it would mirror the way ideas had been stored there in the first place. Memory was especially well served when the rhetor employed the orders of place or time. In fact, chronological order was "properly styled Method" in composition (77). Campbell wrote as though his picture of the mental landscape were like Salvador Dali's: objects retained in memory were strewn about there exactly as they had come into it from the world outside. They were apparently also better remembered if retained in the chronological order in which they had first been noticed.

In essence, then, the reflective combination of memory with method became a theory of composing in Campbell's rhetorical system. Invention consisted in the rhetor's retrospective review of her ideas and the connections made between them; arrangement consisted in composing a discourse where the ordering of parts exactly reflected whatever mental processes had been followed in reaching conclusions.

Thanks to his association of rhetorical reasoning with empirical investigation, Campbell designated analysis as the method that ought to be employed in rhetoric. With this procedure the thinker may "ascend from particulars to universals. . . . The analytic is the only method which we can follow, in the acquisition of natural knowledge, or whatever regards actual existences" (62). Any discourse that resulted from analysis would likewise be arranged so as to move from the particular to the universal. Campbell further recommended synthetic method for teaching, since it was "the shortest way of communicating the principles of a science." But even in teaching, "there is a necessity of recurring to the track in which the knowledge we would convey was first attained"; that is, the arrangement of synthetic discourse should also mimic the mind's movement as it surveyed the field of inquiry at hand.

Invention Within Genres

Because of their interest in method, the new rhetoricians turned away from the classical rhetorical approach that firmly separated invention from arrangement. Rather, they housed their accounts of invention and arrangement within their discussions of specific genres, and they did so for a number of reasons. First of all, their adoption of method obviated the need for separate attention to arrangement, since the method of arrangement would exactly mirror the method used during invention. Second, genre theory took on a new role in eighteenth-century discourse theory. In classical rhetoric, discursive genres had been discriminated according to the setting in which the discourse was to be used—law court, assembly, or ceremony. But in eighteenth-century discourse theory, a new way of discriminating genres developed; henceforth, a rhetor's choice of genre would be dictated by the intention she entertained for each rhetorical act. There would be as many genres, and as many inventional/dispositional schemes, as there were intentions. This obviated the need for a universal theory of arrangement. Third, they needed to devise a theory of invention for a new genre of discourse, one they called narrative or didactic, and for which classical topical theory and the Ciceronian parts of discourse were unsuited. Here again the two sides of method—investigation and presentation—would serve as a means of establishing theories of invention and arrangement that would be special to given genres.

George Campbell was the only one of the new rhetoricians who was explicit about the association of separate aims with distinct genres, although the connection was implicit in the rhetorical theories of Adam Smith and Joseph Priestley. Campbell did not go so far as to identify his "aims of eloquence" with specific genres of discourse, noting only that the appeal to the understanding was purest in mathematical demonstration, while the appeal to the passions was best exemplified in poetry and dramatic writing. He did discriminate two kinds of appeals to the understanding. The first sought to demonstrate some new point to a previously ignorant audience; Campbell called this "instruction." The second sort of appeal to the understanding was to be used with an informed audience when it was necessary to prove "some position disbelieved or doubted by them" (2). Thus, a speaker or writer who wished to appeal to his audience's faculty of understanding should aim either at instruction or conviction.

Campbell associated the other kinds of possible appeals—to the imagination, the passions, and the will—with varying levels of intensity, rather than with distinct genres. For example, an orator could employ figures in such a way as to astonish or delight her audience; but only when she intended to rouse their imaginative faculty in such a way that she "hurrie[d]" her listeners into "love, grief, pity, desire, aversion, fury or hatred" could she be said, strictly speaking, to be engaging in "pathetic" discourse. Campbell was of course quite aware that he was setting up a novel system of classification and that his distinctions among the aims differed from those made in classical rhetoric, which he found wanting for a variety of reasons (4n.5).

Whether he intended this effect or not, Campbell's theory of aims transformed the function of discourse in a fundamental way. His location of the aims of eloquence within the mind of the rhetor served to isolate any speaker or writer, rather decisively, from her audience, to whose minds she had somehow to gain access. She could take comfort in the knowledge that their minds were quite similar to hers, of course, so that any appeal that seemed effective to her should be likewise effective on an audience. But the only link between her mind and theirs—between her intention and their response—was her discourse.

Thus Campbell's innovation focused attention on the shape of discourse to an extent never before necessary. In order to be received properly, any speech or essay would now be obligated, literally, to represent its rhetor's intention. Discourse would now be conceived as a record of its author's attempt to appeal to his hearers' or readers' mental faculties; it was the only bridge between their minds. If any discourse is a representation of an intention, that discourse ought to provide clues as to what that representation was. In other words, the movement of the rhetor's intention ought to be discernible in the shape of the speech or text itself. Further, since there are a variety of intentions, there ought to be classes of discourse that conform to these intentions.

The innovative genre theory developed by two new rhetoricians, Adam Smith and Joseph Priestley, lends credence to this analysis. Both divided the realm of discourse into two large classes: narrative or didactic discourse on the one hand, and argumentative discourse on the other. Both employed method as a means of inventing and arranging narrative discourse.

In an apparent anticipation of Campbell's later distinction between conviction and persuasion, Adam Smith argued that

> every discourse proposes either barely to relate some fact or to prove some proposition. The first is the kind of discourse called a narrative one; the latter is the foundation of two sorts of discourses, the didactic and the rhetorical. The former proposes to put before us the arguments on both sides of the question in their true light, giving each its proper degree of influence, and has it in view to persuade no further than the arguments themselves appear convincing. The rhetorical, again, endeavours by all means to persuade us, and for this purpose it magnifies all the arguments on one side, and diminishes or conceals those that might be brought on the side contrary to that which it is designed that we should favour. Persuasion, which is the primary design in the rhetorical, is but the secondary design in the didactic. It endeavours to persuade us only so far as the strength of the argument is convincing: instruction is the main end. For the other, persuasion is the main design, and instruction is considered only so far as it is subservient to persuasion, and no further. (58)

Although Smith did not make the rhetor's aims the centerpiece of his rhetorical theory, as Campbell did, his remarks in this passage establish that he, too, divided up the realm of possible discourses according to what speakers or writers might intend.[8] The inevitable text-centeredness of this system is apparent in Smith's elimination of any reference to rhetors; it is now discourses that aim to instruct, convince, or persuade. Another innovation appeared in Smith's isolation of didactic discourse as a separate genre.[9] Howell remarks in this context that while "it was not the object of the eighteenth-century to deny the importance of persuasive discourse," its theorists "did feel that the times required an art of impartial exposition to cope with the problem of delivering the new science to the world of scholarship" ("John Locke" 328). Smith and Priestley both rose to this challenge.

Smith's candidate for the appropriate approach to the composition of didactic discourse was synthetic method, which was to be used where "the design of the writer is to lay down a proposition and prove this by the different arguments that lead to that conclusion" (136). If there is only one proposition to be proven, the best method "is to lay down the proposition, and afterwards advance the several arguments that tend to prove it." He warned that the subordinate propositions should never number above five; he preferred that there be only three such propositions since "this number is much more easily comprehended, and appears more complete than two or four" (136–37). Smith apparently chose synthetic method for use with didactic composition because of the traditional identification of synthesis with teaching; he remarked that it is appropriate both "where the design is to deliver a system of any science" as well as in those "as have in view the proof of a single proposition" (138). He ruled out natural method as a means of communicating the fruits of rhetorical or argumentative invention, a procedure to which artful method was better suited.

In this same lecture Smith recommended induction and deduction as methods for the invention of philosophic discourse, associating them with Newton and Aristotle respectively. Apparently he thought that induction was more suited to modern science, while he associated deduction with syllogistic logic. It is difficult to tell whether he intended the term *induction* to refer to a logical or an empirical process, although he displayed a preference for empirical induction. It gives us great pleasure, he said, to see phenomena "all united in one chain" (140).

Yet another innovation is to be found in Smith's creation of theories of composition that would be special to the new rhetorical genres of description and narration. According to Gerard Hauser, description assumed importance in eighteenth-century discourse theory because the new rhetoricians placed a fundamental trust in experience as the surest source of knowledge: "Upholding experience as the basis for belief and action committed its proponents to the proposition that human discourse builds on past sensations, memories, and understanding of circumstances akin to those of the present" (28). Effective description would represent visual, aural, olfactory, gustatory, or tactile experience as faithfully as possible, in the hope that listeners or readers would "respond emotionally and even physically to verbal symbols in a fashion analogous to their behavior in firsthand encounters with actual events" (29).

Smith advocated use of the "direct" method in descriptive composition, wherein the writer described "the several parts that constitute the quality we want to express," and the "indirect" method, which described instead "the effects this quality produces on those who behold it" (63). The indirect method was more artful, Smith thought, because it attempted to describe an internal series of events—an observer's reaction to an object—rather than "the external objects that are the objects of our senses" (64). In descriptive discourse, then, rhetorical effectiveness was to be achieved by stimulating the audience to recreate memories of their own experiences, whether this was done by evoking a picture from the external world or by causing them to remember their reaction to a vivid scene.

Faithfulness to experience was to hold as firmly for narrative discourse as it did for descriptive. The difference was that in narrative authors were to represent events exactly as they had taken place in time, while in description they were to represent objects exactly as they appeared in space. As Smith said, the method of narrative dictated that the order of events be followed, since "the mind naturally conceives that the facts happened in the order they are related, and when they are by this means suited to our natural conception, the notion we form of them is by that means rendered more distinct" (93). He recommended that the order of place be called upon for handling two or more narrative threads, but he noted that neither the order of time nor place ought to supercede that of cause and effect in narrative discourse (93).

Joseph Priestley's *Lectures on Oratory and Criticism* advanced a division of rhetorical genres that was even more innovative than Smith's. For Priestley, rhetoric contained only two genres—narration and argument—because rhetors could have only two objects in mind: "Either we propose simply to relate *facts,* with a view to communicate information, as in *History,* natural or civil, *Travels,* etc. or we lay down some *proposition,* and endeavor to prove or explain it" (6). He looked to method as the means of arranging arguments in both sorts of discourse. Priestley argued that narrative discourse should be ordered in such a way that its progress imitated the most natural associations of ideas made by human minds (35). Consequently, he recommended that authors of narrative discourses follow the order of nature, observing "the order of *time* for *events*, and that of *place*, for the subjects of what is called *natural history*" (34). Didactic composition was also a species of narrative, and for this genre Priestley recommended that writers look to "the nature of the thing," which would direct them how "to divide the subject into its proper distinct parts" (41); that is, the locus of invention and arrangement for this genre were to be found in study of the natural ordering inherent in the subject itself.

Priestley recommended analytic method for the composition of argumentative discourse. He argued that since analysis reflected the natural movement of minds, discourses which represented the typical movement of analysis would perforce present truth. He defined analysis as a tool for the generation of knowledge, "for it is only by comparing a number of particular observations which are self-evident, that we perceive any analogy in effects, which leads us to apprehend an uniformity in their cause, in the knowledge of which all science consists" (42). Synthesis, as the easier approach, was useful in teaching, since "it is easier to show how one general principle comprehends the particulars comprized under it, than to trace all those particulars to one that comprehends them all" (43).

However, analysis might be adopted as a means of communicating the fruits of scientific investigation, Priestley thought. One would merely have to represent the steps involved in the original investigation: "The analytic method of communicating any truth is, properly speaking, nothing more than a copy of the method of its investigation" (56). Priestley did not mean, of course, that every "abortive notion" that entered into the inquiry should be included when its results were being communicated, unless "in consequence of considerable stress having been previously laid upon them, it be requisite to show that such stress was unreasonable" (56). In cases where the investigation was entirely novel, he preferred a method that would approximate mathematical demonstration as closely as possible, letting "the probability grow stronger by degrees" as the writer or speaker systematically excluded competing hypotheses, saving the crucial one for last (57).

Method as a Principle of Arrangement

Method supplanted classical notions about arrangement in eighteenth-century discourse theory, at least insofar as the canon of arrangement included Ciceronian lore concerning the parts of discourse and their relations. Cicero had posited that orations could have as many as six parts, arranged as follows: an exordium, which introduced the case and aroused interest in it; narration, which gave the history of the case to be argued; a partition, which divided the case into its constituent arguments; confirmation and refutation, where arguments for and against the case were presented; and a peroration, in which the orator summed up, aroused pity for her client and indignation at her opponent (*On Invention* 2.20–109). In their least dogmatic formulations, classical dicta about arrangement were rhetorical in focus. By this I mean that classical rhetoricians always considered the relation of their audiences to the discourse being composed. Their inclusion or exclusion of introductions, narrations, partitions, and the rest depended on how thoroughly their audience was acquainted with the case at hand as well as upon their supposed predisposition toward it.

In modern discourse theory, however, arrangement evolved into a rule-governed, text-bound procedure. The rules were not affected by the relationship of a potential audience either to the rhetor or to his subject. All potential members of a modern rhetor's audience were thought to identify with him in the very profound sense that since all were human, all thought alike. In addition, all thinkers processed the information given them by the world in similar ways. Thus, for narrative discourses, for example, arrangement could now be located in the ordering of the facts of the matter, whether these be drawn from history, science, or the arts of grammar or logic. This ordering would naturally reflect the orderly way in which all minds gained information—all persons who investigated the facts would inevitably be drawn to consider similar ideas about them, in a similar order. The rhetor's discourse would save an audience the trouble of pursuing the investigation themselves, since it exactly reflected not only what she found out, but the process by which she came to know it as well. The need to persuade did not present a serious obstacle, then, since the representational force of the discourse would itself be persuasive—audiences would say to themselves, in effect, "Why of course! That's exactly how it is!"

In the case of argumentative discourse, modern rhetoricians firmly tied their preferred arrangements to the movements of the minds that formulated and organized propositions into series. Argumentative discourse would simply represent the mind's placement of propositions in relation to one another. Again, listeners or readers would necessarily be convinced by the naturalness of the logic revealed in the rhetor's discourse.

Among the major treatises produced by the new rhetoricians, Hugh Blair's enormously popular *Lectures on Rhetoric* is relatively conservative, in the sense that it relies more heavily on classical sources than does the work of Campbell, Priestley, or Smith. Nor is it as innovative or as rigorous as these others. Blair was a popular teacher whose eclectic mind put to use whatever rhetorical or logical materials seemed useful to his students.

Because of his eclecticism, Blair's lectures often demonstrated interesting blends of classical and modern thought. For example, in the midst of a Ciceronean treatment of arrangement, he used Cartesian language to recommend that rhetors make a clear and distinct statement of the proposition and its division when "laying down the method of the Discourse" (2.385). Of course Cicero also gave directions for dividing a proposition, but he had derived these from a popular version of Aristotelian logic, which worked in terms of genus and species. Blair's rules for the partition, on the other hand, were similar to those found in Watts and other writers on method: (1) the parts into which the subject is divided should be distinct from one another; that is, there should be no overlap; (2) the division must follow the order of nature; that is, it should proceed from the simple to the complex; (3) the parts of the division ought to exhaust the subject; (4) the terms of the division should be expressed as concisely as possible; and (5) the number of parts should be kept small—no more than three to five or six for sermons (2:389–90). Rules three, four, and five could, conceivably, be attributed to Cicero, but rule one—which required clarity and distinction—and rule two—which required that rhetors be rigorously attuned to nature's habits—betrayed themselves as modern notions.

Blair commented at length on other uses of method. Unlike Smith and Priestley, who worked out elaborate methodical progressions to use in the composition of specific genres, Blair simply recommended method for the composition of all forms of oral discourse: "In all kinds of Public Speaking, nothing is of greater consequence than a proper and clear method." Blair agreed with Campbell that method was an aid to memory, as well as a help in planning. He wrote that "no discourse, of any length, should be without method; that is, every thing should be found in its proper place" (2:237).

Both synthesis and analysis could be used as methods of arrangement, depending on the relation of the audience to the discourse. The analytic was appropriate "when the hearers are much prejudiced against any truth, and by imperceptible steps must be led to conviction," while the synthetic was "most suited to the train of Popular Speaking . . . when the point to be proved is fairly laid down, and one Argument after another is made to bear upon it, till the hearers be fully convinced."

Blair associated analysis with the "hidden method" wherein the "Orator conceals his intention concerning the point he is to prove, till he has gradually brought his hearers to the designed conclusion" that steals upon them "as the natural consequence of a chain of propositions" (2:402–3).

The Methodical Memory Examined

Eighteenth-century discourse theorists utilized contemporary psychological distinctions to authorize the creation of an introspective theory of invention, a theory which located the inventional process squarely within the minds of individual rhetors. Their combined subscription to empirical and rational accounts of mind led these rhetoricians to develop theories of evidence that were consonant with current theories of mind. They also borrowed from logical method to rationalize a new set of generic distinctions that could include scientific discourse, a relatively new phenomenon. They devised a new genre theory based on the notion of aims or intentions, and they developed methodical procedures for carrying out each of these aims. The mirrored appearance of these procedures, graphically displayed within a discourse, would signal the kind of intention the rhetor had desired to embed within it.

These are impressive achievements. Nevertheless, I maintain that an introspective theory of invention is not very useful to writers or speakers. It offers no help to the rhetor who has not already figured out what she wants to accomplish, although she can use methodical tactics in order to make a retrospective evaluation of the logical soundness of her investigation. But a more serious objection can be raised against the introspective theory of invention developed by the British new rhetoricians in that it contains an inherent contradiction. Even though it placed responsibility for the quality of invention squarely in an individual author's mind, introspective invention was never a paean to Romantic notions about individual creativity or originality. Rather, it insisted that the quality of any discourse could be measured by its adherence to a rigorous set of standards derived from psychology and logic. All reasonable persons were expected to be capable of uttering the "natural" forms taken by this discourse, regardless of the fact that on an empirical model of the mind, each person was regarded as having different experiences that might, conceivably, endow her mind with fairly idiosyncratic contents.

The new rhetoric also contained a number of potentially reductive attitudes toward the production of discourse. Among these were the privileging of scientific or logical models of the thought process and the concomitant privileging of original research over its presentation. But the crucial move made by modern discourse theorists was their centering of invention in the minds of individual authors. The reductive potential of this move was not immediately apparent in eighteenth-century discourse theory, which included a variety of rhetorical intentions and permitted selection from an array of genres in which to embody that intention.

Their emphasis on science and logic later led rhetoricians to limit both the possible number of intentions a writer could bring to a rhetorical situation as well as the number of discursive options potentially available to her. Current-traditional rhetoricians eventually concentrated their advice about invention on a single model borrowed from synthetic method and confined the rhetor's selection of genre to didactic discourse, which they called exposition. They further assumed that the inventional process used to create expository discourse could be exactly represented in texts, which were then expected to graphically display the synthetic movement from general to specific. Thus, the expository theme emerged as a sort of ideal text, a standard to which the performance of every writer could be held. Failure to meet this standard would be immediately demonstrable by certain lacks or aberrations in any text.

Even had nineteenth-century rhetoricians not made these reductive moves, one might still object to their basing writing pedagogy on an introspective theory of invention. The pedagogical difficulty is this: on an introspective model, if students' efforts do not meet certain discursive standards, such failures can be laid directly at the door of some mental inadequacy—some lack of experience, failure of memory, or inability to make the required connections between ideas. Quite simply, an author-centered theory of invention holds the quality of an author's mind solely to account for the quality of his discursive inventions. Since language is assumed to be a docile reflection of thought, muddled discourse must be attributed to muddled thinking. No account can be taken of the fact that language sometimes fails—or refuses—to represent an author's intention with accuracy or clarity. Nor can account be taken of exigencies that enhance or interfere with the quality of a discursive production—factors such as ethical, social, or political constraints on what can be said to certain audiences in certain situations, for example.

That methical and associational pictures of the mind at work were themselves historical inventions was soon forgotten by the pedagogues who adapted eighteenth-century discourse theory to their own needs. Rather, these pictures metamorphosed into a set of intellectual prescriptions that were assumed to be natural to all minds. Students were supposed to have natural access to methodical thinking; if they didn't have it, they were encouraged to develop it through practice. And if they still didn't have it, this lack would be demonstrated in the discourse they produced, discourse whose nonadherence to the ideal would bring their teachers to despair of the students' academic success. But the introspective theory of invention associated with the new rhetoric put young writers at a special disadvantage. Since few young people know enough about the world to write authoritatively about it, the quality of their inventions inevitably suffered. This was especially obvious when these were compared, as they often were, to the work of professional writers. Throughout the life of introspective invention in writing classrooms, teachers variously characterized students who could not rise to its challenge as inept, poorly prepared, lazy, or simply recalcitrant. It occurred to only a few teachers that a process they characterized as natural was a highly schematized historical invention whose use was nevertheless prescribed to writers as the natural way to go about composing.

My objections to the methodical memory would be of interest only to historians of rhetoric, then, if it were not that rhetorical theories influence the teaching of composition, just as they did when Aristotle lectured on rhetoric in the Lyceum or when George Campbell discussed drafts of his *Philosophy of Rhetoric* with a circle of scholarly friends in Aberdeen. Countless classical teachers of composition adapted Aristotle's *Rhetoric,* especially the parts about arrangement and style, for use in their classrooms. And countless modern teachers of composition, beginning perhaps with Hugh Blair, adapted Campbell's rhetorical theory to their own classroom needs.

4 Subjects and Objects: Logical and Psychological Models of Invention in Early Current-Traditional Rhetoric

Institutionalized composition instruction in American colleges has been carried on under a number of disciplinary umbrellas. During the eighteenth century, the classical texts of Cicero and Quintilian were commonly resorted to as sources of advice about effective composing. Twentieth-century teachers of composition relied on neoromantic organicism and Deweyan expressionism, among other things, as grounds for their pedagogical practice. Composition teachers have also appropriated findings from allied fields into their instruction; these fields include literary theory, linguistics, general semantics, communications, and cognitive psychology. However, none of these tactics has ever shaken the dominance over American composition instruction exerted by the theory of discourse now known as current-traditional rhetoric.

Current-traditional rhetoric is a direct descendant of the work of the British new rhetoricians. During the greater part of the nineteenth century, their texts constituted a fundamental part of rhetorical instruction in American colleges.[1] George Campbell's *Philosophy of Rhetoric* and Hugh Blair's *Lectures on Rhetoric* were very popular in rhetoric curricula during the latter years of the eighteenth century and the first half of the nineteenth century, although Cicero, Quintilian, and other classical rhetoricians also appeared on many college reading lists. Blair's *Lectures* were included in the curriculum at Yale in 1785 and were widely read in American colleges throughout the nineteenth century. Blair was apparently still in use at a few schools as late as 1890. Campbell's work never achieved the popularity of the *Lectures on Rhetoric*. The *Philosophy of Rhetoric* was apparently deemed appropriate for more advanced students

56

and was ordinarily read as a supplement to Blair. Nevertheless, it was in use at many American colleges throughout the second quarter of the nineteenth century, and it enjoyed some popularity as late as the 1880s.

Richard Whately's *Elements of Rhetoric* was included in rhetoric curricula almost immediately upon its American publication in 1832, and it dominated those curricula throughout the 1850s and 1860s, remaining in use in some schools until about 1900. Warren Guthrie notes that Blair, Campbell, and Whately were "the rhetorical names which almost every student in the nineteenth century colleges knew, and these were the men to dominate American rhetorical theory through 1850" (1948, 61). During the middle years of the century, Campbell's and Whately's texts were ritually buried once a year by junior students at Brown—a sound enough index of their status as curricular institutions.

But American teachers were not slow to see that they had an up-to-date rhetorical theory on hand in the new rhetoric. By 1855 a respectable number of American rhetoricians had appropriated British discourse theory into a series of textbooks that enjoyed success in school and college curricula.[2] Many of their title pages suggest that these texts were intended for private study as well. The authors of these works held varying degrees of respect for their British sources. Some, like Samuel Knox, simply borrowed material from a variety of British authors to compile his *Compendious System of Rhetoric* (originally published 1802). Other works, like John Rippingham's *Rules for English Composition* (originally published 1809), demonstrated their author's organizational preferences while retaining much material borrowed from British rhetorical and logical theory. And still others, like Samuel Newman's *Practical System of Rhetoric* (originally published 1827), while still relying on British sources, demonstrated a good deal of originality as well as points of disagreement with its British authorities.

But despite their derivative character, the first generation of nineteenth-century American rhetoric textbooks represented serious attempts to adapt the principles of British discourse theory into a form suitable for young or inexperienced writers. And although they differ from one another in format, these books are remarkable for their similarities, which might be traced to their influence on one another, as well as to their reliance on Blair and Campbell. Nineteenth-century authors were not so nice about plagiarism as later authors came to be, and so their mutual influence can be surmised from their tendency to quote and paraphrase one another, as well as from the similarity of the discursive precepts they advanced and the practical advice they gave.[3]

Invention was alive and well in current-traditional textbooks written throughout most of the nineteenth century, although it came under fire near the end of that period. Early current-traditional rhetoricians modified the inventional epistemology they found in Campbell and others to suit the needs of their students. They also developed a universal model of the composing process out of eighteenth-century discourse theory, although their terminology and the procedures they recommended differed slightly depending on whether they drew on association psychology or logic.

In this chapter I lay out the philosophical underpinnings that were used to rationalize the current-traditional model of invention. In this I rely on the considerable assistance of a rhetorician named Samuel Newman, from whose *Practical System of Rhetoric* I quote extensively.[4] I also discuss some versions of the composing process recommended by early nineteenth-century textbooks.

An American Rationale for the Methodical Memory

Newman's very full discussion of invention included both a theoretical rationale and practical advice about composing. The *Practical System of Rhetoric* opened with an essay entitled "On Thought as the Foundation of Good Writing," which distilled eighteenth-century speculation about the relation of thought and discourse into a philosophy of composition.

Newman divided the requisite foundations for thought along faculty lines. Its most important aspect involved a writer's address to her readers' powers of understanding; writers appealed to this faculty in readers by sharpening their own reasoning powers. As a second prerequisite, Newman cautioned that writers must exercise and regulate the imagination by cultivating the power of taste.[5] Good taste was requisite for rhetoricians since they often were called on to address their readers' imaginations with the design of interesting or pleasing them. A third requirement, the power of style, was conferred when a writer had achieved skill in using language "for the accurate and perspicuous conveyance of the thought" (15). Thus the aspiring writer needed three capacities: strong powers of reasoning, good taste, and the ability to translate her thoughts into discourse.

Mere possession of the faculty of understanding would not suffice, however; its reasoning powers had to be developed by use and exercise. Mastery of the power of thinking well thus required four capacities in its turn: extensive knowledge, discipline of the mind, a habit of patient reflection, and able use of method. Later in his discussion Newman added a fifth capacity to this list: the power of amplification.

Newman defined knowledge to include both book learning and "an acquaintance with the events and opinions of the day" (16). The possession of a wide range of knowledge was important because things are stored in the mind as "objects of thought," and thought-objects are intimately connected with one another in the mind. Writers could not ponder their opinions about one such object without associating them with other thoughts as well. Persons who could demonstrate variety and connectedness among objects of thoughts marked themselves as capable writers. Thus the acquisition of knowledge was crucial to anyone "who would become a good writer." Such a person "must possess a rich fund of thoughts. The store-house of the mind must be well filled; and he must have that command over his treasures, which will enable him to bring forward, whenever the occasion may require, what has here been accumulated for future use. To make those acquisitions, is not the work of a month, nor of a year" (16–17). The image of the mind as a storehouse filled with treasures would reappear in the current-traditional literature. On a psychological model of invention, of course, the stuff invention works on is taken in from the outside world or from books and is stored in memory until called for. Without such a mental storehouse, invention is impossible.

Aside from a store of knowledge, writers who would strengthen their reasoning powers must possess discipline of mind. The good writer "must be able to examine subjects, and pursue a connected train of thought with power and correctness. . . . A man may have invention, memory and imagination, but if he cannot reason accurately and with power, he will not interest and inform his readers, and thus acquire the reputation of a good writer" (17). No matter what natural capacities writers bring to the process of thinking, these must be put to use. It did no good to be naturally original or creative if the reasoning faculty were not constantly put to work making associations between ideas. His inclusion of this requirement demonstrated Newman's subscription to a popular pedagogy known as mental discipline.[6] This pedagogy, which derived from faculty and association psychology, assumed that minds were like muscles whose faculties could be strengthened by exercise. Practice in making those connections between ideas literally empowered the reasoning faculty. Thus Newman recommended that the student immerse himself in the study of "metaphysical and moral reasonings, and to toil in the wearisome study of the long and intricate solutions of mathematical principles," all of which would "fit him to distinguish himself as an able writer" (18).

Writers must also develop a habit of patient reflection. Newman

worried that students were not in the habit of reflecting on the workings
of their own minds. He wrote that "the attention of most minds is so
much engrossed with the objects and occurrences around them, that
there is little inclination or ability to look in upon their own thoughts
and trace out their connexions and relations" (19). Of course the "inclination" to examine the "connexions and relations" of one's own thoughts
lies at the heart of introspective invention. Newman was explicit about
this: "He who writes for the instruction of others . . . offers to them the
results of his own investigations and reflections."

So far, the message of Newman's text to young readers was no doubt
clear: if you want to be a writer who is worthy of being read, you must
garner all the knowledge you can, continually exercise your mental
faculties on it, and reflect upon the operations of your mind as you do
so. The first level of this inventional scheme, then, mandated a sort of
general intellectual preparedness on the writer's part. To this point,
Newman's analysis of the prerequisites for invention illustrates one of
the central difficulties posed to young writers by an introspective model
of invention. Students were expected to bring a good deal of general
knowledge with them to the composition class. The theory assumed
further that they would have reflected on this knowledge in such a way
as to have made coherence of it and that they would be in the habit of
thinking about their own thinking processes. From the students' point
of view, it must have seemed as though Professor Newman expected
them to carry a great deal of mental baggage along with their other
luggage when they arrived at the gates of Bowdoin.

The fourth prerequisite for success as a writer was attainment of "the
power of methodically arranging . . . thoughts" (21). Possession of the
power of method made the difference between the associational process
used by the ordinary person on the street and that used by persons
who thought "in a more philosophical manner." Newman justified this
difference in quality by noting that "the thoughts in their passage through
the mind, are connected together by certain principles or laws of association." In the nonmethodical mind, "one thought introduces another,
because it has happened to be joined with it, having before been brought
to view in the same place, or at the same time." The person who is
possessed of a methodical mind, however,

> looks at the causes and consequences of whatever passes under
> his observation. When his attention is turned to any subject,
> there is some leading inquiry in view, and the different trains
> of thought which pass through his mind, are seen in their

bearing on this leading object. As a necessary result, he has clear and connected views of whatever subject he examines, and is prepared to place before the minds of others, the conclusions to which he has arrived, with the reasonings by which they are supported. (21)

Method carries the double advantage of serving as an aid to invention as well as arrangement. But most important, it brings order out of potential mental chaos by strictly limiting the mind's connective activity to consideration of some one "leading object."

Newman could easily have found the notion of the leading inquiry in the methodical literature. The publication of Coleridge's essays on method preceded that of the *Practical System of Rhetoric* by about eight years, and Watts' logic text was widely known. But method was part of the intellectual equipment carried about by most educated persons during the early years of the nineteenth century, thanks to its use in logic courses. Newman could also have derived the "leading object" by drawing an analogy with propositional logic, where thinkers were to begin by laying down some proposition that limited the field to be investigated. Whately, whose *Elements* was contemporary with the *Practical System of Rhetoric,* also insisted that if the main proposition were not laid down in the author's mind clearly and in suitable form, the writer would enter on "too wide a field of discussion" (37).

Newman offered two suggestions for attaining the power of method, "or as it is sometimes termed, of looking a subject into shape." Students could study the work of writers "who are accustomed to think with order and precision," paraphrasing the propositions and arguments used into their own language (21). They could also compose plans, "the right division of a composition and the arrangement of its several parts," for their own work as well as for that of others (22).

The final characteristic of the good writer was the power of amplification, which Newman defined as "the power of enlarging upon the positions and opinions advanced." Amplification was important to readers' understanding and reception of a writer's proposition; she had to "exhibit [it] more fully" and "support it by argument" if she wished to "enforce it upon the consideration and observance of others" (22). Amplification was not aimed at persuading readers to accept the proposition; it was only necessary to amplify the proposition in enough detail so that readers could grasp the reasons for the writer's support of it.

Newman's remarks on thought provide a theoretical underpinning for the inventional model that would be put forward not only by him but by other current-traditional authors. Few would provide as careful a philosophical context as he did, however. In general terms, this model consisted of three distinct stages. In the first stage writers gathered a store of knowledge. The second stage of invention involved three steps: first, writers selected a notion or a subject; second, they formulated a proposition about it; third, they divided the proposition into its constituent parts. The last step of this stage was called analysis of the proposition. In the final stage of invention, called amplification, writers elaborated on each of the parts of the proposition. But not all early current-traditional writers agreed about either the terminology or the conceptual structure that underlay this model.

The Subject-Object Model of Invention

Most early current-traditional authors preferred a model of invention explicitly drawn from associationism. Invention was a mental process that began when writers made connections between ideas. In turn, ideas were generated either from experience or from reading. Adherence to this introspective procedure would provide writers with an accurate picture of the part of the world under investigation. This move, which confined invention to exploration of some aspect of writers' accumulated experience of the world, marked a stark contrast to classical inventional theory, in which speakers and writers evaluated the worth of an argument not only in terms of its internal cogency and its suitability to a case, but with an eye toward its potential reception by an audience as well.

Newman's version of this composing process was clear and complete. He advised young writers, first of all, to search their memories and choose subjects with which they were familiar. He insisted further on unity of subject in a discourse. His rationale was that unity was a means of avoiding vagueness (this is reminiscent, of course, of Descartes' insistence on the achievement of a clear notion that would propel the investigation).

Newman then recommended an immediate statement of the proposition that would govern the progress of the discourse: "The first and leading object of attention in every composition of an argumentative kind, is to determine the precise point of inquiry—the proposition which is to be laid down and supported" (32).

His directions for dividing the proposition were borrowed directly from methodical directions for securing "distinctiveness": every division should have a direct and obvious bearing on the leading purpose of the writer; the different divisions should be distinct, one not including another; and the divisions should to a good degree exhaust the subject and, taken together, should present a whole.

Once a suitable division has been accomplished, "the writer now turns his attention to the formation of his plan; in other words, he determines in what order and connection his thought shall be presented" (34). Newman's comments on the plan indicate that he regarded it as a sort of intellectual layout of the details pertinent to each division of the discourse. However, the plan served only a heuristic purpose, insofar as it need not appear, as such, in the finished discourse: "A plan is a species of scaffolding to aid us in erecting the building. When the edifice is finished, we may let the scaffolding fall" (36).

As Newman described it, then, this inventional process had four steps. Writers were to choose a subject, state it in the form of a "leading inquiry" or proposition, analyze it—that is, break it down into its constituent parts—and form a plan whose major heads each represent one of the parts of the proposition.

Paradoxically, given the author-centeredness of their inventional theory, text writers who borrowed their model of the composing process from psychology located the available materials for invention outside writers' minds. If writers were to have ideas at all, they had to widen their acquaintance with the world as fully as possible. And since experience depended primarily on perception, advocates of this mode of invention offered their students goodly amounts of advice about strengthening their powers of observation.

In his *Aids to English Composition* (orginally published 1845), in fact, Richard Green Parker equated "learning to think" with "obtaining ideas" (iv).[7] In order to obtain ideas, he wrote, "it is necessary to cultivate habits of observation; to use the eyes not only in noticing entire objects, but also their different parts; to consider their qualities, uses, operations and effects; together with their relation to other things. The mind employed in such process acquires materials for its own operations, and thoughts and ideas arise as it were spontaneously" (91). On the model of the mind posited by association psychology, minds were empty vessels until they became filled with the information provided them by sensation. Because of this, wide and varied experience was crucial for anyone who would store up enough material to become a writer worth reading. This set of exhortations was often accompanied by intensive analysis of literary pieces that were held up as models of good writing. The combined effect on students' hopes for their easy acquisition of writing skills must have been a little daunting. They were told, in effect, that in time they would know enough to be good writers.

Every day pedagogues like Parker faced a group of young people whose knowledge, defined in associational terms, was quite limited. Thus they set about designing exercises that would force their students to look about them—would force them, in effect, to pay attention to the world and to the experiences it delivered up to their senses. The first exercise in *Aids to English Composition* asked students to enumerate the parts of visible objects, such as houses; in the second, they were to enumerate the qualities and uses of objects; and, in the third, their parts, qualities, properties, uses, and appendages.[8] These exercises were Parker's gesture toward supplying students with ideas about which they could write.

Parker seems to have identified the associational notion of an idea with the logical term *theme*. In any case, he divided themes into two classes, the simple and the complex. Simple themes could be expressed by a single term ("logic," "education," "The Fall of the Roman Empire"), while complex themes "comprehended such propositions as admit of proof or illustration" (203–4). Some of his examples of complex themes were "Logic is a useful study" and "A public is preferable to a private education" (204).

Subjects took on a life of their own in current-traditional composition theory. In his *Advanced Course of Composition and Rhetoric* (originally published 1854), George Payn Quackenbos regarded invention as "the process of evolving thoughts in connection with any particular subject" (325).[9] Apparently subjects were mental representations of objects; that is, the objects in the natural world that submitted themselves to the gaze of the observer were represented in the perceiving mind in exact mental equivalents called subjects. Subjects were supposed to be as easily discriminable from one another as objects were, and they could be developed or covered as well. In keeping with the associational insistence that individual perceptions were housed in the mind as simple ideas and in keeping with the methodical insistence that any investigation should concern only one elemental notion, current-traditional authors insisted that any discourse be limited to only one subject. Hence a subject was a mental representation of some nonlinguistic plane of being, either the things of the world or some idea held in the rhetor's mind. For empirically oriented writers like Quackenbos, the subject was a discursive representation of some object in the physical world or of some area of study that a rhetor had cordoned off for investigation.

The first step in invention proper, then, was to select a subject (such as "houses" or "anger"). As soon as a student had selected a subject to investigate, according to Quackenbos, "the first thing required" was "thought,—careful, deliberate, concentrated thought." Further, this thought was to be original and well directed, "fixed on a definite object, and not allowed to wander from one thing to another." It also had to be "exhaustive thought, embracing the subject in all its relations." While Quackenbos' description of these two requirements was not very clear (or helpful), these two requirements obviously met the methodical prerequisites that any investigative project be marked by unity and complete division of the subject. The first requirement was met by establishing a proposition that displayed unity insofar as it concerned only one idea. The second was met by analyzing the proposition into its constituent parts or heads. Quackenbos called this process "analysis of the subject" and defined it as "a drawing out of the various heads which suggest themselves to the mind as appropriate to the theme of discourse" (*Advanced Course* 326). Only when the student had completed the process of analysis would Quackenbos permit her to embark on the construction of a plan.

Parker wrote that planning, or amplification, consisted in "methodizing, or arranging, a subject; laying it out, as it were, and forming a sort of plan on which to treat it." He thought that this was "one of the most difficult of the departments of composition." He likened the process of amplification to map making, wherein the writer ascertained the boundaries of her subject, "that is to say, the collateral subjects with which it is connected, its dependencies, influences, and prominent traits" (215).

Writers could amplify their discourses by applying analytic procedures such as contrast or repetition. These procedures would generate details with which to fill in each section of the plan. Ideally, the plan installed each member of the division as a separate head, which could then be amplified by any number of means. These early writers were eclectic in their choices of amplifying procedures. They borrowed some from classical rhetoric, some from associational relations, and others from analytic method. For example, Newman recommended definition, statement of particularities, and illustration as means of amplification, although he also included Campbellian versions of testimony and analogy as useful means of development. Parker recommended reason or argument, simile, example, and testimony as means of amplification, while Quackenbos liked definition and illustration.

The empirical approach to subject selection spread the province of invention across two quite separate realms. There was, on the one hand, the world "out there," the world of experience that provided material for invention; there was, on the other hand, the mind "in here," the collection of mental powers that related sensory data to one another that, suitably rehearsed, provided subjects as well as ways of organizing or making sense of the mind's information about the world. Later current-traditional rhetoricians preferred this model of invention to a similar one, which other early text writers adapted from logic.

The Notion-Proposition Model of Invention

One or two early authors explicitly adapted the model of invention found in eighteenth-century logic textbooks for use in composition. As it was promulgated in their textbooks, this inventional process had three steps: selection of a term or notion, analysis of a proposition drawn from the term, and amplification of the parts of the proposition. In analysis of the proposition, the writer divided the proposition into its constituent parts. On this model of invention, which was not initially indebted to empiricism, rhetors needed no storehouse of knowledge drawn from experience. Rather, they began by joining terms together into grammatical sentences, or propositions, just as logicians did. In essence, anyone who could speak the language could perform this sort of invention.

John Rippingham made the indebtedness of this procedure to Watts' *Logick* quite clear when he divided his *Rules for English Composition* (originally published 1816) into three parts: perception, judgment, and argument, which were analogous to the three stages of the reasoning process delineated by Watts. Rippingham cited the *Logick* and paraphrased its inventional scheme as follows:

> Those who undertake to write upon any subject ought necessarily to understand it: they ought also to be able to appreciate whatever they mean to discuss—this is called perception. As soon as the subject is understood, an opinion is formed upon it, which is termed the judgement. The considerations which produce that judgment are designated arguments, and there is wanting only the method of arranging those arguments with perspicuity, to render complete the ability for moral discussion. (ix)

Here perception doesn't seem to have the empirical flavor that it carried in associationism. Rather, perception referred to thoughtful consideration of something the rhetor already knows. This school of logic assumed that thought took place as a process of forming propositions; these could in turn be exactly represented in grammatical sentences.

For Rippingham, the proper inventional procedure was to "define the subject proposed, form an opinion on it, and state the reasons on which that opinion was obtained." For example, if "temperance" were the subject chosen by a student, she would first define it: "Temperance is the restraint of passion" (17). She then would add a predicate to this definition in order to indicate her judgment about it. When cast into discourse, the judgment would result in a proposition suitable for analysis and amplification: "Temperance leads to happiness since it restrains passion." She would then need only to add a list of the reasons which supported her judgment and to develop and arrange these in some appropriate order. Her composition would then be complete.

The inventional scheme borrowed from logic was still popular in textbooks published during the 1850s and 1860s. Henry Coppee's *Elements of Rhetoric* (originally published 1859) favored an inventional scheme entailing the generation of a subject by means of elaborating a logical term (a "single object of apprehension expressed in language" such as "man," "house," "city") into a proposition ("a comparison of two terms, to see whether or not they agree or disagree," as in "John is a hero") (187).[10] If students succeeded in establishing propositions, they could then form arguments, which involved combining propositions with one another in order to deduce a third.

In the rationalist model of invention adapted from logic, an object represented a rhetor's aim, rather than a thing present in the physical world. In this version of the model, then, an object was equivalent to an aim, as in "Her object in this paper is to instruct." Coppee observed that every discourse should contain "but *one* prominent *subject, or theme*" that "will be in some sort dependent upon the *object* of the discourse, or, in other words, upon the *effects* which we design to produce by it" (186). He identified objects with the aims of discourse discriminated by Campbell (189). For Coppee, subjects were discursive representations of simple or complex ideas combined with representations of a writer's psychological aim or object. A subject, when combined with an object, formed a proposition.

In this version of introspective invention, the term *subject* was used in its grammatical-logical sense to name the subject term in a proposition. For logically oriented writers like Coppee, a subject was the headword in a grammatical sentence, rather than a reference to some prelinguistic idea. This distinction, while subtle, would have far-reaching effects on invention. The preference for an empirical definition of subject, as opposed to a rationalist one, opened the way to a theory of discourse that was increasingly rooted in the facts of the physical world.

Invention in the New Dispensation

This inventive scheme had at least three features that rendered it quite distinct from classical notions about invention. Aristotle had assumed that anyone faced with the need to invent arguments could draw on a series of topics or commonplaces that were, in an important sense, the property of all interested parties to the debate. In other words, the topics were available to all members of the community of language users— they were quite literally located in the participants' current or potential discourse. But eighteenth-century discourse theory displaced inventive potential out of communal discourse and relocated it within individual minds. Thus, for the early nineteenth-century rhetoricians who adopted the principles of the new rhetoric, the inventive process was almost wholly reliant on a writer's ability to perform a carefully prescribed set of mental gymnastics. Invention took place in an isolated mental region that was ideally prior to, and separate from, engagement with language. Thus any inadequacy in student discourse could be attributed to its author's mental incapacity or inattentiveness.

Second, invention should proceed apace in spite of any resistance that might be offered by a potentially refractory subject. In this inventional scheme subjects were curiously inert. All alike allowed themselves to be handled through the process of selection, definition, and division. In effect, this theory of discourse presumed an entropic leveling of the features of the natural world. All the world presented itself to any writer as a suitable subject, regardless of depth, complexity, or strangeness, and heedless of a given writer's disposition or education. The objects in a waiting world only required their transformation into subjects by the mind of a writer in order to be made to speak.

Last, the new dispensation regarding invention glossed over the differences that obtain among rhetorical situations. Early nineteenth-century text writers generally assumed that if the process of invention produced discursive fruits that accurately represented the movement of a writer's mind, the resulting discourse would necessarily represent itself clearly to readers' understanding since their minds moved in like fashion. As a result, students were not made to see that rhetorical situations are specific to given occasions and audiences; rather, they were encouraged to assume that a more or less universal inventional procedure could be applied to any subject for any audience on any occasion.

This argument is only implicit in early nineteenth-century accounts of invention. Some of these authors, like Newman, discuss hearers as people who possess passions and wills, but he assumes, as Blair and

Campbell had, that certain well-calculated sorts of appeals would influence all reasonable persons. Other authors were silent on the matter of readers' responses to their students' discourse. No doubt, this unwritten assumption—that all readers are reasonable people—marks out a point of entry for that ubiquitous military persona who stalks the pages of later composition textbooks—General Reader.

The text writers' silence about the role of readers in the construction of discourse marks one crucial site in the current-traditional landscape from which a rhetorical attitude toward composing had disappeared. Rather than rising to speak to the citizenry in a moment of crisis or disagreement, as classical rhetoricians had, modern students of composition would strive to compose texts that exactly represented nature and the movement of the minds who studied its workings.

5 Select, Narrow, and Amplify: Invention in Mature Current-Traditional Rhetoric

Throughout the nineteenth century and well into the twentieth, other teachers followed in the footsteps of Rippingham, Newman, and the others. The list of those who wrote current-traditional textbooks is impressive, not only because of its size but because some authors held impressive scholarly credentials, often in fields other than composition. These writers included Alexander Bain, Henry Noble Day, Fred Newton Scott, Gertrude Buck, George Lyman Kittredge, Charles Sears Baldwin, Henry Siedel Canby, Edith Rickert, Charles Manly, Norman Foerster, Cleanth Brooks, Robert Penn Warren, Rudolf Flesch, Paul Roberts, Richard Weaver, and Frederick Crews. Bain was a psychologist, Day an aesthetician. Kittredge was a Shakespeare scholar, Rickert and Manly were students of Chaucer, and Foerster was a student of American literature. Brooks is a critic, Warren a novelist and poet. Crews is also a critic. Canby was a historian. Buck, Scott, Baldwin, and Weaver were rhetoricians. Flesch was a reading theorist, Roberts a linguist. Hundreds of other current-traditional textbooks were written by scholars or teachers whose most enduring claim to fame lay in their participation in the major textbook tradition associated with American composition instruction.

Despite the scholarly credentials of some authors who wrote current-traditional textbooks, a good deal of evidence suggests that as current-traditional rhetoric matured, its writers gradually lost touch with the theory of discourse from which its model of invention had sprung. During the middle years of the nineteenth century, it was still possible to profess rhetoric in American colleges. Henry Day was familiar with classical and modern rhetoric and with the history of logic as well, as

70

were many textbook authors who were his contemporaries. Alexander Bain was conversant with associationism by virtue of his professional ties; his textbooks also demonstrate that he had read Campbell and Whately carefully.

By the late years of the nineteenth century, however, textbook authors relied on Bain, Day, and other current-traditional authors more consistently than they did on Campbell or Whately, although these two authors were cited well into the twentieth century. Nor did textbook authors draw on new developments in rhetoric, psychology, or logic, preferring instead to retain the textbook model of invention. By the early years of the twentieth century, only minor adjustments were being made to what had become, by that time, a fairly monolithic set of prescriptions for invention.

Most twentieth-century authors preferred to imitate the late nineteenth-century texts that historians now characterize as marking the high point of current-traditional thought. In 1905, Ashley Thorndike wrote in the preface of his *Elements of Rhetoric and Composition* that nearly all textbooks of rhetoric then in use were indebted to the works of those authors who have since been designated the "big four" of current-traditional thought: John Franklin Genung, Adams Sherman Hill, Barrett Wendell, or Fred Newton Scott and Joseph Villiers Denney.[1] And in *College Composition* (1929), Raymond Woodbury Pence noted that Genung's *Working Principles of Rhetoric* (1900), "although nearly thirty years old . . . remains the most complete and authoritative treatment of rhetoric we have" (xiv). Pence also cited Scott and Denney as authorities for his treatment of the paragraph. Wendell was cited as an authority by Mervin James Curl in a 1931 revision of his *Expository Writing* (1914) and by Cunningham and Cushwa in *Reading, Writing, and Thinking* (1943). Wendell's *English Composition* was itself reprinted in 1963.[2] And so on.

During the eighteenth century, as well as the early part of the nineteenth, professors of rhetoric and composition were, for the most part, either clergymen or gentlemen of leisure who were hired by the college president to pass on to their students the best that had been thought and said in Western culture. For example, the second occupant of the Boylston Chair of Rhetoric at Harvard was John Quincy Adams, who drew on his knowledge of classical texts, as well as on his participation in public affairs, as bases for his lectures on rhetoric. (Adams stepped down from the rhetoric chair to assume other duties).

But the gentleman professor disappeared along with the classical curriculum. After the Civil War, a new elective curriculum was gradually put into place in American universities, and the place of the universal scholar was taken over by the specialist, who had spent many years of study—often abroad—to learn his craft. This was true in every academic discipline except English composition, which developed no professoriat of its own. Rather, composition teachers (when they were professors) were recruited from a variety of backgrounds: Genung was a Baptist minister with a doctorate in literature; Hill a journalist with a degree in law; Cyrus Northrop at Yale was also a journalist; Wendell was a dilettante who studied law but did not pass the bar and who did his scholarly work in American literature.

Robert Connors describes the institutional situation surrounding the teaching of English composition at the turn of the twentieth century as follows:

> Bereft of a theoretical discipline and a professional tradition, teachers during this period had nothing to turn to for information about their subject—except their textbooks. After 1910, composition courses were increasingly staffed by graduate students and low-level instructors. Writing teachers became as a result the only college-level instructors who know no more of the discipline than is contained in the texts they assign their students—a sad pattern that still, alas, continues today at too many schools. ("Mechanical Correctness" 69)

In their heyday in the 1880s and 1890s, Hill's and Wendell's texts rivaled the popularity achieved by Whately during the days of his own vogue. As Connors remarks, the lore contained in Hill or Wendell was often the only information that writing teachers possessed about composition.[3] Thus it assumed a degree of authority entirely out of proportion with its intellectual respectability.

While textbooks have always played an important role in composition instruction, this role underwent an important change during the nineteenth century. I suspect that the use to which current-traditional textbooks were put by late nineteenth-century teachers differed a great deal from the use to which Whately had been put in earlier times by teachers who were knowledgeable about rhetoric and its history. The gulf between these two ways of reading textbooks might be expressed as the difference between reading the Bible as the infallible word of God and reading it as an admirable and useful literary work.

Rationalist Invention Breathes Its Last

The notion-proposition model of invention adapted from logic was alive and well in current-traditional texts written during the middle decades of the nineteenth century. It was employed by Coppee and Henry N. Day, as well as by the extremely influential Alexander Bain.

Day employed the propositional model derived from logic in his *Art of Discourse* (1867).[4] His students were first to select a "theme"; second they were to generate a proposition from the theme by adding a statement of their "object" to it. For example, "the immutability of truth" was a theme, rather than a proposition; but "the object of this discourse is to prove the immutability of truth" was an acceptable proposition, since it indicated the writer's aim (58). The next step in invention was to generate the "discussion," that is, "that part of a discourse in which the subject is unfolded" (*Art of Rhetoric* 46). The final step was to compose the "subsidiary" parts of the discourse, that is, the introduction and the conclusion.

Bain's description of his inventional procedure in his *English Composition and Rhetoric* (originally published 1866) is obscure, but it seems accurate to say that it contained the steps usually isolated by rhetoricians who employed propositional logic for this purpose.[5] However, he did give an empirical cast to the subject-object distinction when he remarked that "the feelings and the thoughts of the Mind" were "sometimes called the Subject World, as opposed to the Object or Extended World" (*English Composition: A Manual* 124).

In any case, Bain's students were first to develop a "notion" or general term, apparently by means of collecting related facts under some general heading (his examples were "roundness," "liquidity," "beauty," "poetry," "law") (*English Composition: A Manual* 150). Often, he noted, notions stood "in need of explanation," and for this process he recommended definition, which aimed at rendering the notion intelligible. Definition could proceed by means of listing instances (the method of particulars); indicating the quality opposed to, or excluded by, the one in question (the method of antithesis or contrast); or by dividing the notion into its constituent notions (the method of analysis). Simple notions, such as resistance, motion, line, form, quantity, and the like, were irreducible by analysis, but more complex notions, which were made up of combinations of simple notions, required analysis or enumeration of their parts. Bain exemplified complex notions with the term *circle,* which is defined by means of its constituent notions—plane figures, lines, equality of distance and points (*English Composition: A Manual* 152).

Students were then to incorporate the notion into a proposition, which was to be developed by attaching a predicate to it ("Heat expands bodies," "All matter gravitates," and "Exercise strengthens the body and the mind") (*English Composition: A Manual* 153). Bain noted that the proposition "alone amounts to knowledge." In other words, students had not gained knowledge of a thing until they had formed a proposition about it. The third step involved students in expounding the proposition (that is, in amplification), which they could accomplish by means of repetition, denying a counterproposition, and using examples or illustrations. Bain especially liked these last two methods of expansion when they entailed the use of simile or metaphor, since these devices softened "the rigours of scientific exposition by elements of more pervading human interest" (*English Composition: A Manual* 161). Bain gave no explicit instruction on how any of these steps were to be accomplished, beyond providing students with illustrative examples, usually borrowed from one or another of the sciences.

Bain was not alone in this reticence. No textbook authors gave students advice on how to find the divisions of a theme, nor did they offer much direction on how to draw out the means of amplifying divisions, aside from providing illustrative examples. Perhaps their silence in this regard stemmed from their confidence that these processes of division and amplification described the functioning of all reasonable minds at work, so that students who possessed capable minds would have no difficulty following their prescriptions for invention. In other words, instruction in these processes was superfluous.

To Invent or Not: That's the Question

Mid-nineteenth-century authors of current-traditional textbooks tended to be better acquainted with the history of rhetoric than was the generation who began to publish in the 1870s and 1880s. Because of their knowledge of classical rhetoric, some midcentury authors could worry that attention to invention was on the wane. In his *Elements of Rhetoric* (1850), for example, Henry Noble Day surmised that the current inapplicability of topical invention "to present modes of thought," as well as the "perversion and abuse of ancient systems in the schools of the middle ages" had brought invention into disrepute. But Day put his finger on yet another reason for the seeming disappearance of invention from modern rhetorical theory: "The art of invention . . . is more essentially modified than style by the particular department of oratory or the kinds of discourse to which it is applied" (33).

Day's observation held true for classical rhetoric to the extent that a rhetor's choice of commonplaces might be governed by the rhetorical situation in which he found himself—he could select from an array of judicial topics if he were about to face a courtroom, or he could choose from a variety of deliberative topics about the location of garrisons or the availability of finances if he were arguing policy before a legislative body. And, if a classical orator faced an uninformed audience, he felt somewhat freer to inject elaborate ornament into his discourse than he would when arguing before an experienced magistrate.

Day apparently meant something slightly different, and more distinctly modern, when he made his remark about the putative disappearance of invention from rhetoric. He referred to the modern assumption that the subject matter of a discourse should determine which composing process the rhetor would choose. In other words, since method as presentation was an exact reflection of method as invention, and since the method of invention chosen was dictated by the nature of the subject under investigation, the process of invention would differ from subject to subject. Day's assessment is borne out by the historical fact that at about this time authors of current-traditional textbooks began to devise separate inventional schemes for separate genres of discourse. So invention only seemed to have disappeared from the textbook scene. Actually, it was submerged within discussions of the major genres. Day himself may have provided an influential example in this direction.

Nonetheless Day argued that invention was crucial to rhetoric, since it "respects the soul and substance of discourse—the thought which is communicated." Nor did he have much patience with the argument made by some of his colleagues, that invention was too difficult for young students. Rather, he wrote, "it is in invention that the mind of the learner is most easily interested; most capable of sensible improvement. It is next to impossible to awaken a hearty interest in mere style independent of the thought; as the futile attempts to teach the art of composition as a mere thing of verbal expression has proved" (*Elements of Rhetoric* 34). He deplored the limitation of rhetoric to criticism and style, since the inclusion of invention saved rhetoric from "being degraded to a mere negative, critical system" (v).

But whether or not invention was indeed masquerading as a theory of composition within discussions of separate genres, as Day had suggested, some later nineteenth-century authors abandoned it altogether. Their texts can be called stylistic rhetorics with some justice. Usually they made a perfunctory acknowledgment of the traditional primacy of invention and then moved on to grammar and style.

For example, John S. Hart rationalized granting priority to style in his *Manual of Composition and Rhetoric* (1877) on the ground that invention was "the most difficult part of the subject, requiring no little maturity of mind." Style, on the other hand, had "many details of a simple and positive character, about which the judgement of pupils may be exercised, long before they can enter with profit upon the process of original thought required by Invention" (14). Hart belonged to that late-century group of textbook authors whose subscription to introspective notions about invention caused them to despair of teaching it to students who lacked natural intellectual ability. He remarked that invention was "not a thing to be taught. It is a part of one's native endowment, and of his general intellectual accumulations. . . . No amount of ingenuity or pumping will draw water from a well that is dry" (294).

Of course the author-centeredness of current-traditional rhetoric is the source of Hart's uneasiness about invention. When composition teachers accepted the eighteenth-century notion that rhetorical invention began in the mind, they were bound to accept the unspoken but necessary corollary that the quality of that invention depended on the quality of the mind that produced it. Midcentury authors who were still in touch with classical or eighteenth-century rhetoric and logic had simply adapted or adopted the inventional schemes they found in those traditions for use in their textbooks. And, since they were familiar with the logical-rationalist tradition, neither Bain nor Day struggled with the notion that writers needed some wherewithal or material to write about. In this tradition, writers had "terms" about which to write by virtue of their ability to form propositions.

But by the last quarter of the nineteenth century, some authors were at a loss to understand how modern discourse theory could entertain a theory of invention at all. Like Hart, they were convinced that invention was too difficult to teach, since young people either had the wherewithal or they didn't.

Or, like David J. Hill, they argued that since invention was located in whatever subject was being investigated, it wasn't part of the province of rhetoric at all. Hill excluded invention from both his theoretical *Science of Rhetoric* (1877) and his composition textbook *The Elements of Rhetoric and Composition* (originally published 1878) on the ground that invention was subject specific; that is, analysis of the subject of a discourse provided writers with "what to say" (*Elements of Rhetoric* 3–4). Indeed, "if it were otherwise, Rhetoric would be a universal science, and would have to lay down rules for the lawyer, the preacher, the lecturer, and even the scientific writer." Hill here identified himself as a modern, insofar as he assumed that knowledge is special to given disciplines.[6] His position was in direct contradiction to that taken by Aristotle, who asserted that rhetoric was a universal art of inquiry that could be applied in any sphere appropriate to it.

Elsewhere, Invention Prospers

The popular textbooks of John Franklin Genung constituted an influential late-century exception to the trend toward stylistic rhetoric.[7] Genung paid serious and sustained attention to invention. His discussion of it in *The Practical Elements of Rhetoric* (1885) occupied over 250 pages of text, more than was allotted to style.

Like his predecessors, Genung supposed that the inventive act had several discernible stages: finding material by thought or observation; testing, choosing, and rejecting material; and ordering the material so derived. Of these stages only the first, "what the writer finds, in his subject or in the world of thought . . . is incommunicable by teaching" (*Practical Elements of Rhetoric* 217). Genung elaborated this inventional procedure into six stages that grew out of the basic three; these included preparation, defining a theme, stating it, creating a title, planning, and amplification. But Genung was an anomaly among late-century current-traditional authors in giving detailed attention to invention.

The inventional procedure drawn from associationism and method might have gone the way of the theories of mind on which it was based as these lost favor among psychologists and logicians. However, the introspective model of invention hung on in current-traditional textbooks long after knowledgeable persons in psychology or logic subscribed to the theories that undergirded it.

In their relative ignorance of its historical origins, later current-traditional authors often huddled the three-stage model that had appeared in earlier rhetoric texts into two stages: selection of a subject and development of an outline. Some later authors insisted on one of two intermediate steps: selecting a title or narrowing the subject. Title selection may be a latent fragment of the second step in the earlier model, where writers were to identify an idea or a term on which to concentrate. If this is indeed the case, later current-traditional authors' occasional insertion of title selection into the process of invention constitutes evidence for the gradual shift of inventional focus away from inquiry and onto arrangement. Of course the idea that a title could be preselected for a discourse yet to be written is consonant with the current-traditional assumption that discourse is a representation of stuff that has already been forecast in thought.

Subject Selection

With the loss of associationist thought as a grounding for invention, the technical meaning of an idea as a unit of the thinking process made no sense. Nor were late-century rhetoricians any more in touch with the logical tradition that had insisted that writers begin the inventive process by selecting some term or notion to investigate. Late nineteenth-century text writers simply substituted the empirical notion of subject for ideas and notions; for them, the first step in invention always involved finding a subject to write about. Late-century text writers regularly insisted that this level of invention was beyond the province of instruction, although some were nonetheless willing to give young writers advice on how to go about achieving the state of mental preparedness that was necessary to good writing. A few began by discussing the necessity for the store-houses of writers' minds to be well stocked with the treasures of knowledge, just as Samuel Newman had. John S. Hart described this stage of the process as follows: "When one undertakes to discourse on any particular point, he must hunt up thought in regard to it; and these he will find, partly in his already acquired knowledge, and partly by special study for the occasion; and the more comprehensive is his general knowledge and education, the less of this special study will he have to make when finding materials for discourse." Writers could select "from this general storehouse the thoughts needed for any particular occasion" (293–94).

Other current-traditional discourse theorists subscribed to an empirical epistemology, wittingly or not. As a consequence, many urged their students to sharpen their powers of perception and to learn as much as possible about the world by means of observation and study. John Duncan Quackenbos (the son of George Payn Quackenbos) recommended in his *Practical Rhetoric* (1896) that students strengthen their powers of inference through meditation, reflection, and conversation but that they observe the world around them as well. In acts of reflection, Quackenbos wrote, "the mind turns back on its accumulated store of memory images, and sifts them for material appropriate to whatever is under consideration" (63). He preferred that a student rely on his personal experiences as a source of material, since "facts gathered by his own observation, bits of personal experience artistically woven together, are the most valuable, because the most original material" (67). He suggested that "questions that may naturally be asked regarding the subject open avenues to information, one thought suggesting another, until many related ideas are gathered" (63). Thus he recommended keeping a journal or a copybook as a means of cultivating the powers of observation.

However, the more typical late-century discussion of invention began with advice on how to select a subject. In fact, the matter of subject selection took up a good deal more space in late-century textbooks than it had previously. Apparently students found the process difficult and distasteful. John Scott Clark remarked in his *Practical Rhetoric* (originally published 1886) that "of all the tasks assigned to the average student . . . none has been the subject of so much complaint as that of English composition" (241). Clark attributed this widespread distaste to students' inability to light on a subject for composition that was at once narrow enough to be managed within a short discourse and within their range of interests and capabilities.

Nevertheless, the selection of a manageable subject was crucial in current-traditional invention. David J. Hill made its importance apparent in his *Elements of Rhetoric:* "It is impossible to write clearly unless one has a theme in mind on which the attention is steadily fixed. If there be no subject, words will be strung along loosely and to no purpose, confusion of thought will be evident, and the production will be useless." Here Hill equated the logical notion of theme with the psychological notion of a subject. Regardless of his own confusion, Hill was confident that confused discourse was the necessary (and useless) result of confused thinking. As remedy and safeguard against muddlement, he recommended that student writers ask questions about their subject "until something suggests itself" (6).

Genung, whose discourse theory was always eclectic, also used terminology from both the logical and psychological traditions of invention. Unlike Hill, however, he developed an explanation for his use of both. He determined that "the theme is the subject concentrated by means of directive limitations, upon a single issue, so that it shall contain one principle of division, one definite indication of treatment, one suggestion of scope and limits." In sum, then, the theme was "the whole subject turned in a certain determinate direction." A subject became a theme, in short, after it had undergone the methodical processes of definition and division. Genung illustrated the difference between a subject and a theme by borrowing a passage from one of John Henry Newman's lectures: "fortune" was a subject; but "fortune favors the bold" was a theme (*Practical Elements of Rhetoric* 250).

Narrowing the Subject

Once a writer had selected a subject, most textbook authors recommended that she narrow its scope. John Scott Clark conformed to the mainstream of late-century text writers when he simply substituted the process of narrowing down a theme for the older procedure of stating a proposition. His example of the narrowing process ran as follows: "The

Arts—The Fine Arts—the Growth of the Fine Arts—the Growth of the Fine Arts in America—the Growth of the Fine Arts in America since 1870" (243).

All writers of the period insisted that the scope of the discourse be kept within manageable limits, recommending that this be achieved by a clear statement of the theme or title of the discourse, along with persistent narrowing of the subject. Earlier writers' recommendation of division as the starting point for analysis of the proposition may have given rise to the late nineteenth-century preference for narrowing the field of inquiry—that is, for setting consecutively smaller limits on it— as a means of invention. A latent fragment of synthetic method may also linger on in this advice, which was directed at forcing students to become ever more specific as the invention of their discourse proceeded.

Analysis and Amplification

Early current-traditional rhetoricians had recommended that writers divide their chosen subject into its constituent parts. They called this analysis. Then each of the divisions of the subject was to be·amplified into a separate discussion. This was called amplification. But later writers in the tradition collapsed analysis and amplification into a single process called outlining. To put this another way, by 1890 or so the analytic technique of dividing the proposition into its constituent parts was taking on a graphic character. Analysis of the proposition had been transferred out of the generating mind and onto the page, where it joined amplification—the writer's graphic articulation of the joints of the discourse. Together, these processes melded into outlining.

Analysis is as old as the logical hills, of course. Ultimately, the procedure that modern logicians and rhetoricians called analysis of the proposition can be traced at least as far back as Plato's insistence in the *Phaedrus* that rhetoricians begin by defining and dividing the issue under discussion (265d–266b). The more immediate history of this double movement lay in Descartes' insistence that any inquiry be marked by clarity and distinction. Methodical logicians evolved procedures for insuring that these two prerequisites would be met in the statement of a proposition, and I have mentioned a number of these (see Blair's commentary on the process in chap. 3, for instance).

Modern composition theory was fairly consistent in assuming that minds worked by isolating wholes (that is, by achieving clarity) and dividing them into their constituent parts (thus achieving distinction). But Genung was almost alone among late nineteenth-century discourse theorists in making explicit the initial dependence of invention on clarity and distinction. Indeed, he stands out among late nineteenth-century text writers, and certainly among the big four (or five), by virtue of his regular provision of rationales for the discursive strictures he recommended to students.

Whether or not Genung was familiar with the literature on method, his account in the *Working Principles of Rhetoric* of the two directions taken by invention certainly resembled Coleridge's accounts of unity and progression. He wrote that invention worked in two opposite directions: concentrative, where "it thinks its material inward to one controlling comprehensive proposition," and distributive, which "thinks outward along the various lines and radiations of the thought" (420). He associated these two mental movements with the formulation of the theme and planning, respectively. And in the *Practical Elements of Rhetoric,* he argued that two procedures, "exposition intensive, or definition" and "exposition extensive, or division" governed the analysis of ideas "as to their depth or intension and their breadth or extension." The means of definition was logical (that is, it was drawn from scholastic logic), but it could be amplified by iteration, exemplification, and analogy. His treatment of the division, on the other hand, was governed by the rules of method: the division must be logically complete, correct, selective, and thorough (387–401).

Unlike Genung, many later current-traditional authors condensed their advice about the analysis and amplification of propositions into a single process in which analysis became the process of naming and listing the major divisions of a subject and amplification became a list of directions for developing each of the major divisions. In a further development, amplification of the constituent parts of the proposition became methods of development for paragraphs and essays. In both cases amplification also lost its inventional character and returned to the province of arrangement, from whence it had been briefly snatched by the intrusion of method into composition theory.

I suspect that this development had something to do with the assumption that the parts of a discourse and their relationships represented normal processes of thought. Mature current-traditional theory consistently moved in the direction of text-centeredness, confident that certain graphic features of a text would literally represent an author's intention. Thought itself was considered to move in discernible patterns that related wholes to their parts in a variety of ways.

A somewhat muddled expression of this congeries of assumptions appeared in J. B. Fletcher and G. R. Carpenter's *Introduction to Theme-*

Writing (1893) in connection with their discussion of exposition. They defined thinking as "the process of arranging our perceptions according to their different kinds" (96). This must refer to the process of analysis, specifically to that portion of it which divided and classified the parts of a notion or idea. If so, our authors here identified thinking with analysis. An expository discourse simply made the products of analysis—its classifications—manifest. Fletcher and Carpenter recommended that students engage in a number of mental processes as means of gathering material: definition (asking what a thing is), exclusion (asking what it is not), and analogy (asking what it is like). Here we see processes that had formerly been recommended as a means of analysis—that is, as inquiry procedures—now being touted as ways of finding material to write about.

Planning-Outlining

John Duncan Quackenbos' treatment of outlining suggests that the discursive outline was intended as a representation of a mental filing cabinet. In a section of his text significantly entitled "Importance of Analysis," Quackenbos observed that "when a specialist sits down to write a book . . . he mentally sees his subject in its logical entirety, and grasps the plan of presentation that will render it most intelligible and attractive to his group of readers" (74). A written outline, then, was a graphic representation of the categories contained in the memory. The discursive outline simply was a graphic representation of the processes of analysis and amplification. The workings of the methodical memory could now be put on display for all to see! That this was the case is established by Quackenbos' choice of associational principles as a means of determining the heads of an outline: "Having determined which of the many thoughts should first be presented to the reader's mind, [the writer] will next find one that is associated with it through the relation of cause and effect, or resemblance or contrast, of contiguity in time or place. This he will assign the second position in his skeleton, and so on" (72).

It is difficult to determine exactly when planning—an inquiry process—began to metamorphose into outlining—a graphic display of the writer's intention. In his *Outlines of Rhetoric* (originally published 1877), Joseph Henry Gilmore recommended a heuristic procedure for planning and amplification: write down answers to How shall I maintain or illustrate my proposition? as fast as possible; test the answers for truth, significance, and value; combine the surviving points; arrange these according to their mutual relation and relative importance (33).

Genung thought of outlines as aids to readers as well as writers. He also relied on "the laws of association" as means of "designing a practical aid to the reader's memory," although he recommended as well that the outline be characterized by "natural stages of progress": definition, development, and solution. In the *Working Principles of Rhetoric,* he defined the outline as "a list of the main thoughts drawn up in tabular form, and with the division so expressed and numbered that their relation to the theme and to each other is clearly determined" (433). With his usual good sense Genung cautioned that the outline should serve the writer as a tool for revision and should appear in the finished discourse only as a framework to aid the reader. Genung's discussion pointed up the potential for outlining itself to serve as an inventive procedure. Nonetheless even his influential example could not keep it from slipping into the province of arrangement in many textbooks composed near the century's end.

As late as 1911, Fred Newton Scott and Joseph Villiers Denney drew on the principles of association in their *New Composition-Rhetoric* to give directions for outlining, although they labeled their principles as logical rather than as psychological (441–43).[8] They recommended grouping the facts if they were contiguous in time or space, had the relation of contrast or antithesis, or were related to one another as cause and effect. They preferred this method of planning since it brought together topics that were "closely associated in thought" (29). Interestingly enough, Scott and Denney equated association with contiguity. This may indicate that they were using *association* in a general, nontechnical sense to refer to any relationship that exists between items that appear next to each other in space or time.

Outlining was given a real boost by the publication of Barrett Wendell's long-lived *English Composition* (originally published 1891), which hit on a way to display the heads of discourse in graphic array.[9] Wendell devised a system for organizing topic headings onto cards, which the writer then studied and sorted like "a hand at whist." A few minutes' shuffling of the cards, Wendell wrote, had "often revealed to me more than I should have learned by hours of unaided pondering." Wendell noted that, during thought, "ideas that really stand in the relation of proof to proposition frequently present themselves as co-ordinate," while "the same idea will sometimes phrase itself in two or three distinct ways, whose superficial differences for the moment conceal their identity; and more frequently still, the comparative strength and importances, and the mutual relations, of really distinct ideas will in the first act of composition curiously conceal themselves from the writer" (165). For

Wendell, then, outlines did not merely reflect thought—they could straighten it out as well.

Wendell's references to coordination and subordination indicate that the outline was descended from synthetic method, probably via Bain's principles governing paragraph development (see chap. 7). Martha Ball, the author of *Principles of Outlining* (1910) recommended outlining because it subordinated "everything else to precision and clearness in reproducing the framework of the thought which it sets forth." Ball commented that the difference between an outline and an "ordinary connected composition is practically the difference between a diagram which shows plainly how one part of the object represented is related to another, and a picture in which the various parts are subdued by a thousand enveloping details" (1). All of this is suffused with the methodical hope that thought can somehow be transferred into a graphic discursive display. And even though her sample outlines reflect the movement from general to specific usually associated with synthetic method, Ball aligned the process of outlining with analysis, which she identified as an aid to memory—just as George Campbell had done (3–4). By this time, it must be said, the term *analysis* was regularly associated with the process of division. Its eighteenth-century affiliation with associationism, where it had referred to a methodical process that repeated the connections made between ideas, simply disappeared from current-traditional thought.

In late current-traditional theory, outlining enjoyed a lively history on its own hook. Whole chapters of textbooks were devoted to it, and it developed a lore of its own. Generally twentieth-century text writers allowed that there were three sorts of outlines—topic, sentence, and analytical. The latter was to be developed according to methodical principles of division, which became thoroughly geometrized in the later tradition. According to one successful current-traditional textbook, the sections of an analytical outline were to be divided according to "one and only one principle"; the divisions "should be mutually exclusive" and "exhaustive"; that is, the "sum of the parts should equal the whole" (Espenshade, Gates, and Mallery 20). Except for its prescriptive tone, this account does not differ a great deal from Blair's commentary on the uses of method in dividing a proposition into its constituent parts.

Twentieth-century textbook authors agreed that the purpose of the outline was to forecast the argument of a discourse. But they were also fascinated with its etiquette (see fig. 2). They cautioned their readers to take care in numbering, indenting, punctuating, and composing headings. For example, the words *introduction* and *conclusion* were not

```
I.  ....................................................................
    A.  ..............................................................
        1.  ..........................................................
            a.  ......................................................
            b.  ......................................................
        2.  ..........................................................
            a.  ......................................................
            b.  ......................................................
    B.  ..............................................................
        1.  ..........................................................
            a.  ......................................................
            b.  ......................................................
        2.  ..........................................................
II.  ...................................................................
    A. etc.
```

Fig. 2. Outline Etiquette in Late Current-Traditional Textbooks (a "dummy form" sentence outline from Brooks and Warren 521– 22)

appropriate headings, nor were writers ever to make a division where only one part existed, so that an *A* would have to stand alone without a companion *B*.

When I study these mid-twentieth-century remnants of method, I am inevitably reminded of the relentless dichotomous divisions of which Peter Ramus was so fond. For example, Ramus partitioned Cicero's biography into "Life" and "Death." Of course, the second half of the division had no subheadings. One wonders if his current-traditional progeny would approve.

Muddled Models of Invention

In some late nineteenth-century current-traditional texts, the fairly distinct stages of invention that I discriminated above—selection and narrowing of a subject, analysis and amplification—got muddled together into a relatively inchoate process. This was the case in some of the most influential current-traditional textbooks ever composed.

In the preface to his *Principles of Rhetoric and Their Application* (1878), Adams Sherman Hill remarked that rhetoric "does not undertake to furnish a person with something to say."[10] Rather, it "shows how to convey from one mind to another the results of observation, discovery, or classification" (iv). His definition of rhetoric as an art of presentation placed Hill firmly in the camp of those who subscribed to a modern model of knowledge generation. It assumed that individual minds function in isolation from one another and that the knowledge they generate is derived either from empirical or logical investigation. The results of such investigations are then reflected in discourse. So much for invention.

As it was for David J. Hill, so it was for the infinitely more influential Adams Sherman Hill—since thought was prior to rhetoric, its province included arrangement and style alone. Adams Sherman Hill buttressed his position with an appeal to the authority of Coleridge, whose primary rule for a good style, according to Hill at least, was "not to attempt to express ourselves in language before we thoroughly know our own meaning" (*Principles of Rhetoric* iv). Hill limited the first half of the *Principles of Rhetoric,* "Composition in General," to the choice and arrangement of words, sentences, and paragraphs; the second half of the book dealt with the kinds of composition. Nor did he adopt the practice of giving attention to invention within the kinds. In the later *Foundations of Rhetoric* (1892), Hill limited the province of rhetoric to style, and a fairly narrow theory of style at that. He mandated that good writers aim at clarity of expression, syntactic correctness, and brevity (i).

In the *Principles of Rhetoric* Hill's fullest reference to invention appeared in the context of his discussion of exposition, where he wrote that "it is necessary to choose a subject which can be adequately treated within the prescribed limits, to frame the title in words that express or at least suggest the exact subject, and to make (either on paper or in the mind) a general plan of the whole. . . . [T]o secure clearness in detail, it is necessary to present each part distinctly" (310). Here Hill condensed invention into an exceedingly brief procedure that conflated and confused the stages of invention delineated by his predecessors. The choice of subject was now determined by a prescribed discursive length; the choice of a theme was now encapsulated in the choice of a title for the text; division and amplification had dwindled into the creation of a plan or an outline of the proposed contents of the discourse; clarity and distinction were secured by attention to the separate parts, rather than during analysis of the proposition. Hill's offhand description of a process that had formerly been treated as a series of distinct inventive stages was couched in language that suggested that invention was of little importance to composing.

Wendell recommended an extremely condensed model of invention to his readers simply because it was "what writers do." His comments on invention in *English Composition* retained echoes of the three-stage process recommended by his early nineteenth-century predecessors, although Wendell presented the steps as if they were matters of common sense. His pages assured writers that the process of invention worked like this: "An idea presents itself . . . in general form." Subsequently, the writer's "first task—and often his longest—is to plan his work: he decides how to begin, what course to follow, where to end. His next task is to fill out his plan; in other words, to compose, in accordance with the general outline in his mind, a series of words and sentences which shall so symbolize this outline that other minds than his can perceive it" (116). The writer's final task, Wendell wrote, was revision; yet this was to be done only on a small scale, given that "words and sentences are subjects of revision; paragraphs and whole compositions are subjects of prevision" (117). Here again, the outline acted as a forecast of a discourse yet to be written. Apparently, Wendell thought that the prior arrangement of parts was a fairly predictable process, while the process of getting words to represent mental entities was altogether less predictable. In any case, revision took place only at the sentence level, thanks to the forecasting wizardry of the outline.

The collapsed model of invention recommended by Hill and Wendell was also put forth by Scott and Denney, although they cited Ben Franklin as the source of their scheme for invention in both *Composition-Rhetoric, Designed for Use in Secondary Schools* (1897) and its first revision, *Composition-Literature* (1902). Franklin's role in this innovation was a popular bit of inventional folklore; Erastus Otis Haven and John Duncan Quackenbos also attributed the composing process they recommend to Franklin. In *Rhetoric: A Text-Book* (1873), Haven quoted a letter dated 2 November 1789 in which Franklin suggested that before writing on any subject, a writer should "spend some days in considering it, putting down at the same time, in short hints, every thought which occurs" to him. When the thoughts had all been collected, the writer was to determine which of them was "properest to be presented first to the mind of the reader, that he, being possessed of that, may be better disposed to receive what you intend for the second" and so on (327). That Franklin invented this model of invention is doubtful. However, text writers probably found it useful to appropriate his considerable authority to prop up their own commentary on invention.

Elsewhere, Scott and Denney adopted the position that the production of discourse was analogous to the growth of an organism.[11] In *Composition-Rhetoric* they used a metaphor from botany to describe the relation of paragraph to theme, which was that of seed to plant: paragraphs were embryonic themes. They were more explicit about this reference in a later edition of *Paragraph-Writing: A Rhetoric for Colleges* (originally published 1891) when they wrote that "organic structure" was characteristic of every work of art where "the design is apparent in all of the details." As far as discursive art was concerned this meant that "every sentence does its share of work toward making the meaning clear" (2).

Despite their avowed subscription to these other models of composing, Scott and Denney's commentary on invention is vaguely reminiscent of those found in the work of earlier, more self-conscious logicians. They posit that any writer begins with a "first vague conception" (*Composition-Literature* 49). This sounds a bit like Coppee's insistence that invention begins with a notion or theme. Subsequently,

> instead of beginning to write, he therefore begins to ponder, turning the idea over and over in his mind and looking at it from all sides and from various angles. As he does so the idea grows clearer. It separates into parts, and these parts again separate, until there are numerous divisions. As he continues to reflect, these divisions link themselves one to another to form natural groups, and these groups arrange themselves in an orderly way. In the end, if he thinks long enough and patiently enough, he finds that the first vague idea has grown into a symmetrical structure. (*Composition-Literature* 49–50)

However foggily, this progression reflects the inventive steps of making mental associations, formulating and dividing a notion, and amplifying it. But the really remarkable thing about this passage, as well as those from Hill and Wendell, is not their blurring of earlier distinctions; it is rather that, in their hands, invention has been transformed into a fairly unconscious and spontaneous mental activity. It is as if the writer's mind would naturally follow the procedure dictated by method if only she would relax and let it pursue its natural work.

The Paradigm Emerges

The procedure for invention that evolved in mature current-traditional thought proved remarkably stable during the twentieth century, although it was flexible enough to admit minor innovation. It could be reduced to only two steps—choosing a subject and making an outline—or it could be elaborated into as many as seven stages. In *A Manual of English Composition* (1907), John Hays Gardiner, George Lyman Kittredge, and Sarah Louise Arnold recommended selecting "a definite and manageable subject" that had both unity and coherence. They revived the logical advice that writers ought to formulate a proposition and state it clearly, although they called it "the key-sentence"; its functions were to render thoughts clear and compact and to help reduce a mass of topics to intelligible order (171). For aid in outlining, they borrowed a page from Wendell's text, recommending the use of cards on which the writer's notes could be recorded. Their subscription to a belief in mental representation was reflected in their commentary on outlining: "The various topics which you have noted, should correspond to the natural divisions of the subject"; for each division there should be "a group of related facts." Writers were to arrange topics in their natural order, number them, and find subtopics for each (168).

The continuity and stability of the multistage inventional process was exemplified by its continued presence in the many editions of a successful current-traditional text written by A. Howry Espenshade. Espenshade produced revisions of his *Essentials of English Composition and Rhetoric* (1904) at regular intervals throughout the first half of the twentieth century (later, when he collaborated with Gates and Mallery, the book was called simply *The Essentials of English Composition*). The inventive model recommended in a late edition of this textbook would have seemed familiar enough to Genung.

The 1945 edition of the *Essentials of English Composition* acknowledged that "the practical writer outside the classroom" had no difficulty in selecting a subject: "He already has something to write about; it is for this reason only that he wishes to write." Because he lacks a pressing rhetorical exigency, however, "the student of composition . . . who is writing in order to gain command of his pen, and to secure some degree of clearness, force, and ease" commonly faces "some difficulty" in choosing a subject (Espenshade, Gates, and Mallery 3). Thus the authors recommended that students find suitable subjects to write about before "entering upon a course in English composition"; the sources of such subject matter were reading and research, the students' observations, experience, opinions, convictions, impressions, and—somewhat surprisingly—their imaginations. Espenshade and his collaborators wrote that the "imagination is, or may become, a constant and unfailing source of good writing. Out of it have come the drama, the epic, the novel, in fact, all great literature, which has somehow made itself more real and permanent than life itself." But after this brief brush with literary excellence they immediately returned to more solid ground, putting imaginative writing firmly off limits to students. Since imaginative writing demanded "penetration, insight, control" the student writer who wished to cultivate his imaginative faculty "should found his imaginings upon the known" (6). Thus Espenshade and company banished student flights of fancy to the borderlands of composition; the heartland was more appropriately inhabited by the facts that constitute everyday knowledge.

Because of their novice status, students of composition were also to avoid the trite, obvious, or trivial. Such subjects were to be left to those who possess "talent of a high order" and who can "transmute common place material into literature" (Espenshade, Gates, and Mallery 10). Espenshade and his colleagues had minimal expectations for the discourse that students would produce. Given their subscription to the introspective theory of invention—which depends for its quality solely on the furniture that equips a writer's mind—these low expectations indirectly reflected a low estimate of students' capabilities. Not once did Espenshade (or any other current-traditional author) pin the blame for their low expectations on the inventional model they prescribed, probably because they assumed that it reflected the natural way of doing things.

After students had developed a fund of suitable subjects (outside of class), Espenshade recommended that the topic be restricted in order to avoid its being given too broad or general treatment. When students chose a title, they were not to make the mistake of assuming that it was an antecedent argument for the theme: "The title is not the real beginning; it should not be taken for granted in the opening sentence" (Espenshade, Gates, and Mallery 12).

So much for invention proper. The authors next devoted an entire chapter to outlining. They acknowledged that an outline may have generative power: "The very act of planning a composition will often suggest new and valuable material. It is frequently true that a writer knows only vaguely what his ideas on a subject are until, in his effort to plan his composition, he is obliged to take account of stock" (Espenshade, Gates and Mallery 15). In the planning stage writers were to ask themselves questions such as: What are the main ideas of this subject? What ideas are of coordinate rank and what clearly subordinate? What is the logical order of the divisions? How much assigned space should be given to each main topic?

Of even greater interest, given this text's publication date, the organization of the plan was to be governed by what can only be read as lingering fragments of associationist psychology: its divisions were to be arranged according to "(1) continuity in time or contiguity in place, (2) the relation of cause and effect, (3) similarity and contrast, (4) relative value" (20). Espenshade's treatments of amplification in exposition and argument were thoroughly conventional; in fact he chose a citation from Genung with which to open the chapter on exposition.

More or less elaborate versions of the multistaged inventional scheme appear in current-traditional textbooks written throughout the first eighty years of the twentieth century. Authors of the major handbooks published during the 1930s, 1940s, and 1950s relied on it, as did a host of others. So did Norman Foerster and J. M. Steadman, Jr., in *Writing and Thinking* (1931), Rudolf Flesch and A. H. Lass' *Way to Write* (originally published 1947), Cleanth Brooks and Robert Penn Warren's *Modern Rhetoric* (1949), and early editions of Frederick Crews' *Random House Handbook* (originally published 1974).

Flesch and Lass' text presents a typical example of midcentury manifestations of the model. They recommended making plans, listing, reading, making notes, and conversing as means of collecting ideas. Their readers were then to engage in three processes: "1. When you have collected your ideas, make a list of them. 2. Sort your ideas out in groups. Leave out those that don't belong. 3. Then put your ideas in order" (42). Here is Wendell's advice for outlining, sans the handy cards.

The robust good health of the select-narrow-amplify model continues into very-current-traditional textbooks. One important difference from their predecessors exists in works composed since 1975, however. Most have appropriated some of the techniques recommended by teachers who advocate process pedagogy—techniques such as freewriting, clustering, brainstorming, and the like.[12] But most text writers have randomly inserted these techniques into the select-narrow-amplify model. They most emphatically have not adopted the theory of composition that stimulated the development of process pedagogy and that suggests that thought may be a product of the writing process itself.

A good example of this adaptive strategy can be found in Winkler and McCuen's *Rhetoric Made Plain* (5th ed., 1988). Their subscription to current-traditional epistemology is announced in the opening sentence of their second chapter: "You begin a writing assignment by first thinking about it. You do the actual writing later." But, they admit, there is a preparatory stage that inserts itself between thinking and writing; they call this prewriting. The goals they set for prewriting come as no surprise to any student of current-traditional thought: "Ideally, you are after three goals in the pre-writing stage: to narrow the broad subject into a manageable topic; to compress the topic into a suitable controlling idea; and to word the controlling idea into a thesis that predicts, controls, and obligates" (22). Writers can figure out how to narrow their subjects by talking to themselves about it, freewriting, making a cluster diagram, or listing. And if they need help with amplification, there's a whole chapter devoted to outlining.

Even though their text is more thoroughly informed by the notion that textbooks ought to help students get through the writing process, Woodman and Adler preserve the mature current-traditional model of invention in an almost pure form in *The Writer's Choices with Handbook* (2d ed., 1988). Writers are to choose a subject, explore it by brainstorming, clustering, or using the classical topics or Kenneth Burke's dramatistic pentad, and limit it by establishing a purpose and developing a thesis. Subjects can be selected more easily if students use the library and keep a journal. Even more interesting, Woodman and Adler recommend that students first of all undertake an introspective tour of their memories. They treat the memory as a "filing cabinet," just as their current-traditional precursors had, and they use the same language to describe it: "All writers possess a storehouse of accumulated experience from which to dig out an appropriate subject" (27).

In their *Writing: A College Rhetoric* (2nd ed., 1988), Kirszner and Mandell begin by supposing that writers "may have any one of a variety of aims, or more than one aim, in mind" (3). We should not be surprised to find that the aims include conveying information and convincing or persuading, since these were among the aims discriminated by George Campbell. We might be surprised to discover, however, that Kirszner and Mandell include an assortment of other aims as well: writers may also intend to give pleasure, express personal feelings, evaluate, discover, affirm, or "analyze, explain, speculate, theorize, question, define, advise, change, influence, argue, suggest, classify, amuse, criticize, describe, discredit, motivate, recount, debunk, inspire, or satirize." There would seem, in short, to be nearly as many intentions as there are conceivable rhetorical situations. But, lest this plethora of potential aims intimidate students, the authors quickly assure their readers that "your primary purpose is generally to convey information" (4). We're back on solid current-traditional ground.

Kirszner and Mandell recommend a variety of techniques to help students move toward a thesis: freewriting, asking questions, keeping a journal, brainstorming, and the like. But there is a crucial new development here. Even though students are to engage in all of these heuristics as a means of finding a thesis, they are now encouraged not to narrow their topic, but to generate a multitude of material from which they can choose. Nevertheless, the thesis is still used to bring order out of this chaos, and it must be composed before actual writing begins (34).

The authors of this text also demonstrate their with-it-ness by acknowledging that the thesis statement may change during the composing process: "Remember that as you write you will constantly be changing and sharpening your thesis. It is entirely possible, then, that you could begin your essay with one thesis in mind and end up having said something else. If this happens, be sure to revise your essay so that it is consistent throughout and clearly supports the thesis you have decided on." Should any student be so bold as to ask, "Well then, what's the point of writing a thesis at all, if it changes all the time?," our authors are prepared with an answer: "As you proceed through the writing process, you will arrive at new insights about your material, and the final version of your thesis, and your paper, will be the better for it" (35). Unlike their earlier counterparts, they stop short of suggesting that writers who submit themselves to such discipline will also "be the better for it."

We've come a long way from Samuel Newman's advice about thought, but we haven't strayed altogether too far. Invention is still a matter of forecasting, of predicting, what will follow in writing. The forecast is drawn from an introspective review of what a writer remembers about what she knows and what she thinks about it. Composing occurs in a neat linear fashion that is precisely mirrored in an outline. Writing itself has become almost irrelevant, since it only fleshes out the material encapsulated in the outline.

Coda: Writing with an Aim, Ahem, Purpose

The first edition of one of the most popular current-traditional textbooks ever issued appeared in 1950. This was James McCrimmon's *Writing with a Purpose: A First Course in College Composition.*[13] McCrimmon's text, the ninth edition of which is dated 1988, is a primary piece of evidence for the continuity of current-traditional composition theory to the present time. The inventional procedure prescribed by the first edition of *Writing with a Purpose* nicely exemplified the paradigm espoused in late current-traditional thought. By 1950, it was to be used for the composition of discourse in any genre.

McCrimmon charged writers to choose a subject from their inventory of experience, narrow it into a topic, and state it clearly in a sentence. The discourse was to be developed by means of chronological, spatial, or analytical order. These orders derive respectively from narrative, descriptive, and analytic method—although as the last term is used here, it refers to a process of sucessive division into parts. To put this another way, by the time McCrimmon wrote the first edition of *Writing with a Purpose,* the inventive step formerly called analysis of the proposition had evolved into a choice between means of amplification. Analysis had been joined by means of amplification borrowed from two separate and distinct genres—narration and description (see chap. 6).

McCrimmon devoted an entire chapter to outlining, which aided in organizing reading, testing plans, and determining purpose. Outlining was helpful in this last regard since, "like the housewife who finds out how she wants her furniture arranged by moving it about the room," writers could save themselves "a good deal of trouble" if they could see, "without all this experimenting" how their material should be arranged (93). Here McCrimmon's advice is in keeping with the status of the outline in mid-twentieth-century current-traditional rhetoric: its composition precedes and predicts the composition of the discourse proper; in effect, it substitutes for the experiment of composing itself.

McCrimmon's governing thesis was that "the most useful approach to the problems of composition is through a serious concern with purpose. A clear grasp of his intention becomes the only criterion by which a writer can wisely choose between alternatives." He rightly noted that such choices "cannot be intelligently made apart from some frame of reference." The appropriate frame of reference chosen by McCrimmon, however, was neither audience nor rhetorical occasion. Rather, it was the author's purpose. McCrimmon expressed the hope that his approach would help students to develop control over their writing, and he hypothesized that "a concern with purpose, by subordinating types of writing to an analysis of the particular needs of particular assignments," would make the composition course something more than a series of hypostasized exercises (vii).

McCrimmon justified his choice on the ground that consciousness of purpose would enable students to exert control over their compositions.

> Except in an elementary sense, the notion of purpose is foreign to most students of freshman composition. They have had little experience in analyzing a writing problem or in thinking out what they want to do before they begin to write. . . . In short, they have not yet developed enough self-confidence to understand that within certain limits they are not only free, but have an obligation to make their own judgments about what forms and usages are appropriate to their particular needs (vii).

Whether this is a complaint about current-traditional pedagogy or about students' ineptitude is not altogether clear.

The irony posed by McCrimmon's supposedly revolutionary thesis was that modern thought about discourse had identified a writer's aim as the starting point of invention ever since Campbell published the *Philosophy of Rhetoric* in 1776. Thus McCrimmon's choice of purpose as the basis for his text, laudable as his own purposes may have been, nevertheless mired his work firmly within current-traditional thought and offered his readers no escape from the submissive composing posture that its strictures forced them to assume. The difficulty McCrimmon overlooked was, of course, that when classroom exercises in writing center on an author's purpose apart from her desire to communicate with some other human being, they are bound to be rudimentary and mechanical. Current-traditional pedagogy treats writers' purposes as though discourse can be generated in a rhetorical vacuum, isolated from the social or intellectual contexts that ordinarily guide writers' inventional choices.

Thus even though McCrimmon made an accurate diagnosis of the central difficulty of current-traditional writing instruction, he was unable to circumvent it. Current-traditional pedagogy removes writers' right to control their discourses, to choose whichever style, arrangement, or inventional procedure seems to them to suit the occasion. Instead, it displaces their authority onto a set of prescribed rules that strictly govern the inventional process; equally restrictive rules force writers to select from only a few mandated genres and prescribe the way that every discourse is to be arranged, down to the very order in which sentences are to follow one another.

In this chapter I have traced the gradual hardening of discursive arteries that characterized invention during what I call the mature period of current-traditional rhetoric—from about 1870 to about 1900. In the following two chapters, I trace the fortunes of the genre theory inherited from eighteenth-century discourse theorists and chart the mutation of arrangement into the methods of development. While I relied on early and mid-nineteenth-century texts for much of my discussion about the development of the current-traditional theory of invention, much of my evidence in the next two chapters will be drawn from late nineteenth- and twentieth-century current-traditional textbooks. The reason for this is the increasing text-centeredness of the tradition as it lapsed into old age.

6 EDNA Takes Over: The Modes of Discourse

The history of current-traditional invention can be read as a continuing transfer of inventive authority away from writers and onto texts. Eighteenth-century rhetoricians centered their inventional theory on the introspective mind of a sovereign self-aware author. They posited that authors had access to the contents and processes of their minds by means of a retrospective survey of their memories. But nineteenth-century text writers discovered that their students were not readily capable of engaging in reflective analyses of their thought processes. Early on, they provided students with exercises that would force them to engage in closer observation of their surroundings. Increasingly, however, text writers fell back on the assumption that the art of introspective analysis could not be taught. They expected students either to bring this art to the classroom or to develop it by means that were not susceptible of instruction. They told students to become more aware of their environment, to enhance their powers of observation, to keep notebooks.

What was susceptible of instruction, however, was the shape that discourse ought to assume if it were to represent a writer's introspective analysis. Eventually then, interest in the contours of a text itself superceded the introspective process as the focus of current-traditional instruction in invention. Teachers could see the texts that students produced; students' texts were the only available evidence that they were thinking straight. Thus their teachers concentrated attention on how a text ought to look when it reflected straight thinking.

Of course they had precedent for this in eighteenth-century rhetorical theory, where discourse had been assumed to represent the discovery

96

process. But as current-traditional pedagogy matured, its text writers lost interest in discovery altogether. What did interest them was arrangement. But arrangement is not quite the right word to describe their focus on texts; what they were interested in was the shape of a discourse—how its parts would be articulated and displayed on a page.

Samuel Newman and the Kinds

When Samuel Newman came to the portion of the composing process that classical rhetoricians would have called arrangement, he opened his remarks instead with a discussion of genre. There is precedent for Newman's association of arrangement with genre in eighteenth-century composition theory. For example, John Ogilvie's *Philosophical and Critical Observations on the Nature, Characters, and Various Species of Composition* (originally published 1774) has as its thesis that composition can be studied in two lights, first "as the result of a peculiar combination, and propensity of the faculties of the mind: in another, as an art, distinguished by particular characters, divided into various species" (1.1–2). Ogilvie proposed "to point out the spheres of the intellectual powers in this art, to mark the signatures by which each is discriminated." In other words, an author's intention could be signified or marked by the structural features of her text. Ogilvie carried out his program by discussing the role of each of the mental faculties in several species of composition: philosophical essays, scientific writing, poetry, criticism, and so on.

But early nineteenth-century rhetoricians' concern with genre ultimately stemmed from George Campbell's discrimination of the ends of eloquence into four (or five) categories, depending on a speaker's or writer's intention. In later current-traditional theory, however, Campbell's association of the aims with rhetorical intent was lost, and his intentional categories would instead be identified with a set of generic distinctions.

Newman was apparently the first to associate a writer's aims explicitly with the genre of discourse that would result from her having a specific intention.[1] If one accepts a faculty model of the mind and if one subscribes to the notion that method represents mental movements in discourse, it is an easy leap to the supposition that a writer who wishes to appeal to one of the faculties, say, the passions, can first devise a formal strategy that is peculiarly suited to stimulating emotional responses and, further, that this strategy can be embodied in the finished text. In other words, a leap is made from a discourse classification based on an author's possible range of intentions (moving the will, stimulating the passions and so on) to a classification that assumes that there are sets of formal textual features that represent and distinguish kinds of aims from one another.

Newman named five genres, which he discriminated according to the "object, which the writer has primarily and in view," just as Campbell had done (28). Newman's "kinds of composition" were didactic discourse, which aimed at instruction (textbooks, for example); persuasive discourse, which influenced the will (sermons, legislative discourse); argumentative discourse, which was addressed to the reasoning powers; and narrative and descriptive discourse, which appealed to the imagination. Description stimulated the imagination, for example, because it placed "before the mind, for its contemplation, various objects and scenes" (28–29). Didactic writing was the kind of discourse whose aim in Campbell's scheme was called conviction. Newman's distinction between persuasive and argumentative discourse reflected Campbell's distinction between pathetic and persuasive discourse, given that in the former kind writers attempted to influence the wills of their hearers, while in the latter they addressed their readers' "reasoning faculties" by concentrating on "the statement of proofs, the assigning of causes" and the like (28).

Newman's identification of Campbell's aims with specific genres had two general effects on later composition theory. First, his innovation helped to switch the focus of invention away from rhetorical situations and onto genres. The primacy awarded to a rhetor's purpose in modern rhetoric lent an importance to generic distinctions that was absent from classical rhetoric. Ancient rhetoricians usually discriminated three genres of discourse; these were defined by the different rhetorical situations that obtained in courtrooms and assemblies or on ceremonial occasions. Rhetors could choose their inventive strategies from a separate list of topics designed for each of these situations, although some topics were common to all. However, the classical canons—invention, arrangement, and so on—were organized according to the sequence of steps that occurred in rhetorical inquiry, and ancient teachers recommended that these be followed regardless of the situation. In other words, in classical rhetoric the process of inquiry was separate from and prior to generic considerations.

As I demonstrated earlier, early current-traditional rhetoricians took pains to develop an inventional process that was distinct from, and more universal than, the processes delineated for separate genres. However, only a few midcentury rhetoricians clung to this practice. In later nineteenth-century discourse theory, the procedural aspect of composing was often confined within the generic constraints that were thought to be appropriate to certain intentions. Too, the initially universal three-stage composing process eventually became identified with a single genre: exposition. And in yet another reversal of its fortunes, the inventional process associated with exposition assumed something like the primacy earlier enjoyed by invention in general, since exposition was virtually the only genre that interested current-traditional rhetoricians. But by the turn of the twentieth century, its procedural character had nearly disappeared. Late current-traditional rhetoricians removed invention from the chronology of memory and relocated it within the spatial interstices of the outline.

The second general effect of Newman's identification of Campbell's aims with specific genres was that the number of discursive kinds approved for study was drastically reduced from the generic plethora that had been studied by eighteenth-century discourse theorists. Hugh Blair had considered the composition not only of oratory and sermons, but of history, philosophy, and poetry. Adam Smith commented on the composition of history, poetry, demonstrative and epideictic discourse, didactic composition (philosophy, scientific discourse, biography, and history), and oratory. Newman gave separate and brief attention to the writing of letters, essays, history, biography, fiction, argument, and oratory, in addition to the Campbellian genres mentioned above. Parker and George Payn Quackenbos were similarly eclectic with regard to genre. Two chapters of Quackenbos' *Advanced Course* were given over to prose composition and poetical composition. In the chapter on prose composition, Quackenbos identified the parts of composition as description, narration, argument, exposition, and "speculation" ("the expression of theoretical views not as yet verified by fact or practice") (354). He also listed six leading divisions of prose composition: letters, narratives, fiction, essays, theses or argumentative discourses, and orations. The first set of generic distinctions is derived from the new rhetoric, while the second includes remnants of older rhetorical theories.

Henry Day's work illustrates that genre theory was still a malleable field of discussion at midcentury. In the *Elements of Rhetoric* Day classified the kinds of discourse with his usual innovative verve. He divided the kinds according to the aspect of discursive situations that they chiefly emphasized—form, subject, or audience. This scheme yielded three major categories: poetry, which "represents for the sake of the form"; representative discourse, which "represents for the sake of the theme itself"; and Oratory, which "represents for the sake of the effect on an audience" (28). Day betrayed his allegiance to classical rhetoric when he announced that oratory was "the proper form of discourse in its strictest and fullest import," while all other forms were "abnormal" or "derived." "Derived forms" included "epistolary composition" and his new category of "representative discourse." These were derived forms because they dropped "the idea of a direct effect on another mind" (27). Despite this, Day's assumption that all discourse was representative placed him squarely within the tradition of the new rhetoric, which always regarded discourse as the reflection of an author's introspective tour of her memory.

But this is the last we hear of this unique classification in either of Day's major treatises on rhetoric. When he got down to the business of discussing specific genres, he preferred a Campbellian classification based on the "objects" of discourse—that is, on their aims or ends. The four genres thus discriminated bore Day's colorful terminology: they were "Explanation, Conviction, Excitation, and Persuasion" (42). Despite their new names, the four can be equated with Campbell's aims: explanation and conviction appealed to the understanding, while excitation agitated the feelings and persuasion moved the will.

Day's explicit commitment to faculty psychology would eventually be dropped from current-traditional textbooks; his four genres would remain. They got new names though, and these were given them when Alexander Bain's *English Composition and Rhetoric: A Manual* appeared on the current-traditional scene.

Bain Shapes Up

While Day clung to the notion that invention deserved separate attention, he also devised distinct inventional systems for each of his preferred genres. Bain, however, silently shifted his discussion of invention and arrangement into his discussion of the kinds of discourse. Nowhere did he devote separate attention to either invention or arrangement.

As Campbell had done, Bain derived his generic scheme from association psychology, but he gave the scheme a reductive twist. He insisted that the associational laws of thought were reflected in the principles of discourse. In other words, rather than simply tying certain aims to specific genres, as Newman and Day had done, Bain thought that these aims ought to be graphically manifested by the composer's choice of genre. Thus a reader of a discourse that displayed the generic features prescribed for exposition could simply assume that its author was appealing to her understanding.

Bain tried eclecticism. He melded the classical ends of discourse discriminated by Cicero—to inform, to persuade, and to please—with respective appeals to the mental faculties of the understanding, the will, and the feelings. Information appealed to the understanding, persuasion to the will, and pleasure to the passions. This blend yielded five categories of discourse corresponding to these three ends: exposition, description, and narration appealed to the understanding, while persuasion moved the will and poetry excited the passions. In fact, this scheme condensed the available discursive appeals discriminated by Campbell and Newman, insofar as it eliminated appeals to the imagination.

But Bain had only begun streamlining. He eliminated separate appeals to the will by positing that this faculty could be moved only through appeals to the understanding or the feelings—"hence, there are at bottom but two Rhetorical ends" (*English Composition: A Manual* 1). He associated invention solely with appeals to the understanding, and thus with three genres of discourse—exposition, narration, and description. He connected poetry to another canon altogether—style—by means of which it aroused the passions. Persuasion was left in the precarious position of straddling invention and style, since it appealed now to the understanding and now to the passions.

Persuasion was "the original subject of the Rhetorical art," Bain noted, but it presented "great difficulties to the teacher" because of its entanglement with logic (*English Composition: A Manual* vi). Poetry also demanded "a full share of attention, both on its own account, and also as supplementary to other departments, all which cherish, as a secondary aim, matters of interest to human feeling" (*English Composition: A Manual* vii). Bain borrowed from classical rhetoric, as well as from eighteenth-century discourse theory, for his discussions of persuasion and poetry.

Thanks to Bain's influential example, perhaps, current-traditional genre theory eventually coalesced into the familiar four-part division: exposition, description, narration, and argument—EDNA for short. Attention to poetry, oratory, and other genres such as history, biography, and letter writing continued throughout the nineteenth century in textbooks written by rhetoricians with classical training. But these genres eventually disappeared from mainstream current-traditional texts. The preference for exposition, narration, and description can be explained, of course, by their appeal to the reason rather than to the more ineffable faculties of the passions and the will. Argument probably hung on because it bore the authority of the classical tradition. In any case, many text writers discussed it in classical terms.

Expository Invention

Kitzhaber mentions Bain's claim that he invented the modes of discourse (191). That Bain invented the modes is doubtful. What he must be credited with, however, is a definitive and influential discussion of the genre he called exposition.[2]

Bain's rationales for exposition, narration, and description were very similar to those appearing in the lectures of Priestley and Smith. Unlike them, however, Bain eliminated historical and philosophical writing from the province of didactic discourse, limiting it to scientific writing. Of course, the association of didactic discourse with science was authorized in eighteenth-century discourse theory by Smith and Priestley, as well as by Campbell in his connection of rhetorical reasoning to empirical investigation.

Bain firmly identified exposition with science and logic. Since exposition was "the mode of handling applicable to knowledge or information" in the sciences and since "the property that alone gives value to anything called knowledge, or information" was that "it shall be true, or certain, Science is further characterized by the attribute of Generality or comprehensiveness." While Bain admitted that knowledge could consist of facts ("Rome was sacked by the Gauls"), generalizations were "at once the glory and difficulty of science" (*English Composition: A Manual* 147).

Bain's admiration for science stemmed from his faith that scientific method—which gathers isolated facts under an appropriate general head—mimics the movement of minds in discovering nature. But the advantage of science is that it rehearses this move in a very precise fashion. Bain thought that universal use of scientific method would produce universal knowledge. If "the pains, usual in science, had been expended in testing the truth of . . . the partially correct maxims" that were advanced outside of science, "we should have the whole reality" (*English Composition: A Manual* 148). In fact, human beings' inability to remain consistently logical was the only reason for the existence of other kinds of discourse. "To a mind perfectly rational," Bain wrote, "scientific or logical evidence is conviction; Logic and Rhetoric are the same" (*English Composition: A Manual* 187). That is to say, if all minds were reasonable ones, exposition would suffice as the mode in which discourse could be conducted, and persuasion would be unnecessary. Or, in yet other words, if all persons were perfectly reasonable, appeals to the will would be unnecessary, and the world could dispense with rhetoric altogether.

Bain adopted the proposition-analysis-amplification model of invention for exposition, and he chose his preferred means of analysis from propositional logic as well. He identified three means of analysis: definition, which classified objects according to some common property and applied a general name to them ("roundness," for example); induction, which noticed the "regular concurrence of two natural properties, disclosed by a comparison of particular concurrences" and expressed these in a "general Law, Proposition, or Affirmation"; and deduction, whereby a proposition resulted from the application of "a more general proposition already established" (*English Composition: A Manual* 148). His preferences among means of amplification were not generally adopted by later textbook authors, however.

In fact, the appropriate means to employ in the amplification of an expository proposition was a matter of some discussion throughout the last half of the nineteenth century. Day suggested that explanatory discourse could be developed by narration, description, analysis, exemplification, or comparison and contrast (*Elements of Rhetoric* 55). With the exception of narration, description, and analysis, these methods have counterparts in standard classical lists of the topics. For example, the list discussed by Quintilian in the *Institutes of Oratory* includes definition, division, similarities, consequences, causes, comparisons, and genus-species (5.10).

In his eclectic way, Day listed means of amplification for exposition that had historically been associated with method—narration, description, and analysis—along with those associated with the classical topics—exemplification, comparison, and contrast. Narration and description were to be used when perceived objects could be viewed as a whole. Since narration represented events as they occurred in time, it was to move either according to chronological sequence of events or, in more sophisticated discourse such as history, according to speculations about cause and effect. Description represented perceived objects in terms of their relations in space and was to begin with some prominent point and proceed to successive points (*Elements of Rhetoric* 58–60, 65–66). Analysis was to be used when an object was regarded as consisting of parts. Its means were partition and division, depending on whether the discriminated parts of the theme were considered as similar or were simply juxtaposed in time or space (*Elements of Rhetoric* 71–72). Exemplification, comparison, and contrast were appropriate when the object could be regarded as a class that represented a single species or through "its resemblance or opposition to others of the same class" (*Elements of Rhetoric* 55).

Precedent for the use of classical topics as a means of amplification occurred in seventeenth-century rhetorical manuals such as Thomas Hobbes' *Briefe of the Art of Rhetorique* (originally published 1637). Hugh Blair also mentioned comparison, illustration, cause-effect, and exemplification as means of explicating a text. Robert J. Connors quotes an interesting passage from Blair that associates the topics of classical invention with the *narratio,* or explication section of a secular speech, and opines that this "may well be a 'missing link' between the topics of classical invention . . . and the 'methods of exposition' " ("Aristotle to 1850" 202). However they got there, some of the methods of exposition may be the only relics of classical rhetoric to have made their way into late current-traditional lore.

These processes, whether borrowed from classical rhetoric or from method, had a checkered history once they found their way into current-traditional rhetoric. Early on, they were recommended as a means of amplification for any discursive proposition. However, after Day's example perhaps, they appeared in mature current-traditional texts as the exclusive province of exposition. Later still, after EDNA was rejected as a means of organizing textbooks, the methods of expository amplification identified by Day evolved into methods of development that were appropriate to composition in any genre. And, in very-current-traditional textbooks, they are relegated to the composition of paragraphs.

Scott and Denney may be indirectly responsible for this last development. They retained definition and division as "logical" principles of invention in *Paragraph-Writing.* However, they presented other processes of expository inquiry as organizational devices that could be employed in the composition of any paragraph, no matter what its generic affiliation. In other writers in the mature tradition the means of amplification could include methodical division (also called analysis or partition) and description, as well as classical exemplification, comparison and contrast, and, more rarely, analogy and antithesis. In late textbooks, the means of development became minigenres in their own right. Assignments often set students to composing such things as an essay of comparison or a paragraph of description.

Very-current-traditional texts have settled on a fairly standard list of the means of development that can be used to amplify any kind of discourse. As general means of development, these texts prefer description and narration, along with means of development that apparently evolved out of classical rhetoric: definition, cause and effect, classification, comparison and contrast, exemplification, and something variously called process or process analysis. In the latter method of development, students are to rehearse the steps involved in accomplishing some process, such as assembling a bicycle, in strict chronological order.

Process analysis may be descended from analytic method. It faithfully repeats the chronological order in which the stages of some process, located in the physical world, occurs. If it is descended from analytic method, it has been much reduced from its status there as a means of inquiry that reflected the mental connections that thinkers made between associated ideas. In mature current-traditional texts, analysis usually referred to the division of a proposition. Somewhere in the late tradition, analysis may have become confused with chronological order (descended from narrative method), since chronological, spatial, and analytical order were often listed there as means of dividing an outline into its constituent parts. Or process analysis may be the invention of some text writer whose work remains obscure to me. In any case, this method of development is consonant with current-traditional epistemology, insofar as it dictates that discourse is a perfect representation of events that occur in the physical world.

Narrative and Descriptive Invention

Narration and description readily assumed status as separate genres in mature current-traditional theory, although the methodical rationales that lent them this status had disappeared from its purview by the late nineteenth century. Bain's treatment of narration and description, like that of Smith and Priestley, was borrowed from method.[3] As Bain used it, the term *narration* signified a distinct category of discourse in which events were related in the order in which they occurred in nature or in history. Thus it differed from Priestley's use of the term to designate a larger category, also called didactic discourse, which Bain instead labeled *exposition*. Bain's use of narration was like that of Smith, who employed it to refer to the methodical technique of organizing events in their natural chronological order.

Bain echoed Priestley's advice that the method of narrative dictated that such discourse should follow the order of events as they occurred over time (*English Composition: A Manual* 130). He also gave advice on how to handle "concurring streams of events" by defining a principle action and subordinating others to it (*English Composition: A Manual* 133). The method of description, on the other hand, was "to include, with the Enumeration of the parts, a comprehensive statement, or general Plan, of the whole," which could be "furnished, in many instances, by the Form, or Outline" of the object to be described (*English Composition: A Manual* 118). Writers of description were to move from their general impression of the object to its particular parts, thus appealing to the natural associative powers of the mind that always followed the order of nature.

Later authors followed Bain's example. Typically, they defined narration as the category of discourse which presented "successive related events occurring in time," as Scott and Denney did in *Paragraph-Writing* (70). For some, its province included history, biography, and fiction. Other authors even provided advice on the selection of subjects and the collection of material for history writing. For example, Erastus Otis Haven suggested that students write the history of their town or school; he urged them to read "the history of some personage, take abundant notes, and then write out a sketch without once consulting the book during the writing" (324). Students were ordinarily cautioned to adhere to the order demanded by the chronology of events when composing narratives, unless some overriding concern suggested the use of some other ordering principle, such as cause and effect. As David J. Hill put it in *The Science of Rhetoric* (1877): "Events are not mere isolated links, but form part of an endless chain of antecedents and consequents, each of which is a cause of its consequent, and an effect of its antecedent. A narrator rises in dignity in proportion as he becomes a philosopher, and explains the events he narrates. This requires a constant reference to the actual sequence of events in time" (89). Many writers observed that narration was to follow the methodical principles of unity, selection, and completeness. Unity demanded that all parts of the narrative should be related to each other. Some writers, like Scott and Denney, suggested that this could be accomplished by the maintenance of a unifying point of view or culminating point that "is kept in view all the time and nothing is admitted which does not carry the narrative forward towards it" (*Paragraph-Writing* 72). Selection required that only details that were directly relevant to the point be included, while completeness insured that no necessary details were left out.

Description was ordinarily defined as the presentation of some object or, less often, some mental state or character, whether these be real or fictional. The composition of descriptions was to be governed by the end in view. As many text writers noted, description was often a smaller component of other genres, such as scientific writing or narrative. Many writers suggested that description ought to begin with some general impression made by the object, while others argued that objects should be described according to some logical order. *Logical* as used in this context usually implied division or classification (that is, analysis). For example, if a student wished to describe a tree, she should move from top to bottom, or she should classify its parts into trunk, branch, leaves, fruit, and so on.

The inventional procedures recommended for narration and description hung on in current-traditional textbooks long after EDNA had disappeared from them as an organizational device. In late current-traditional textbooks, they became means for development of paragraphs or whole essays; that is, they metamorphosed into principles of arrangement that were recommended indiscriminately for any discourse whatever. For example, in *The Complete Stylist and Handbook* (originally published 1966), Sheridan Baker recommended a hodgepodge of arrangements for the middle of discourses. These included the orders of space, time, and cause and effect, natural divisions, and inductive and deductive order. As might be expected, given their history, the orders of space and time were to supply an exact representation in discourse of the writer's movement through a piece of geography or some chronology of events. But Baker appealed not to history but to nature for a rationale for these operations. He wrote that "like space, time is a natural organizer, ancient and simple" (38).

Argumentative Invention

The tenacity of eighteenth-century theories of evidence in current-traditional textbooks is remarkable. Usually they were presented in connection with argumentative discourse. But since argument went out of vogue in mature and late current-traditional rhetoric, induction and deduction were appropriated for use in discussions of expository discourse and then adapted as means of development for all discourse. Argument has resurfaced as a genre deserving separate attention in very-current-traditional textbooks, and they divide their treatments of evidence between it and the inventional procedure they recommend for all discourse. Thus both rationalist and empiricist accounts of evidence continued to appear in textbooks published long after EDNA itself had gone out of favor as an organizational device and long after the work of the eighteenth-century theorists from whom these accounts were borrowed had faded into relative oblivion.

Bain included a lengthy discussion of argumentation in *English Composition: A Manual*. For him argument was that genre that was necessary to move unreasonable persons to action. His treatment was orthodox, borrowed as it was from Campbell, for the most part. Campbell's influence (or Bain's own interest in association psychology) was apparent in his definition of oratory as an aim-oriented art, while his discussions of persons addressed, appeals to the feelings, and demeanor of the speaker were all quite similar to Campbell's. For Bain, oratory operated in three spheres: the pulpit, the assembly, and the bar. Persuasion was affected when a speaker could assimilate "the object desired with the principles of action of those addressed," that is, when she could make her aim coincide with the wills of all members of her audience (223). Bain made one important departure from British discourse theory in order to yoke narration, description, and exposition into service as persuasive proofs, along with appeals to the feelings and some classical advice about argument.

Bain began his discussion of argumentation with the announcement that all evidence operated according to the associational principles of similarity or dissimilarity, since the arts of persuasion aimed either at "strengthening or loosening the bonds that cement ideas in the mind" (*English Composition: A Manual* 186). Despite this rather eccentric innovation, his list of the kinds of evidence would have been familiar to readers of Whately, although Bain abandoned the nice conceptual distinction between logical or rational processes of reasoning (called intuitive by Campbell and a priori by Whately) and its more empirical companions (see fig. 3). Bain discussed analogy, mathematical probability, induction and deduction as though all were roughly equivalent as means of proof. Like Campbell's, his discussions of analogy and chance were grounded in association psychology rather than in logic. He argued, for instance, that the rhetorical plausibility of analogical arguments resided in their containing "the foundation circumstances of all reasoning, a resemblance of particulars" (*English Composition: A Manual* 191).

When he came to the persuasive use of deduction and induction, however, Bain shifted his commentary from psychological to logical grounds. The weight of deductive evidence lay in its formal validity, since deductive arguments "imply the thing to be proved" (*English Composition: A Manual* 188). Although Bain's meaning here is not entirely clear, it seems likely that he is referring to Whately's principle that a priori arguments simply assume the truth of the major premise. If so, Bain adopted a rationalist basis for his treatment of deduction.

While both Campbell and Whately had discussed several means of reasoning from particulars, neither used the term *induction* to apply to all of its forms. Bain, however, gave a systematic treatment of induction. He was assisted in this by the publication of John Stuart Mill's *System*

Campbell (1776)	Whately (1828)	Bain (1865)	Adams Sherman Hill (1878)
Intuitive			
Intelligence			
Consciousness			
Common sense			
Deductive	A Priori	Deduction	Antecedent Probability
Demonstrative			
Moral	Non-A Priori		
	Example		Example
experience	experience	Induction	
analogy	analogy	Analogy	analogy
	contraries		
	real/invented		real/invented
	Sign		Sign
testimony	testimony		testimony
	fact/opinion		fact/opinion
			authorities
	progressive argument		progressive argument
probability		Probability	

McCrimmon (1980)	Baker (1981)	Winkler and McCuen (1988)
Types of Premises		
Fact/Judgement		Facts
Expert Testimony	Testimony	Witnesses/Authorities
Types of Inferences		
generalization	Examples	Experience
analogy	Analogy	
causal relation		
	Probability	

Fig. 3. Parallels in Modern Treatments of Evidence

of Logic in 1843. Mill's *System of Logic* discriminated five inductive methods, which, he maintained, described the way in which causal relationships were discovered and demonstrated (in other words, Whately's a priori evidence was actually derived inductively!). Mill insisted further that his methods were fundamentally important in scientific investigation. As a result, Bain was able to ally even logical induction with empirical investigation. He provided his readers with brief descriptions of four of Mill's methods—agreement, difference, residues, and concomitant variation—although he made no suggestions about how to employ the methods in the invention of discourse. Nor did he discuss their appropriate rhetorical uses. He did, however, make the questionable observation that Mill's Method of Concomitant Variations was the same mode of reasoning that Whately had designated "progressive argument."

Bain's sophisticated discussion of argument—even though laced with his own eccentricities—relied on classical rhetoric, as well as on contemporary logic. Despite this influential example, argument became gradu-

ally less important as current-traditional rhetoric matured, partly because
of its presumed difficulty. But of all the genres included in EDNA,
argument is the least amenable to the epistemology that undergirds
current-traditional rhetoric. For one thing, it requires rhetors to think
about the needs and desires of audiences; for another, it relies on nonem-
pirical forms of evidence for the most part. To put this another way, it
is difficult to treat argument as though it were representative discourse.
Nevertheless, it maintained a marginal hold on mature and late current-
traditional textbooks, and the methods of development associated with
it hung on here and there as well. The treatments of argumentative
evidence that appear in mature and late current-traditional textbooks
are illuminating, insofar as they display their authors' attempts to fit
argumentation into a conceptual structure designed to explain the workings of more methodical kinds of discourse.

While Adams Sherman Hill adopted some aspects of Whately's discussion of evidence for his *Principles of Rhetoric,* he made one very
important departure. As Campbell had done, he limited rhetorical evidence to empirical means of investigation. But he used Whately's no-
menclature to identify its constituent parts: antecedent probability, sign,
and example. And when he considered the relative weight of fact and
opinion in testimony, Hill concluded that "the real distinction is between
matters into which fact most largely enters, and those into which opinion
most largely enters" (202). He apparently meant that in some cases, only
expert testimony was acceptable, since it approached the status of fact,
while the testimony of the person on the street only amounted to opinion.

In other words, Hill transmogrified Whately's careful discussion of
the argumentative weight carried by fact and opinion into a distinction
regarding the quality of the credentials possessed by those who give
testimony. Opinion could be accepted as fact when the person who
expressed it was an authority. Otherwise, opinions are suspect. Hill's
discussion manifested the growing modern distrust of "common" knowledge, in which classical rhetoricians—and Richard Whately—had
placed their confidence.

Hill relied on Whately and Mill for his comments on analogy, over-
looking the fact that the two logicians disagreed about the nature of
inductive evidence. He borrowed his initial definition of deduction from
a nineteenth-century historian of science, William Whewell (also a vocal
opponent of Mill), and ignored the fact that his own later discussion of
deductive evidence, borrowed this time from Whately, contradicted his
earlier definition.

Late current-traditional textbooks contain accounts of evidence that are similar to those that appeared in their precursors, but later accounts are even more reductive. Later authors overwhelmingly preferred the sort of simpleminded empiricism that was filtered out of Campbell's and Whately's more balanced discussions of evidence by nineteenth-century rhetoricians like Hill. And the later authors almost invariably associated the sorts of evidence that Campbell and Whately would have identified as empirical (facts-opinions, testimony) with expository discourse. After EDNA's demise, they recommended using facts and testimony as support for the composition of any discourse that maintains a thesis—in essence, for all discourse.

Late and very-current-traditional textbooks divide evidence into two classes, just as Campbell and Whately did. Usually they name these *evidence* and *reasoning*. I interpret this distinction as a reductive appropriation of the categories that Campbell would have distinguished as *moral* and *deductive*—evidence provided by the senses, on the one hand, and evidence derived solely from the intellect on the other. Winkler and McCuen, for example, assert that there are four kinds of evidence: fact, experience, witnesses, and authority. Of course Campbell never mentioned facts at all, and his discussion of probability has disappeared. Winkler and McCuen associate reasoning, on the other hand, with the composition of argumentative discourse, under which head they include their treatments of induction and deduction. Rationalist sorts of evidence (what Campbell called intuitive or demonstrative and Whately called a priori) have simply disappeared.

Non-a priori evidence has been markedly reduced from the multifaceted nature assigned to it by Whately. It usually contains discussions of only testimony and facts. Testimony is further reduced in many contemporary texts to citation of experts or authorities from books or scholarly publications. This in itself is testimony to current faith in "expert opinion," a notion that would have seemed quite strange to Bishop Whately. Expertise is a product of the modern proliferation of scientific knowledge and the consequent specialization of technical proficiency. Recent texts award fairly spacious treatment to the quality of testimonial, just as the Bishop did. But where he had been concerned with witnesses' proximity to events in question and with their veracity, later textbook authors were only concerned about professional credentials: they warned students that authorities must be capable, current, and respected. In the world described by current-traditional rhetoric, people don't tell lies or distort facts—especially if they possess professional credentials of one sort or another.

In keeping with their fondness for empirical evidence, late current-traditional authors preferred facts as a means of proof. In 1945, Espenshade and company remarked that "good arguments employ as many specific facts as their authors can suitably include. New facts interest the reader, but above all else, they supply the missing elements in the foundation for proof." Like Bain, he thought that "if the reader had had all the facts or had been thoroughly conversant with the principle involved, there would probably have been no occasion for argument" (Espenshade, Gates, and Mallery 362).

An even more compelling assertion for the inclusion of facts in any discourse appears in very-current-traditional texts: facts are incontestable. Sheridan Baker defined facts in *The Complete Stylist* as "the kinds of things that can be tested by the senses . . . or by inferences from physical data so strong as to allow no other explanation" (107). For Frederick Crews, writing in the *Random House Handbook* (originally published 1974) facts and figures were "statements and numerical data that are beyond any dispute." As such, facts were the "most compelling" kinds of evidence, in that arguments based on them seem "to have sprung directly from unquestionable findings" (98).

In the scientistic world described by traditional composition textbooks, disagreement revolves around the lack of empirical knowledge. Or, to put it another way, no respectable person will fail to see the truth of an argumentative proposition that has been sufficiently shored up by a list of facts, despite any vagrant opinions she might previously have held. Unlike Whately, contemporary text writers preferred facts to opinions as a means of assembling evidence, since opinions lack empirical verifiability and are only "held" by people. Indeed, Baker was willing to buck the weight of twenty-five hundred years of rhetorical history to insist that "the central business of argument" consisted in the "testing of opinions to discover the facts" (*Complete Stylist* 107).

Recent text writers were confused by analogy; they were hard put to imagine how such a device could compete with facts as a kind of evidence. Nonetheless, most included analogy in their discussions of evidence, perhaps because it had been part of evidential theory since Whately put it there in the early nineteenth century. Of course analogy was a form of proof in classical rhetoric, where it differed from simple comparison in that it compared systems or procedures rather than particulars. To argue, for instance, that the circulation of knowledge within a culture is like the circulation of blood in bodies is to create an analogy. The similarity lies in the systemic or procedural resemblance, rather than in any likeness betweeen the two items named.

Cleanth Brooks and Robert Penn Warren conflated analogy with induction in the third edition of their *Modern Rhetoric* (1970). Analogical reasoning worked as follows: "If two instances are alike on a number of important points, they will be alike on the point in question" (202). Apparently they distinguished analogy from induction on the ground that in induction any number of instances may be adduced for comparison, and not just two. And in the eighth edition of *Writing with a Purpose*, McCrimmon treated analogy as a simple inductive comparison, since "from the premise that two very different things are alike in some significant way, the argument concludes that an inference about one will also apply to the other" (221).

Other late and very-current-traditional text writers think that analogies should be perfect—a strange state of affairs in which they would cease to be analogies at all. In *Writing: A College Handbook* (1982), Hefferman and Lincoln treated analogy as a fallacy, since "no analogy presents a perfect likeness"; thus any argument based on analogy was suspect (90). Baker was also suspicious of "false analogy," where not all the details were exactly comparable (*Complete Stylist* 116).

The uses to which induction and deduction were put in current-traditional textbooks were very different from the meanings they carried in the rhetorical and logical systems from which they were borrowed. Induction referred to two distinct kinds of inquiry in eighteenth-century discourse theory. Empirical or psychological induction, which Campbell associated with moral reasoning, took place when minds piled up a record of sensory impressions; rhetors could intuit a generalization from the similarity of their impressions of like instances. On the other hand, logical or rational induction—as espoused by Whately—depended upon establishing the appropriate relationships among particular premises in order that the rhetor could infer a generalization from them. In logic, however, induction was never defined only as the enumeration of particulars that could be subsumed under a generalization—it was the relation among the particulars that was important.[4] Induction could also involve inference of particulars from the existence of others. Nor was deduction defined as a simple matter of moving from the general to the less general. Instead logical deduction, again, involved the appropriate placing of general and particular premises in their proper relationships in order to deduce new propositions.

Current-traditional text writers probably inherited empirical induction from Campbell's identification of it with moral evidence, which he named as the kind of evidence that was appropriate to rhetoric. This is the category that Whately had railed against as a misunderstanding of the more rational kind of induction conducted in logical investigations.

Nevertheless, empirical induction—the piling up of experiential particulars to generate a generalization—was firmly associated with didactic discourse early in its history (as in Smith's *Lectures on Rhetoric and Belles Lettres*), which explains its occasional association with exposition in the later tradition.

However, late current-traditional textbook authors seem to have confused induction and deduction with analytic and synthetic method insofar as the the latter terms referred to the arrangement of arguments in order of increasing or decreasing generality, rather than as indicators of two distinct processes of logical inquiry.[5] Genung's discussion of induction and deduction in the *Working Principles of Rhetoric* is reminiscent of method as a means of arranging discourse. Induction repeated "the order of investigation wherein the final goal is a new and hitherto undiscovered truth"—a description that sounds very like methodical accounts of analysis as presentation. Deduction, on the other hand, was "the order of enforcement" that demonstrated "new applications or illustrations of principles already known and conceded"—that is, synthesis. In keeping with methodical teaching, Genung argued that deduction moved from generalization to particulars, from principles to facts, or from a known truth to its novel application (446–48). Despite his conflation of induction-deduction with analysis-synthesis however, Genung still treated both as means of inquiry.

Other late nineteenth-century text writers treated induction and deduction not as dynamic processes but as contrasting ways of ordering the placement of ideas on a page, from particulars to the general in the one case, and from generalization to specifics in the other. Scott and Denney's treatment in *Paragraph-Writing* was typical. "In deductive reasoning," they wrote,

> the general principle (stated usually at the beginning) is applied in the particulars; in inductive reasoning the general principle (stated usually at the end) is inferred from the particulars, as a conclusion. In a deductive paragraph, as would be expected, the sentences applying the principle to the particular case in hand, usually follow the topic-sentence, which states the principle. In an inductive paragraph the sentences stating the particular facts usually precede the topic-sentence, which states the general conclusion. (48–49)

In other words, movements that in logic had denoted distinct methods of inquiry came in current-traditional rhetoric to name two different ways of displaying those movements on a page.

More recent discussions of induction and deduction also demonstrate a limited conception of these two operations. Among those late authors who treat them as processes of inquiry, many confined induction to the species of empirical argument denigrated by Whately—that which assembles a progression of data in order to point to a generalization under which all could be subsumed. For example, Hefferman and Lincoln simply equated induction with the assembly of relevant examples. And deductive reasoning caused nightmares for authors of late current-traditional textbooks. By the late twentieth century, the rationalist philosophy in which rhetorical deduction was embedded had thoroughly disappeared from the logical terrain surveyed by current-traditional thought. This philosophy posited that some notions could be accepted without proof, since they derived from innate ideas, from postulated axioms, or from propositions widely accepted by thinking persons (that is, from "common sense"). But in a world dominated by an empirical epistemology, it was difficult to account for the genesis of major premises out of whole nonexperiential cloth.

Nevertheless, many text writers included deduction in their discussions of support for a thesis. I suspect that deduction hung on in current-traditional theory because of the binary thinking that characterizes it. Deduction had to be included simply because it had always been paired with induction. Of course, when it was confused with synthesis, which it often was, deduction also provided an alternative means of arranging discourse, from general to specific. As I demonstrate in the next chapter, this order was much preferred to its opposite by late current-traditional authors.

Cleanth Brooks and Robert Penn Warren's *Modern Rhetoric* (originally published 1949) is one of the few current-traditional textbooks that improved with age. In the first edition of that work, they offered a definition of generalization (induction) that looked a lot like Whately's argument from rhetorical example in an empirical disguise. For them, generalization moved "from a number of particular instances to the general conclusion that all instances of the type investigated will be of this same sort" (158). This is a limited, empirical, view of the inductive process. But Brooks and Warren included fairly sophisticated discussions of both induction and deduction in the popular third edition of *Modern Rhetoric*. Their treatment of deduction was supplemented with Venn diagrams, and they included a discussion of Mill's methods of induction in an appendix entitled "Causal Analysis."

In the fifth edition of *Writing with a Purpose* (1972), McCrimmon presented a treatment of deductive reasoning that was also remarkably sophisticated. He even included a classically derived discussion of syllogisms and enthymemes. In the *Rhetoric,* Aristotle defined an enthymeme as an argument based on probable rather than certain premises (1.2.1357a). Syllogistic reasoning, where premises were relatively certain, was appropriate to logic and science, while enthymatic reasoning, with its smaller degree of certainty, belonged to rhetoric. But in McCrimmon's discussion, as in many others, Aristotle's distinction between logical and rhetorical syllogisms was lost. Enthymemes were treated as partial or weak-kneed syllogisms that were missing a premise or two, rather than as arguments appropriate to an entirely separate realm of probability.

McCrimmon later abandoned deduction altogether in favor of something he called causal relations, which was a redaction of the empirical argument from sign (1982, 229). In his eighth edition, he described an inquiry process he called generalization; it drew "a conclusion about a whole class from a study of some of its members" (225). This is vaguely reminiscent of mature discussions of logical induction. In fact, McCrimmon's choice of the phrase "causal relations" leads me to suspect that his discussions of induction throughout various later editions of *Writing with a Purpose* represent a reductive appropriation of Mill's laws of induction. Be that as it may, induction and deduction are both present in the ninth edition, but they are treated solely as means of arrangement. McCrimmon likes induction because it "reflects the history of your investigation," which is the same justification that Campbell and Priestley offered to explain their preference for analytic method. Deduction gets three paragraphs in the ninth edition, but now its major premises have to be supported by "specific evidence" (141–42).

Sheridan Baker's definition of induction and deduction was somewhat more typical of very-current-traditional thought, and he unabashedly identified them with invention and arrangement, respectively:

> Induction and deduction are the two paths of reasoning. Induction is "leading into" (*in + ducere,* "to lead"), thinking through the evidence to some general conclusion. Deduction is "leading away from" some general precept to its particular parts and consequences. All along, you have been thinking inductively to find your thesis, and then you have turned the process around, writing deductively when you present your thesis and support it with your evidence. (*Complete Stylist* 115)

It is difficult to see how an investigation that proceeded inductively— even in the simplistic empirical version of induction, which involves the movement from particular instance to particular instance in order to reach a generalized conclusion—can then be exactly represented in a chain of deductive reasoning, which often does not involve the use of particulars in the empirical sense at all. That Baker did not equate deduction with syllogistic reasoning became clear when he defined the deductive premise as "a hunch, a half-formed theory" that suggested further experimental tests. The difference, now, between an inductive hypothesis and the major premise of a deductive argument is very small: it is the difference between "making a hypothesis instead of merely borrowing an honored assumption" (*Complete Stylist* 115).

Baker almost sounded like a classical rhetorician when he described the major deductive premise as a sort of maxim, "a kind of weathered hypothesis, a general idea so well fitted and durable as to seem part of the natural order of things." But his unremitting preference for empirical investigation resurfaced when he offered deduction as the brand of reasoning that must be resorted to when questions of value or quality were at stake; in these cases, alas, "factual induction finds little to grasp." Indeed, neither induction nor deduction were to be trusted "when the numbers or words they employ generalize too far from the skin of physical and mental actuality" (*Complete Stylist* 118).

Very-current-traditional textbooks continue to recommend induction and deduction for argumentative discourse. Some have even reintroduced the classical distinction between syllogisms and enthymemes, based on the relative certainty of the premises. On the down side, however, very recent discussions of deduction are quite reductive, usually introducing only the categorical syllogism. Many textbooks still discuss both induction and deduction as though they were means of arranging discourse rather than distinct means of inquiry. Too, their discussions focus more on fallacies than they do on the construction of effective inductive or deductive arguments.

The rich evidential heritage passed on to current-traditional rhetoric by Campbell and Whately had tried to account for a variety of reasoning processes, those that were purely intellectual as well as those that depended on empirical observation. Campbell and Whately also discriminated among the kinds of proofs appropriate to distinct sorts of deliberation. Deductive reasoning was to be used in mathematics and theology, for example, while induction found its niche in some kinds of scientific investigations. But some current-traditional texts were content to reduce this evidential wealth to a single process—they urge students to provide teachers with a disinterested assembly of relevant facts.

Aside from their massive reduction of eighteenth-century evidential theory to a few misunderstood terms and relations, what is missing from late current-traditional treatments of argumentative evidence is any sense that writers conceptualize or synthesize their opinions out of the available materials. Even more serious, from my point of view, is their omission of proofs that rely on common wisdom. On the one hand, there are facts; on the other, there is opinion. No connection exists between these two realms. Opinions further occupy a distinctly second-class status in relation to facts, the truth of which is universally acknowledged (by reasonable people, at least). Current-traditional rhetoricians never recognize the possibility that common opinions exist. They don't acknowledge that communities render judgments on such matters as abortion and flag burning. Rather, they reject the notion of communal opinion, preferring to define opinions as individual assessments about the way the world works. If opinions issue from the pens or mouths of ordinary persons, then, such opinions are both unassailable and unimportant since they are inevitably tied up with the character of a given individual. As such, they can't be changed, since their alteration would require the alteration of an entire personality. Nor are opinions very important, since they are held by single individuals.

The Fortunes of EDNA

In the *Practical Elements of Rhetoric,* John Franklin Genung employed EDNA as part of the organizing principle of part of his discussion of invention. He divided invention into five parts: description (invention dealing with observed objects); narration (dealing with events); exposition (dealing with generalizations); argumentation (dealing with truths); and persuasion (dealing with practical issues or oratory). He retained this scheme in the *Working Principles of Rhetoric,* although he dropped persuasion from his discussion of the kinds in that work. But by the turn of the twentieth century, most current-traditional textbooks had dropped EDNA as an organizational device altogether.[6] The genre theory employed by later current-traditional text writers was much less inclusive, for two reasons. First of all, parts of EDNA now had their own courses and textbooks. Texts dealing exclusively with expository writing began to be published with some frequency in the early decades of the twentieth century. Maurice Garland Fulton's *Expository Writing* (1912) is a successful example. George Pierce Baker's popular *Principles of Argumentation* (1895) revived a brief vogue for argumentation, and courses devoted exclusively to narration and description had appeared at some colleges.

Second of all, by this time, the rules for composing exposition had come to be confounded with those used in the composition of all discourse. To put this another way, as far as later current-traditional textbooks were concerned, all discourse (with the occasional exception of argument), was to be governed by the select-narrow-amplify model of invention, and hence all discourse needed to display a thesis and support for it. Most of the prescriptions that were appropriate to the composition of all discourse were taken from nineteenth-century treatments of exposition.

But EDNA is not dead. It still puts in an occasional appearance as "the forms of discourse," as it did in the third edition of Brooks and Warren's *Modern Rhetoric*. But mostly it has gone on to bigger things. Exposition and argument still serve as methods of organizing current-traditional composition programs and syllabi—exposition the first semester, argument the second. An exception to this rule occurs when the research paper—exposition all grown up and happily married to testimony—occupies students' time during their second semester of composition instruction. Narration and description still survive in the almost universal very-current-traditional recommendation that they be used as methods of development for paragraphs or even whole essays. And students are still writing expository themes and paragraphs of description day after day, all across the land.

7 The Methodical Memory on Display: The Five-Paragraph Theme

A popular conceit among eighteenth-century rhetorical theorists characterized the relation between thought and its expression as analogous to that between soul and body. George Campbell employed the analogy in the *Philosophy of Rhetoric* as follows:

> In contemplating a human creature, the most natural division of the subject is the common division into soul and body, or into the living principle of perception and of action, and that system of material organs by which the other receives information from without, and is enabled to exert its powers. . . . Analogous to this, there are two things in every discourse which principally claim our attention, the sense and the expression; or in other words, the thought and the symbol by which it is communicated. These may be said to constitute the soul and the body of an oration, or indeed of whatever is signified to another by language. For, as in man, each of these constituent parts hath its distinctive attributes, and as the perfection of the latter consisteth in its fitness for serving the purposes of the former, it is precisely with those two essential parts of every speech, the sense and the expression. (32)

Campbell's metaphoric distinction between an inner core and an outer envelope endured within current-traditional thought. To supply only one example of its many appearances, I quote Day in the *Art of Discourse:* "No process of art is complete until its product appears in a sensible form; and language is the form in which the art of discourse embodies itself, as sound furnishes the body in the art of music and color in that of painting" (208). In the modern rhetorical systems I am examining here, language was treated as a pliant medium that exactly represented thought. Thought, the "soul," "interior," or "core" of discourse, always preceded, and was superior to, language, which was a secondary, fallen, exterior embodiment of what was really important.

Because language had only one function—to mirror thought—the function of arrangement came to be very like that of style in current-traditional rhetoric. Both served to externalize the internalized process of invention. Where arrangement made graphic the larger movements of mind, such as analysis or synthesis, style made graphic its connections between simple ideas. Indeed, early current-traditional rhetoricians acknowledged this likeness between the two canons by submerging their treatment of arrangement within that given to style. For example, Alexander Jamieson included arrangement in his general remarks on style in his *Grammar of Rhetoric and Polite Literature* (originally published 1818).[1] Samuel Newman also placed his very brief treatment of arrangement in the *Practical System of Rhetoric* under the heading of style.

Thus many current-traditional authors maintained that rhetoric, and hence composition, had only two canons: invention and style. Arrangement, suspended as it was between the binaries of thought and expression never quite found a comfortable home in their textbooks. Occasionally it was submerged within invention, as when various sorts of aims were associated with their respective orders of development within genres. Of course this was made possible by the two-faced nature of method, which could both direct the progress of thought and exactly represent that progress in discourse.

Despite all of this, current-traditional authors were very concerned with arrangement, even though they no longer gave that name to the disposition within a discourse of its larger parts or divisions. Two developments characterized mature current-traditional treatments of the arrangement of discourse on a page: the hardening and reduction of methodical principles into the trinity of unity, coherence, and emphasis and the emergence of what I call the "nesting approach" to composing.

Early Commentary on Arrangement

In *On Invention,* Cicero discriminated six parts that could appear in any rhetorical discourse: the introduction, which readied audiences to receive the argument; the narration, which gave the history of the case; the partition, which announced the issues that would be addressed and the order in which the rhetor would address them; the confirmation and refutation, which presented the rhetor's arguments for the case and against those offered by opponents; and the peroration or conclusion, which excited enthusiasm for the rhetor's argument or set the audience against the case advanced by opponents (2.20–190).

The arrangement of any discourse was determined by the rhetor's assessment of the rhetorical situation for which she was preparing. For example, the composition of an introduction was determined by her guess about the attitude of the targeted audience toward her ethos and the case at hand. Were they hostile? Did she need to be conciliatory? Or were they receptive, so that she could begin more directly? If the audience were familiar with the case, the rhetor could dispense with the narration of its history; if the audience were uninformed and there was no skilled opponent, a refutation was unnecessary. In other words, the composition and arrangement of the parts of the discourse were determined by the rhetor's informed guess about how listeners or readers would react.

Current-traditional discourse theory, on the other hand, painted listeners and readers as curiously docile. They were never hostile or inattentive—they were just interested. Writers needed only to arrange their discourse, then, in a fashion that would ease the reading process—that would, in fact, reflect the way any reasonable person might have written it, according to the natural dictates of the rational mind.

Alexander Jamieson was among the few current-traditional rhetoricians who drew on Cicero's six-part division of the oration for his principles of arrangement. However, he updated the classical treatment by adding some methodical refinements to his discussion of the partition—just as Hugh Blair had. While Cicero had only recommended that the partition be stated briefly, clearly, and concisely, Jamieson noted that the division of the subject ought to follow "the order of nature"; otherwise it should be "concealed." He recommended natural method (analysis) for general use since it moved from the simple to the complex and was appropriate for any discourse, such as a sermon, where "division is proper to be used." In this case, the parts of the division must be "really distinct from one another." They should begin "with the simplest points, such as are easiest apprehended." Taken together, the "several members of a division ought to exhaust the subject." Their terms ought to be absolutely clear, and "unnecessary multiplication of heads" was to be avoided (249). Observance of these careful methodical procedures, Jamieson thought, would insure that any similarly rational reader could follow the writer's train of thought.

This is the last we hear of Ciceronian arrangement in mainstream current-traditional textbooks, however. Newman's treatment of arrangement, which occupied perhaps a single page of his textbook, was suffused with methodical principles much like those advanced by George Campbell. Newman suggested that the arguments in a discourse ought to be arranged synthetically, since this method was more natural given that "men usually assert their opinions, and then assign the reasons on which they are founded." However, "if what is asserted is likely, either from its being novel, or uncommon, or from its being opposed to the prejudices of the reader, to disaffect him, and to prevent his due consideration of the arguments brought forward, it is better to . . . defer the formal statement of the proposition maintained to the close" (37). This is analysis, couched in the "concealed" or "hidden" method of presentation recommended by Blair and Watts.

As Campbell and Priestley had done, Newman made some comments on transitions. As generic lines altered, conventional classical means of marking the major sections of discourse were not so ubiquitous nor so familiar to educated readers as they once had been. Newman noted that transitions were not so important in argumentative discourse, "where the different parts are connected by a common reference to some particular point" (38). Since argumentative discourse was the genre to which classical lore about arrangement was most often applied, its conventions regarding the disposition of its parts were well known, and thus argument needed fewer explicit transitions.

Transitions were crucial, however, in those sorts of discourse that followed the newer analytic approach. Newman wrote that transitions were to be "natural and easy, that is, in agreement with the common modes of associating the thoughts" (38). They were most skillfully employed when they represented resemblance, cause and effect, or contiguity as to time or place. Newman's interest in transitions as a means of representing mental patterns of association marked his work as indebted to the new rhetoric, insofar as the accurate linguistic representation of mental connections had become crucial to readers' ability to follow an argument. Later current-traditional rhetoricians identified the methodical principle of coherence with the ability to make appropriate transitions between the parts of discourse.

The Gang of Three: Unity, Coherence, and Friend

Method came into its own in mature current-traditional rhetoric as a means of amplification. Textbook authors set forth dispositional formulas that prescribed which formal features ought to characterize every finished piece of discourse. Some of these formulas were derived from method.

As I noted earlier, advocates of method employed it during the discovery process in the hope of reducing the intrusion of unpredictable factors that might extend the investigation forever. The concept of unity (also called clarity) allowed investigators to impose arbitrary limits on the area roped off for investigation. A second concept, called variously distinction, division, or progression, insured that the investigation touched systematically on every point that could be deemed relevant to the notion under study. That unity and progression were part of the history of logic was never acknowledged by the current-traditional rhetoricians who adopted it as an inflexible principle of amplification. They took great pains to establish unity as a natural and necessary principle of discourse at every level from the sentence on up to whole compositions.

The importation of method into current-traditional rhetoric as a means of amplification owed a good deal to two influential midcentury rhetoricians, Henry Noble Day and Alexander Bain. Throughout his explication of the means of amplification in the *Elements of Rhetoric,* Day insisted on the absolute observance of two requirements: unity and completeness. In explanatory discourse, the principle of unity required "that the conception which forms the theme, be one. This one conception, however, may be simple or complex; may embrace but one individual or a class" (53). This passage indicates that, for Day, unity meant representation in discourse of a single idea as this term was used in association psychology—that is, of an idea that had resulted from a simple perception or a combination of perceptions.

But Day had a fetish about unity, which was apparently a self-evident principle of discourse for him. In his discussion of invention in general, he argued that "unless the object of speaking be distinctly perceived and that object be strictly one, the inventive faculty has no foothold at all, or, at least, no sure standing and all of its operations must be unsteady and feeble" (44). Unity was to be secured in discourse, then, not only by selecting a single subject for development, but by choosing but "one leading object to be effected" (43). Elsewhere, Day argued that since discourse was a rational procedure, any "discourse can hardly with propriety be called one which has more than one general theme. The unity of a discourse in which, indeed, lies its very life, requires that there be but one thought to which every other shall be subordinate and subservient, utterly forbids the introduction of two or more co-ordinate thoughts" (38). To take Day's remarks quite literally, every discourse is to represent one whole thought and the relation of its parts, since this thought in its turn represents a combination of the rhetor's aim with her mental representation of some object perceived in nature. Observance of the principle of unity apparently insured that all discourses that observed it would be eminently readable, since they announced themselves as representations of single thought units.

By the time Day wrote the *Art of Discourse*, the laws of unity and completeness had been joined by two others—selection and method. Unity, selection, completeness, and method were to govern amplification in every genre, although he gave them their fullest explication in connection with explanatory discourse.

In his later work Day took even fewer pains to justify the necessity of unity than he had previously. He noted that unity was "founded in the nature of all discourse as a rational procedure" (60). He then referred his readers to two other sections of his text, in each of which he made a circular argument for the necessity of unity. Since unity required that a discourse have only one subject, it was important that writers center their discourse around a single thought, so that their work would have unity (44, 51).

The law of selection reinforced unity in that selection was "grounded in the necessity of excluding some of the infinite variety of subordinate thoughts or views through which the general theme may be developed" (Day, *Art of Discourse* 60). The law of completeness was also mandated by the rational nature of discourse and provided for a "full exhibition of the theme for the object proposed" (62). The laws of unity, selection, and completeness, taken together, repeat Descartes' injunction that any investigation be characterized by clarity and distinction. The laws mandated that writers concentrate on a single whole, that they divide it into its constituent parts, and that all of the resulting parts be enumerated.

When unity, selection, and completeness were used as means of amplification, they repeated methodical advice for analyzing the proposition, now applied on the scale of the whole discourse; that is, the organization of the entire discourse would now repeat the analytic moves that were appropriate to establishing the proposition and its parts, and thus the structure of whole essays would now reflect the structure of their propositions on a larger scale. Here Day employed the micro-macrocosmic vision that was characteristic of method: smaller parts repeat and fit neatly into larger parts.

What was left, then, was to provide some advice about progression, which Day did in his discussion of the law of method. The law of method had to govern invention since to proceed methodically was to exert the activity of the mind "freely, fully, and successfully," that is, "as it proceeds in accordance with the laws of its own nature." He was further confident that the laws of the mind were consonant with those of nature, "so that the mind . . . must be proceeding at the same time in accordance with the principles of truth." Nonetheless method, however natural, had to be studied and applied in discourse so that it could form and strengthen "those habits of methodical thinking" that were the indispensable condition of all rational progress. "A mind trained to habitual activity in method has reached its true maturity of training. Without this, it is essentially deficient in its culture" (*Art of Discourse* 61). The constant study and practice of discourse could be justified on the ground that it immersed its students in the exercise of method; method in turn exercised the mind along its natural lines and thus strengthened it.

To some extent the four laws of method supplanted the classical list of means of amplification that Day had formerly favored. The resulting discussion looks a lot more like Watts' list of rules for method as presentation than anything derived from classical rhetoric. Day could have found an early connection between method and the amplification of scientific discourse in Priestley's *Lectures on Oratory and Criticism*. It seems more likely, however, that the connection suggested itself simply because explanatory discourse took science as its subject, and thus method, as the discovery process that took nature as its model, was appropriate to it.

However, Day was not alone in utilizing methodical means of amplification. Alexander Bain also derived his famous principles for the formulation of acceptable paragraphs from method.[2] His innovative departure from tradition in this regard did not lay in the principles themselves but rather in his interest in paragraphs, which had received virtually no modern attention prior to the publication of the first edition of *English Composition and Rhetoric*.

Bain justified his attention to paragraphs by means of "an old homely maxim," borrowed from the methodical tradition, which posited that smaller units of discourse should always bear a microcosmic relation to larger units. As he put it: "Look to the paragraphs and the discourse will look to itself, for, although a discourse as a whole has a method or plan suited to its nature, yet the confining of each paragraph to a distinct topic avoids some of the worst faults of composition; besides which, he that fully comprehends the method of a paragraph, will also comprehend the method of an entire work" (151). Like Day, Bain authorized the micro-macrocosmic view of discourse that characterized late current-traditional thought.

Bain defined "the Paragraph" as "a collection of sentences with unity of purpose" (142). His requirements for their formation can be summarized as follows: paragraphs must have (1) coherence, which demanded explicit reference and use of conjunctions; (2) parallel construction, which mandated that sentences that express ideas roughly equal in weight be presented as grammatically equivalent to one another; (3) a clear statement of the topic in the opening sentence; (4) an absence of dislocation, which required that sentences succeed one another in some logical sequence, the preferred descent being from the general to the particular; (5) unity, so that the writer could make her purpose immediately apparent to readers and avoid digression; (6) due proportion between principal and subordinate statements (142–52).

Bain's concern for the major requirements of method—unity and progression—is apparent in these principles. Every paragraph was to represent one whole thought and the relation of its parts, since this representation in its turn represented some object in nature. Observance of the principles insured that all paragraphs would be eminently readable, since they announced themselves as representations of a single thought, idea, or notion.

Unity was secured by observance of the fifth and third principles. Each paragraph would be opened by a sentence that stated its contents in general form. This sentence came to be called the topic sentence, and it owes its genesis to synthetic method. Given the ubiquitous assumption in methodical theory that larger units of discourse reflect the structure and movement of smaller ones, Bain may have derived his principle of the topic sentence by analogy with the proposition that was to govern the direction of the entire discourse—just as Day had done. The presence of the topic sentence gave further assurance that unity would be observed in the paragraph that followed.

Progression required that all parts of the discourse be explicitly related to one another. Bain refined this principle to insist that sentences within a paragraph be ordered by means of some discernible sequence, preferably from the general to the specific. Bain's second and fourth principles— parallel construction and logical sequence—are reminiscent of synthetic method, where they were standard means of division. His preference for a descending order of generality could have been dictated by methodical tradition, which usually recommended synthetic method as a means of arranging material that had already been discovered. Or he could have chosen synthesis out of concern for his audience; synthetic method was always the recommended movement for discourse aimed at learners, and *English Composition and Rhetoric* itself employs a synthetic movement. Of course, Bain's avowed allegiance to science—which he defined as the production of useful generalizations—could also have dictated the precedence of generality.

Observance of the first principle secured surface coherence in any paragraph. This would be represented by the selection of appropriate transitions, which announced the logical relation of each sentence to those that preceded and followed it. Principle six, which required that writers show a due awareness of the relationships that obtain between levels of generality, was a traditional methodical means of insuring distinctiveness. This last principle was refined by Bain's imitators into a rule requiring that all discourse demonstrate something called mass or proportion or emphasis.

My hunch that Bain derived these principles out of method is lent support not only by the interesting analogies that obtain between his rules and older lists of laws governing presentational method such as Watts', but by some affinities with other contemporary applications of the law of method, such as Day's. For example, the methodical interest in a clear statement of the "leading inquiry" or proposition is apparent in his second principle. What is new is Bain's systematization of a long conceptual tradition governing patterns of inquiry into inflexible rules for paragraph development. In a sense, his principles of the paragraph complete the process I have been tracing, a process that shifts the ultimate responsibility for the ordering of discourse away from the steps gone through during inquiry and onto the way that discourse is supposed to look on the page.

Bain's principles were widely adopted by later current-traditional textbook writers, perhaps because his was the first popular composition textbook to pay extended attention to paragraphs as separate units of composition. Certainly current-traditional textbook authors have more often treated his principles as rules to be employed in the amplification of paragraphs than in essays, which were usually to be amplified by the expository means of development. At the very least, Bain's application of methodical principles to the development of paragraphs exacerbated the emerging tendency of nineteenth-century composition theory to concentrate on the shape of discourse, rather than on its contents or on the persons who compose and read it.[3] His rules for paragraph formation must also have accelerated the tendency of school rhetoric to assume that universal rules could be generated for the composition of almost any discourse, regardless of its occasion.

Scott and Denney adapted a conflation of Day's and Bain's methodical principles in order to forge their "laws of the paragraph" for *Paragraph-*

Writing. The law of unity required "that the sentences composing the paragraph be intimately connected with one another in thought and purpose. . . . [U]nity forbids digressions and irrelevant matter" (4). The law of selection mandated that "of all which might be said on the subject treated, only those points be chosen for mention in the sentences which will best subserve the purpose of the paragraph," while the law of proportion dictated the scope, length, and placement of important points within the paragraph (6). The law of sequence, that is, of method, required "that the sentences be presented in the order which will best bring out the thought" (13).

Scott and Denney did add a new law to the list: variety. This law required "that as much diversity as is consistent with the purpose of the paragraph is introduced." Lest the law of variety be thought to contradict the law of unity, Scott and Denney hastened to add that variety was a matter of length, structure, and order, rather than of thought (*Paragraph-Writing* 15). Here again, the rigid current-traditional distinction between thought and language surfaced. "Artistic" flourishes, such as variety, were always associated with language, and as such, were always subservient to the rules mandating clarity and distinctiveness of thought.

As they had done in the case of the expository means of development, later current-traditional textbook authors recommended a variety of methods for paragraph development. There could be as many as four of these—as in Day—or five or six—as in Scott and Denney or Bain. But mature current-traditional theory more consistently condensed the principles governing the development of paragraphs into three.[4] Genung reduced the paragraph principles to unity, continuity, and proportion, and his influential example may have established the tripartite tradition, although Barrett Wendell may have been complicit in this as well. In his discussion of the whole composition, Wendell extended the principles of unity, coherence, and mass (proportion) to the composition of all discourse at all levels, since the trains of thought they represented were typical of all minds (153–54). Wendell marshaled the principles as first lines of defense against the confused and disordered state in which ideas presented themselves to writers.

In the methodical tradition, of course, unity was treated as a self-evident principle of discourse, and as I have tried to demonstrate, it was crucial to such thinking. The ubiquity of unity as a primary principle of discourse was no doubt reinforced by teachers' fear that students would bite off more than they could chew in a short discourse; Whately's dictum that no discourse should "enter on too wide a field of discussion" is the primary example (37). But in current-traditional rhetoric, unity came to be conceived as an end in itself to which the flow of all parts of the discourse, even sentences, was to be subordinated.

Continuity or coherence was also necessary to method, since discursive coherence represented the connections made between mental ideas; that is, the connective logic of the mind could be repeated in discourse by selection of the appropriate transitions. This was especially true when the method chosen was analysis, where the connecting links between the parts of the discourse depended upon the associative movement of the writer's mind, rather than on some predetermined or conventional form. Writers employing this method would have to take special care to cue their readers into the movement and relation of their ideas by means of explicit linguistic transitions.

Emphasis, or proportion, may also have derived from method. As formulated originally by Bain, emphasis meant placing generalities in a dominant position so that their relation of primacy over the particulars that supported them was absolutely clear. Barrett Wendell generalized this rule somewhat; he defined emphasis (he called it mass) as the discursive feature governing the relative placement of ideas on the page, no matter what their level of generality. He lamented that sometimes the achievement of coherence interfered with the principle of mass, but he solved this difficulty by announcing that coherence was more important at the beginnings of paragraphs than at their conclusions, where mass assumed predominance (180).

During the twentieth century, unity, coherence, and emphasis increasingly controlled the process of amplification in general. They were to be applied in the composition of all discourse at all levels, no matter what its kind. In some textbooks unity and coherence even got chapters all to themselves. Their observance was often recommended in negative terms. Writers could violate the principle of unity by failing to cover everything associated with the main idea of a paragraph or composition, or they could commit the sin of digression. There were also two ways to violate the principle of coherence. Sentences could follow one another in some illogical order, or the writer could fail to include transitions that signaled the appropriate relations between sentences. The recommended "logical" orders were usually the means of expository amplification, although in some writers these were limited to three orders, all drawn from method: chronology, spatial arrangement, and analysis. Transitions were to announce and track such movements—the inclusion of words and phrases such as *moreover, besides, on the contrary,* or *in conclusion* would constantly cue readers into the method underlying the paragraph or discourse.

In very-current-traditional textbooks, the principles have returned to their original province—the paragraph. They are now generally identified as unity, coherence, and completeness. Very-current-traditional textbooks emphasize that paragraphs are not just any old random assemblage of sentences: "A block of words on a page is not a paragraph merely because it looks like one; it must also *function* like one" (Winkler and McCuen 94). Paragraphs are predictive—for writers as well as readers. Their topic sentences (usually placed at the beginning of the paragraph) announce to readers what will happen in the following sentences, thereby securing unity for the paragraph. Certain transitional words announce the relation of every sentence to those that precede and follow it, and hence coherence is assured. The textbooks sometimes offer question-begging advice about completeness. Writers know that their paragraphs are complete when enough sentences have been supplied to support the topic sentence. Others supplement this advice by calling on the limits of readers' ability to endure hardship. For example, Packer and Timpane say that readers will call it quits when "they find it difficult to retain the overall shape of the argument, or their eyes and mind begin to tire" (170). They do give writers a rule of thumb for estimating completeness, however; paragraphs shouldn't require more than ten sentences, nor should they spread over a whole page.

Discourse as Nesting Behavior

The current-traditional preoccupation with the paragraph as an independent unit of discourse is a very curious phenomenon. Scholars have attempted to account for it by connecting it to the rise of literacy (after all, spoken discourse does not break itself into paragraphs). A historical rationale can also be found in the enormous influence exerted on current-traditional rhetoric by Bain's *English Composition and Rhetoric,* which spawned Scott and Denney's equally influential *Paragraph-Writing.*

But many current-traditional authors adopted a pedagogical rationale to justify their preference for paragraphs: since paragraphs were shorter than essays, they could be composed with more ease, especially by younger students. Scott and Denney rationalized the entire project of *Paragraph-Writing* in just this way: the paragraph exemplified the principles of discourse in "small and convenient compass so that they are easily appreciable by the beginner" (iv). A student could also "write more paragraphs than he can write essays in the same length of time; hence the character of the work may be made for him more varied, progressive, and interesting" (v). Nor did Scott and Denney overlook the advantage of paragraph exercises to teachers, who would have shorter compositions to evaluate than if they assigned whole essays.

I think that current-traditional focus on the paragraph had a great deal to do with the tradition's reliance on method. Scott and Denney would not so casually have substituted paragraph writing for essay practice were they not confident that the same principles were at work in both. Paragraphs were a little handier than whole essays as ways of reflecting the movement of minds. The topic sentence with its accompanying details, whose internal relations were rigidly controlled by the principles of coherence and emphasis, constituted a tidy graphic display of unity and progression. Nor can there be any doubt that current-traditional rhetoricians regarded paragraphs as representations of complete thoughts, just as sentences were. For example, in *Writing and Thinking* (originally published 1931) Norman Foerster and J. M. Steadman charged that "scrappy" paragraphs resulted from "a mere fragment of the full-formed idea that lies in the mind but that we are too lazy to call forth" (68).

Paragraphs came into their own because of the methodical habit of viewing the universe of discourse as a collection of increasingly larger repetitions of its smallest elements. After about 1880, textbook authors began to organize their texts according to what might be called the constituent units of discourse: words, sentences, paragraphs, whole compositions. The constituent units of discourse often named chapters or sections of traditional textbooks, as they did, for example, in Adams Sherman Hill's *Principles of Rhetoric*.

In its maturity, current-traditional rhetoric tended to see a composition as a nest of Chinese boxes, in which the smaller parts of discourse— words and sentences—were contained inside, and reflected by, the structure of increasingly larger parts—the paragraph and the essay. In treatises on method, this microcosmic to macrocosmic view of discourse was often illustrated by analogy with the study of grammar, which began with letters, syllables, and words since these were the smallest discernible units and supposedly the least difficult to understand. Once they had mastered these, students were allowed to move on to the study of sentences.

Adams Sherman Hill provided an influential example in the direction of treating larger levels of discourse as reflections of smaller ones. In the most effective arrangement of words, he wrote, "the position of every verbal sign would exactly correspond to that of the thing signified; the order of language would be the order of the thought, and would distinctly indicate the relative importance of every constituent part of the composition" (*Principles of Rhetoric* 129).

Although Hill cited Lord Kames as his authority here, associationism and method seem to be the sources of this line of thought. To recap briefly: the mental entities called ideas were connected in the mind by means of mental operations called associations. Hill apparently thought that ideas and operations ought to be representable in the syntax of the sentence, where the grammatical subject represented an idea and the predicate represented whatever operation was applied to the subject. Thus sentences could represent complete thoughts, just as they did in logical propositions. And, just as "every sentence should contain but one principal assertion; every paragraph should discuss the subject in hand from but one point of view; every essay or discourse should treat of but one subject, and of but one proposition relating to that subject at a time" (159). This is an argument for observance of the principle of unity at all levels of discourse. Hill was equally insistent on the observance of coherence at all levels beyond the sentence: "If a sentence can be put in one place as well as in another, there is a defect somewhere" (157).

Wendell found the principles of unity, coherence, and mass in sentences, paragraphs, and whole compositions. He was able to do this because he firmly separated words from ideas and awarded priority to ideas. In *English Composition* he wrote that once we know "what ideas we wish to group together, the task of finding words for them is immensely simplified" (29–30). Apparently ideas took form in the mind already equipped with unity, which always characterized the immaterial ideas for which material words stood. Coherence was the province of both ideas and words; that is, the associative operations of the mind lent coherence to ideas, while discursive transitions lent coherence to discourse. Mass, however, applied only to words, and, as I already noted, sometimes the achievement of mass got in the way of coherence (34, 180).

Here again a current-traditional writer had difficulty in getting language to lie down and behave itself. Despite his assured tone, Wendell had no little difficulty when he applied his three principles to composition of the sentence, where they were "constantly hampered by good use." He wrote this peculiarity off as a result of the vagaries of English grammar (120). Good use never stood in Wendell's way when he set about the business of applying his three principles to the production of discourse at all levels.

Later current-traditional authors imported the principles into their discussions of syntax in an attempt to demonstrate that individual sentences could display unity, coherence, and emphasis. The principles also appeared in some twentieth-century textbooks as principles of composition for essays and paragraphs. In sum, later current-traditional textbooks created a grammar of discourse, where whole discourses were reflective sums of their parts. Just as sentences combined subjects with predicates, paragraphs named their subjects in an opening sentence, to which its body bore one or another of a series of predicated relationships. Whole compositions, in their turn, displayed thesis statements that were analogous to topic sentences; the ordering of the paragraphs and their relation to the whole composition and to each other mirrored the ordering of sentences within a paragraph and their relation to each other. Wendell provided his readers with a fine statement of the nesting theory of arrangement when he wrote that "a paragraph whose unity can be demonstrated by summarizing its substance in a sentence whose subject shall be a summary of its opening sentence, and whose predicate shall be a summary of its closing sentence, is theoretically well massed" (129). Here is method with a vengeance; Peter Ramus would feel right at home.

Because they adopted a word-sentence-paragraph approach to composition, textbooks often postponed work with essays, preferring to begin with grammar and syntax and moving through the composition of paragraphs to whole essays. The difficult character assigned to essays assumed, of course, that the bigger parts of discourse were harder to write—an assumption that seems to contradict the assertion that all parts of a discourse display the same principles.

The tendency of current-traditional composition theory to structuralize concepts that were formerly means of invention and to disperse them graphically within a theme as components of its arrangement saw its most striking manifestation in the paradigm discourse espoused by many twentieth-century current-traditional textbooks—the five-paragraph theme. This ideal discourse was a standard to be imitated whenever students wrote. The standard was formal rather than conceptual; that is, a set of static relations dictated the placement on the page of certain structural features of the text. The five-paragraph theme had a paragraph of introduction, three of development, and one of conclusion. Each of the developmental paragraphs was initiated by a topic sentence summarizing the body of the paragraph.

If there was a conceptual movement within this paradigm, it was from general to particular. By virtue of this synthetic movement, the parts of the discourse fit neatly into one another. Just as essays contained thesis and body paragraphs that specified the thesis, paragraphs contained topic and body sentences that specified the topic of each paragraph. The model five-paragraph theme could be laid out on the page with the aid of colored lines, boxes, and arrows. Discourse had shape. Shape was clarified by analogy to funnels, pyramids, or keyholes. (I borrow these metaphors from Sheridan Baker's *The Practical Stylist* [1962]).

Of course the five-paragraph theme is a graphic representation of the introspective model of invention I traced in earlier chapters. This paradigm appeared as a methodical process for arranging didactic discourse in Adam Smith's lectures in the 1760s. It was still appearing in current-traditional textbooks written two hundred years later. But by the middle years of the twentieth century, the synthetic process was more often treated as a graphic structure than a means of invention.

The five-paragraph theme was the most thoroughgoing scheme for spatializing discourse that had appeared in rhetorical theory since Peter Ramus' method of dichotomizing division rendered all the world divisible by halves. Indeed, it is no doubt indebted to method, as this entered traditional composition theory via Bain's paragraph principles and Day's laws of amplification, and was translated to twentieth-century textbook authors in the guise of Wendell's three principles of discourse. The five-paragraph theme was prescribed to students in the absence of a historical context; it was simply touted as the way things are done. The intellectual contexts originally recommended for the use of synthesis had disappeared from the tradition entirely, as had the psychological arguments that made it analogous to the movement of the human mind in acts of communication.

Writing Instruction as Socialization

In 1936, I. A. Richards was invited to Bryn Mawr to lecture on rhetoric. In those lectures, subsequently published as *The Philosophy of Rhetoric* (1936), he fired several well-aimed salvos at textbook exemplars of both the new rhetoric and current-traditional rhetoric. Accusing them of "poking the fire from the top," he dismissed much of the advice they gave as irrelevant to rhetorical practice. Most telling of all, he launched a direct attack on the current-traditional notion that language could be separated from thought: "An idea or a notion, when unencumbered and undisguised, is no easier to get hold of than one of those oiled and naked thieves who infest the railway carriages of India. Indeed an idea, or a notion, like the physicist's ultimate particles and rays, is only known by what it does. Apart from its dress or other signs it is not identifiable" (5). Richards' critique seems to have had little impact on the current-traditional juggernaut. He may have put his finger on one reason for its longevity when he characterized its strictures about discursive deportment as "the Club Spirit." As he noted, the club spirit enlisted language as a servant of manners, specifically those of "a special set of speakers. . . . Deviations from their customs is incorrectness and is visited with a social penalty as such" (78).

Current-traditional concern with mannerly discourse can be explained in part by the institutional circumstances in which college composition has always been taught. At least one introductory composition course has been required of students entering American colleges ever since the late nineteenth century.[5] At the turn of the twentieth century, the huge numbers of students who were required to take one or two introductory writing courses simply swamped the resources of most college and university English departments, which were just then emerging as representatives of an independent academic discipline. The immediate solution to the numbers difficulty was to develop a composition course that could be taught to many students at once, through lectures and readings. And if the theory of composition used were highly formalized, the work of grading papers could be simplified, since harried teachers could ignore the content of their students' themes and would only need to assess the degree of their conformity to the formal features prescribed by the lectures and the textbook. Students needed only to demonstrate that their writing conformed to standards that had been devised as measures of their work before they ever set foot inside the academy.

But herein lies an irony. Of all the subjects commonly taught in university curricula, composition is no doubt the skill least amenable to standardized instruction. Writing is best taught and learned through individual effort and attention. As Wallace Stegner pointed out in 1950, "anyone writing honestly creates and solves new problems every time he sits down at his desk. Nobody can solve them for him in advance, and no teacher had better try" (431).[6] And yet current-traditional pedagogy rests on this very assumption—that students' inventional processes can be forecasted, their difficulties anticipated, and their inadequacies named, in advance.

I am prepared to grant that the authors of current-traditional textbooks imported standardized techniques into writing instruction in order to render its demands on teachers less onerous. No doubt the textbooks composed by Wendell and the others were attractive because they provided a list of universal prescriptions that made evaluation of students' papers a routine matter. Wendell's text supplied teachers and students of composition with a small set of discursive principles that could be applied at any level of discourse with the same degree of analytical rigor. His system articulated three unequivocal rules that would determine how any completed discourse should look. Teachers had only to measure each student's discourse against the standardized ideal discourse in order to gauge a given paper's relative success or failure.

However, late nineteenth-century attempts to standardize composition instruction may have sprung from motives other than that of relieving composition teachers from some of the burden of paper grading. Evelyn Wright argues that socialization was a hidden agenda in most language arts instruction during the late nineteenth century. According to Wright, elementary schoolteachers were held "responsible for saving children from grammatical-rhetorical sins by which their personal character was judged"; that is, students' failure to meet universally imposed standards of good form was interpreted as a sign of inadequate moral development rather than an indication that the standards might have been insufficiently considered" (332).[7] And as Wright remarks in connection with a series of popular elementary textbooks, "When rules of courtesy or school deportment are smuggled into English lessons as if they are an intellectual discipline or a law of language or of thought, then the lesson obscures the social issues and apotheosizes middle-class manners by associating them with the sentence definition" (333). In other words, language arts instruction was efficiently (because silently) geared to include those whose manners and class it reflected. Those whose manners were not middle-class either adapted or were excluded.

Wright's analysis holds for college-level textbooks as well. The textbook series she excoriates in the passage above was written by Gardiner, Kittredge, and Arnold, whose college-level text, *A Manual of English Composition* (1907) was singled out for attack by Richards. In his review of the history of nineteenth-century rhetoric, Donald C. Stewart asserts that "late nineteenth-century composition theory and practice was less a response to the social and educational needs of the time and more a reflection of a select class's wrong-headed attitudes about the importance of usage and superficial editorial accuracy" ("Introduction" 230). That current-traditional textwriters saw their work in terms of the socialization of their charges was usually not acknowledged explicitly in their text books, but it came through loud and clear nonetheless. As Stewart noted, it showed up in their discussions of correct usage, which was consistently presented as the mark of an "educated person." It was also implicit in their pervasive assumption that unremitting practice in a prescribed discursive format would not only encourage the practice of straight thinking but would virtually insure it.

The formal standards the textbooks imposed on student writers reflected ethical and social values fully as much as intellectual ones. A discourse marked by unity, coherence, and emphasis, stringently construed, would of necessity reflect a strong sense of limitations, of what was possible, as well as a grasp of the proper relations of things within the universe.

The discursive imperatives imposed by these limitations was felt so strongly by James Fernald as to lead him to remark in his textbook that no distraction, no matter how beautiful, was to be admitted into a discourse: writers "must have the moral courage severely to cut down or cut out what is good and beautiful, if it leads away from the main theme and plan." To do so, Fernald continued, was to make the necessary "sacrifice to unity" (416).

True enough, rejection of the approved conventional form could produce discourse that was fragmented or digressive. But the authors of many current-traditional textbooks were concerned with more than wayward discourse. As one set of authors remarked in 1922, "It is desirable to preserve in composition the graces of social life: quietness of manner, moderation in the expression of judgments, the tone of persuasion rather than that of command—in a word, the group of civilized qualities that may be summed up in *urbanity*" (Thomas, Manchester, and Scott 13). The institutional project of current-traditional rhetoric, it seems, was to produce quiescent, moderate, and solicitous student discourse. I suspect that, as with most things in life, current-traditional rhetoricians got just what they asked for.

8 So What's Wrong with Current-Traditional Rhetoric, Anyway?

Recent studies of college writing programs suggest that current-traditional rhetoric is alive and well. At least half of such programs in the country—perhaps more—follow its pedagogy. Current-traditional textbooks are still being published; most go into at least two editions, and many enjoy five or six. Advertisements for the more successful textbooks list the names of as many as three dozen colleges and universities that have adopted them for use in their introductory composition program. At a large institution, where a text is mandated for use by all students and teachers in the required composition course, this can mean sales of six or seven thousand copies a semester. The numbers can be figured in another way. There are an estimated thirty-three thousand composition teachers in this country.[1] If half of them use current-traditional pedagogy, whether by choice or through institutional mandate, and if each of them is assigned one hundred students (a conservative estimate), something more than a million and a half students are introduced to the principles of current-traditional rhetoric every academic semester.

Undeniably, current-traditional rhetoric is a very successful theory of discourse. Surely its very success indicates that current-traditional rhetoric works. My answer to this is simple: yes indeed, it works. But its work does not lie in teaching people how to write. Rather, current-traditional rhetoric works precisely because its theory of invention is complicit with the professional hierarchy that currently obtains in the American academy. Since subscription to the methodical memory imposes severe limitations on writing instruction, the only other ready

139

explanation for its tenacity is its compliance with certain institutional needs. And its limitations are not only pedagogical; they also inhere in its subscription to an outmoded epistemology. Its continued use raises a serious ethical question as well. I deal with the pedagogical limitations of the methodical memory in this chapter and take up the epistemological and ethical questions in the following chapter. Both chapters attempt to answer the question posed by the title of this one.

The Intellectual Poverty of Textbooks

The most influential current-traditional textbooks ever written are among the most pedantic and intellectually poverty-stricken examples of the tradition. I refer specifically to some of the textbooks composed by the "big four." Their combination of success with simplification and prescription should tell us something about the institutional circumstances that generated their textbooks.

The members of the big four were all respected scholars; most were well read in logic and rhetoric. Some drew explicitly on the germinal texts of the new rhetoric in their textbooks; others cited their reading in logic and belles lettres. For example, Adams Sherman Hill cited Campbell, Whately, Coleridge, and a number of nineteenth-century logicians in the *Principles of Rhetoric*. Scott and Denney concluded the influential third edition of *Paragraph-Writing* with a review of sources that reads like a who's who of current-traditional thought—it includes Campbell, Kames, Blair, Whately, Day, Bain, Boyd, George Payn Quackenbos, Haven, Hart, Adams Sherman Hill, David J. Hill, Clark, Carpenter, Wendell, Genung (106). In his massive texts, Genung quoted nearly every writer regarded as worth reading by educated persons during the nineteenth century. The textbooks composed by all of these writers demonstrated their awareness that they were working in a scholarly tradition with a history. (The exception is Barrett Wendell's *English Composition*, which presents the principles of unity, coherence, and mass as though Adam had discovered them at work in the Garden.)

Nevertheless, the textbooks of the big four seem curiously disconnected from the tumultous intellectual climate that spawned the new rhetoric. They show no interest in debating the theory of mind enshrined there; nor are they interested in discussing the relative claims of empiricism and rationalism, or of any other epistemology, for that matter. Even more disturbing, they seem similarly disconnected from contemporary developments in psychology, rhetoric, or logic.[2] Indeed, a critic of school rhetoric noted in 1897 that "although philology, sociology, and psychology stand ready to make contributions of methods and conclusions, students of rhetoric have been much slower than students of more progressive sciences to avail themselves of such aid" (Smyser 141).

A tendency toward self-reflexivity became especially marked in the works composed by the big four during the 1890s: Genung's *Working Principles of Rhetoric* (1900), Adams Sherman Hill's *Foundations of Rhetoric* (originally published 1892), Scott and Denney's *Paragraph-Writing* (1891), and Wendell's *English Composition* (originally published 1891). For example, the *Working Principles of Rhetoric* is much less fully rationalized than Genung's earlier *Practical Elements of Rhetoric* (1886), and its treatment of invention is much reduced. And for the first time, Genung cites the work of his colleagues in the tradition: he borrowed Hill's principles of style, reduced the literary types of discourse to EDNA, and quoted Wendell several times with approval. I suggest that the tendency toward simplification that marks the relation of the *Working Principles of Rhetoric* to the *Practical Elements of Rhetoric,* or that of Adams Sherman Hill's *Foundations of Rhetoric* to his earlier *Principles of Rhetoric* (1878), testifies to the truly desperate situation in which teachers of composition found themselves near the century's end.

The composition course was invented out of whole cloth in response to late nineteenth-century hysteria about the low levels of literacy manifested by entering college students. But composition had no subject. Nor did it have a cadre of professors who had devoted their professional careers to its mastery. Its teachers were recruited from the ranks of willing persons who could speak and write English reasonably well. These people had to be taught a subject matter as quickly and efficiently as possible.

Given this institutional situation, the textbooks that survived were not the most innovative or subtle or exploratory; they were those that were the most teachable. Robert J. Connors puts it this way:

> With the advent of Freshman Composition, the melee of competing theory that had been "written rhetoric" was radically simplified. A criterion of choice had been found: teachability. The complex taxonomies and systems of the mid-century period melted away, and in their place a few skeletal concepts remained, embroidered differently by different writers but essentially the same. Between 1885 and 1900 the core of what we now call current-traditional rhetoric was shaped and made smooth by the mechanisms of a modernized, centralized textbook marketplace. ("Rhetorical History" 234)

The singular contribution of the textbooks published late in the century by the big four, then, was that they packaged vagrant remnants of the intellectual traditions that had spawned current-traditional rhetoric in such a way that the whole shebang could be efficiently memorized, taught, and studied.

Because of this, mature current-traditional rhetoric was characterized by three features: self-reflexiveness, confusion about its intellectual heritage, and increasing prescriptiveness. Take, for example, Adams Sherman Hill's *Foundations of Rhetoric*. This text reduced the aims of good writers to three inflexible principles:

> (1) to use no word that is not established as a part of the language in the sense in which they use it, and no word that does not say what they wish it to say so clearly as to be understood at once, and either so strongly as to command attention or so agreeably as to win attention; (2) to put every word in the place fixed for it by the idiom of the language, and by the principles which govern communication between man and man—the place which gives the word its exact value in itself and in its relations with other words; and (3) to use no more words than are necessary to effect the purpose in hand.
> (iii)

Reading between the lines with a historically informed eye, I suggest that the three principles derive ultimately from Hill's use of George Campbell's discussions about grammatical purity and perspicuity in the *Philosophy of Rhetoric*. In fact, Hill's discussion of correctness is a much reduced redaction of Campbell's remarks on purity.

Campbell's lengthy discussion of these matters had cited copiously from contemporary authors and was couched in descriptive terms. Hill, however, metamorphosed Campbell's descriptive account into a prescriptive list of five qualities that were to operate in the choice of every word and in the composition of every sentence: correctness, clearness, force, ease, and unity.[3] The same five qualities were to operate in the composition of paragraphs, as well (Adams Sherman Hill, *Foundations of Rhetoric* 305). Invention proper had no place in the foundations of rhetoric. Hill tied the composing process up into three neat graphic bundles—words, sentences, and paragraphs. Invention now came down to the making of choices between correct and incorrect renderings. The binary logic of the *Foundations of Rhetoric* surfaced repeatedly in chapter and section headings: "words and not words," "sentences good and bad," "correct and incorrect sentences," "long or short," "periodic or loose." Hill's nested lists of principles, combined with his simple either/ or strategy, would have made his dicta easy for teachers to remember and to implement in a lecture or during the evaluation of student papers.

For another example, take Scott and Denney's *Paragraph-Writing*. While carefully researched, this text simply reduced the materials found in earlier examples of the tradition to a compact, well-organized set of current-traditional dicta that were to be applied to the composition of paragraphs (a move which would mitigate attention to essays or whole compositions in successive textbooks). Scott and Denney "purposely omitted" the "study of Elegance, or Beauty" from their text on the ground that "students need first of all to learn the beauty of unified thought and the beauty of clear statement" (vii–viii). Indeed, the third edition of *Paragraph-Writing* was a theoretical treatise on the composition of unified and clear paragraphs. It even contained an appendix entitled "Theory of the Paragraph." The body of the text applied a hodgepodge of terms and concepts from classical rhetoric, new rhetoric, logic, and older current-traditional texts to two new kinds of compositions: the isolated paragraph and the related paragraph.

The point is this: apparently neither Hill nor Scott and Denney saw any reason to question the epistemology that underlay the tradition they inherited. They merely reorganized it and enlarged upon some of its less well-developed implications. If they invented new principles or entities, such as the isolated paragraph, they did so by following up tendencies that were already well established in the tradition.

Early twentieth-century textbooks—those composed under the direct influence of the big four—also preserved isolated fragments of the old as well as the new rhetoric within their pages, along with scattered bits of advice originally drawn from psychology and logic. But this advice consisted of little more than rearrangements of a terminological and conceptual residue. Twentieth-century textbook authors borrowed terms at random from associationism or method or classical rhetoric in order to rationalize the prescription of this or that piece of current-traditional arcana. They used terms such as *idea* or *analysis* with no apparent awareness that these once had had quite specific technical meanings with specific conceptual systems.

In his *Expressive English* (1918), for example, James Fernald recommended a liberal mixture of remnants of associationism, method, and stylistic advice as criteria for forming a plan. Fernald's list of means for planning included the Genungian requirements of unity, division, and sequence (which Genung in turn could have found in Day or Blair or in the literature on method). Fernald housed the steps of finding and stating a thesis under the principle of unity, while sequence (coherence) was to be secured by following "the natural laws of association of thought" or a cause and effect movement (shades of associationism) (417). Fernald then added two other principles to his list of required features of the plan. Proportion (Wendell's "mass") included the advice that material be ordered according to time or space, procedures that ultimately derived from eighteenth-century methodical discussions of narrative and description, respectively. Proportion in the plan was also to be governed by the principle of force, which Fernald presumably borrowed from Hill's theory of style. The last requirement for a plan was climax, which was a traditional methodical technique for keeping an audience in suspense (as in Blair for example), although it was often imported into discussions of style in the late nineteenth century.

R. A. Jeliffe recognized the traditional role of definition and division as the initial procedures to be undertaken by the writer of exposition in *A Handbook of Exposition* (originally published 1914). As some earlier textwriters had done, he identified division with analysis, that is, with the breaking of a subject into its parts, while definition, as the fixing of boundaries, was synthetic (25–27). This was, of course, a version of Genung's "exposition extensive" and "exposition intensive." But Jeliffe thought of these two processes as "the inverse and the complement of one another," in that "after analyzing a subject into its parts, division frequently and rightly generalizes on the basis of that analysis; and Definition, while synthetic in the main, as frequently classifies a subject in order that it may the more readily construct its generalizations" (29). Jeliffe apparently thought that definition/division and synthesis/analysis were simply different sets of names for the textbook version of induction and deduction, which, by this time, had become identified as obverse movements from the particular to the general and vice versa.

In other words, during the early years of the twentieth century, current-traditional rhetoric became a self-generating textbook tradition that drew on similar earlier or contemporary works for inspiration. Its prescriptions, as definitively delineated by the big four, became the subject matter of composition. And, since it had no ties to rhetorical theory— let alone to logic or psychology or ethics or politics or epistemology— the textbook tradition became increasingly prescriptive, as well. The longer it fed on itself, disembodied from developments in related fields or in the culture at large, the more authoritative its prescriptions seemed. Suggestions became precepts, and casual observations about inquiry processes metamorphosed into sets of inflexible rules that were to govern the composition of any discourse at all. Footnotes citing previous authorities simply disappeared.

Since no corrective was offered from outside the tradition, its discursive rules could be presented to students and teachers as though they had metaphysical status; their rightness was simply asserted. For example, Henry Pearson insisted in *The Principles of Composition* (1897) that "the basis of authority for the principles of Unity, Coherence, and Emphasis lies in the fact that they represent what the common experience of mankind has found to be the best way of expression." Thus it was incumbent on young writers "to accept the principles of composition without question" (7). Of course Pearson knew that "the common experience of mankind" actually represented the composition theory promulgated by Barrett Wendell, who had been his teacher at Harvard. (Bishop Whately might have been amused to learn that while late current-traditional authors rejected a priori evidence as a means of proof, they were nonetheless willing to present their entire theory of discourse as though it had been derived in this fashion.)

Since textbooks are intended to initiate novices into a field of study, they tend to simplify and universalize its tenets; that is, textbook authors choose, organize, and represent the supposedly fundamental tenets of any field of study as though these had always existed in the coherent form in which they appear in the textbook. The big four did exactly this. They borrowed bits and pieces of a rhetorical theory, melded it with some features of an eighteenth-century theory of mind, and organized the whole into a coherent package. Subsequent textbooks painted an increasingly neater and tidier picture of the ideal discourse.

Authors of textbooks usually condense or omit altogether the historical debates that led to the formulation of the discipline they introduce to students. Thus they overlook the local and time-bound nature of the speculative investigations that unearthed the principles they present. For example, the urtext of modern rhetoric, George Campbell's *Philosophy of Rhetoric,* was composed in the midst of the heady intellectual excitement generated by the work of the empiricist philosopher David Hume. Reverend Campbell and his colleagues in the Aberdeen Philosophical Society found Hume's arguments very compelling. Nonetheless, Campbell's religious convictions led him to reject empirical skepticism as the sole available means of investigating the world. Thus he tinctured Hume's skepticism with a solid dose of rationalism.

But the many textbook authors who adapted Campbell's work to their composition textbooks during the nineteenth century presented his theories of mind and language as though they were not the products of a single mind working in a specific time and place. Rather, remnants of his rhetorical theory were advanced as timeless givens—ways of thinking about discourse that had always been subscribed to by thoughtful persons. In this way, textbook authors simplified the results of Campbell's speculative inquiry and at the same time hardened some of its more obvious features into precepts. Current-traditional textbooks are still written as though the discursive rules they promote were not the product of history, but of nature.

This tendency was exacerbated in the case of composition textbooks by a curious feature of the discipline's history to which I've already alluded. In a complete reversal of the way things develop in most academic disciplines, textbooks created and maintained the theory of discourse that was used to teach writing. This necessarily enhanced the stability of current-traditional composition theory. As certain textbooks met with success because of some new, more teachable, pattern of organization, they would be copied by other writers hoping to cash in on the huge sums that could be made from a best-selling textbook. Textbooks that departed too radically from tradition would not sell, and thus soon fell into oblivion.

Nor was an author's unique voice or perspective any longer required. During the heyday of current-traditional rhetoric, its textbooks had carried the mark of their authors' personalities—Genung's thoroughness, Hill's assertiveness, Wendell's flamboyant irresponsibility. But individual voices soon disappeared from the pages of current-traditional texts. By the early decades of the twentieth century, traditional theory was so unequivocally established that a version of it could be put together by almost anyone who made a study of its most successful examples. Multiple authorships also became common in twentieth-century textbooks. In some cases, scholars of reputation were persuaded to put their names to textbooks mostly written by others.[4] The stability of current-traditional composition theory during the twentieth century has made it possible for the success of popular textbooks to outlast their original authors' interest in them. In fact, some books outlived their authors altogether. In this case new writers were called in to compose subsequent editions. The tradition had become so stable that the loss of an influential author's voice became inconsequential.

Hence none of the current-traditional textbooks published during the twentieth century added much of significance to the theory of discourse on which they were based. There were occasional exceptions to this generalization, of course.[5] But most authors of traditional textbooks adopted the conventional wisdom that cautions, "If it ain't broke, don't fix it." So far, I haven't established that current-traditional rhetoric was—or is—"broke," even today. What I have established, I think, is that its institutionalization in the academy was due to a set of circumstances unique to composition instruction.

What is wrong with current-traditional rhetoric is that it has very little to do with learning to write. Just as its initial success was stimulated by institutional needs, its continued maintenance by the academy has a good deal more to do with institutional circumstances than it does with the appropriateness of its theory of discourse for writing instruction.

Full Frontal Teaching

There is a hard irony to be faced when we consider the development of current-traditional pedagogy. Current-traditional textbooks were popular originally because they gave untrained teachers something to teach. As current-traditional thought prospered, that "something" became the core of the composition course. It dictated the organization of syllabi and of whole composition programs (exposition during the first semester, argument or the research paper during the second). Its prescriptions were identified as the ones that governed the writing done for English classes and for other courses as well. In the current-traditional classroom, teachers required students to read the textbooks they assigned; they lectured about the prescriptions given in the textbooks; they analyzed finished essays to show how their authors had adhered to textbook prescriptions; and they asked students to complete textbook exercises that drilled them in current-traditional prescriptions about grammar, diction, and style. Almost never did they model the writing process for students; almost never did students actually write in class.

Some wag has christened this approach "full frontal teaching." In current-traditional pedagogy, students don't perform: teachers do.

The current-traditional model of invention played an important role in the development of this pedagogy. The model can fairly be described as the construction of a mental forecast of what was to appear on paper. Since this forecast consisted of a retrospective review of the writer's thought processes and since these processes were assumed to be natural to all normal persons, the model tacitly assumed that any thinking student should be able to get her writing right on the first go-round. She needed no assistance with invention proper; indeed very little could be given her. What teachers could do was lecture about how a finished discourse should look, if it were to accurately reflect the uniform, "natural," composing process put forward in current-traditional theory.

The model also collapsed the composing process into a neat linear progression: select, narrow, and amplify. This gave rise to the ubiquitous current-traditional assignment: "From the following list, choose the topic that most appeals to you. Construct a thesis, develop support, organize your ideas, and draft an essay—in that order" (Packer and Timpane 44). Such an assignment generates all the enthusiasm of a visit to the dentist for a root canal. More to the point, it seriously distorts the nature of the writing process as this is practiced in the world outside of the current-traditional classroom. The notion that writing itself might generate ideas, instead of the other way around, was simply not to available to teachers whose only model of invention was the one promulgated in current-traditional textbooks.

Since invention was a matter of forecasting what would appear in writing, current-traditional textbooks identified revision with the correction of mistakes—the stage of writing that professional writers refer to as editing. Writers revised, not to reenvision what they had written, but to pretty up their work so that it met current-traditional standards of correctness. Unless they were writers themselves, composition teachers who used this model of invention could not conceive of writing as a process of tentative starts and stops, wrong turns, successive drafts, and extensive revision over time.

In other words, current-traditional pedagogy is not instruction in writing. It is instruction in a theory of composition. These are two very different things.

To instruct students in a theory of discourse would not necessarily be a bad thing, were it not for the fact that current-traditional pedagogy anticipates the composing process, dictating its progress before it even begins. It stands in for writing; it substitutes discussions of current-traditional arcana for the writing process. It distances teachers from their students' composing processes; it mediates between them and their students' writing.

In fact, students and teachers using the current-traditional model of invention may defer writing altogether, since the current-traditional theme can substitute for writing itself. Often, students in a current-traditional writing program adopt what Jasper Neel calls "anti-writing" as a survival strategy (84). They dash off version after version of "Three Reasons for Stopping X"—formally perfect five-paragraph themes that demonstrate their authors' mastery of the discursive principles prescribed by their textbooks (see fig. 4). Composition becomes a series of exercises wherein students demonstrate their mastery of textbook trivia.

Three Reasons for Stopping X

X is one of the most important problems in today's modern society. There are three main reasons why X should be stopped. This essay will explain those reasons.

First, a lot of people X because it is the popular thing to do. They do not realize how harmful it can be in their later lives. All young people should realize that the best thing to do is have fun later when it will last. Doing the popular thing now because it is fun is a big mistake, because this sort of fun doesn't last.

Second, a lot of people don't realize that taking the easy way now is a bad idea. The way to have a bright future that will last is to work hard now and wait until later to X. For example, Horatio Alger did not X a lot when he was young. Instead, he worked hard for a bright future, and he ended up with a wonderful family, a good job, a lot of money, and a beautiful home.

Third, the Bible says young people should not X. The Bible has been around a lot longer than those who X. If young people will be patient like Job was and if they work hard like he did, they will end up with children and all the good things life has to offer.

In conclusion, I feel that people should not X. We should elect leaders and hire teachers who do not X. Because X is popular, and the easy way, and against the Bible, you can see X should be stopped.

Figure 4. The Ideal Five-Paragraph Theme (Neel 84)

But there is a more serious problem with anti-writing. This sort of prose establishes no voice, selects no audience, takes no stand, makes no commitment. It can be produced by anyone, anywhere, at any time, on demand. Neel reads the message sent by anti-writing as follows: "I am not writing. I hold no position. I have nothing at all to do with discovery, communication, or persuasion. I care nothing about the truth. What I am is an essay. I announce my beginning, my parts, my ending, and the links between them. I announce myself as sentences correctly punctuated and words correctly spelled" (85). The five-paragraph essay simply imposes itself between a writer and her text. Like a boorish guest at a party, it muscles its way into any conversation that she might want to begin.

The Usurpation of Discursive Authority

Despite its intellectual emptiness and its artificial pedagogy, current-traditional rhetoric has lived long and prospered. I suspect that its popularity in the academy is no accident. The reason for this is that the current-traditional theory of invention usurps students' authority over their discourse.

Herein lies another irony. Modern thought subscribed to the notion that discourse is self-authorizing; that is, the very existence of a well-formed discourse was supposed to validate its writer's claim to have discovered something about the world. This program was potentially liberating, since it opened the possibility that anyone could produce discourse that would command the attention of the rhetorical community.

As a consequence, both the new rhetoric and current-traditional rhetoric were governed at the outset by a democratic impetus to make writing available to everybody (or least to those middle-class males who could afford to attend school). The students who listened to Adam Smith or Hugh Blair did so in order to learn how to speak and write English according to standards that would admit them to polite and/or professional circles. This democratic impetus carried over into current-traditional rhetoric. Alexander Bain, its germinal figure in many ways, wrote *English Composition and Rhetoric* with the aim of "methodizing composition," of putting the bones and sinews of writing on public display for everyone's potential appropriation. Bain insisted that the "principle vocation" of the composition teacher was to condense the principles of writing so that he could "impart in a short compass, what, without him, would be acquired slowly, if at all" (v). But the promise of current-traditional rhetoric to deliver discursive mastery to all students was eventually compromised by a paradox inherent within the theory itself.

Classical rhetoricians had explicitly acknowledged the reality that a writer's authority depended to some extent upon her reputation in the community. This reality was occulted in the current-traditional theory of invention (although it must always have been operative in teachers' evaluations of students' performances). There, a writer's appropriation of discursive authority was necessarily tied to invention. Strictly speaking, if she is to establish an authoritative voice, a writer must be able to choose the rhetorical situations she will address. Further, she must be free to select a voice, a stance, her material, and her arguments. She must also be permitted to give free play to the composing process as her writing develops over time. She should not be constrained by generic considerations other than those placed on her by cultural convention.

Of course, the current-traditional theory of invention denies all of these choices to student writers. I take some examples of this denial, selected at random, from very-current-traditional textbooks. Kirszner and Mandell assure their readers that "writing is not an orderly, predict-able sequence of steps." Just two sentences before this, however, they insisted that "you will have to establish a focus for your writing, find material to write about, decide on a tentative thesis, and then move on to draft and revise" (14). Another text points out that "the writing process is a continuing development, a growing through time. . . . But in most cases the writing process occurs in four stages: generating ideas, settling on a subject and thesis, getting the ideas written, getting the writing right" (Packer and Timpane 7). Another very successful text insists that every piece of writing have a thesis statement and lists nine errors that writers of thesis statements can commit. The thesis must not be a fragment or a question. It should not contain irrelevancies. It should not "contain phrases like 'I think' or 'in my opinion,' because they weaken a writer's argument" (Winkler and McCuen 40). And so on.

Winkler and McCuen's sanction against phrases like "I think" under-scores an additional feature of current-traditional composition theory—its effort to kill off individual voices. In addition to prescribing inven-tional choices, current-traditional rhetoricians created a standard autho-rial voice for student-written discourse—a voice that could be put on for any occasion. As Richard Ohmann observed in *English in America* (1976), traditional composition textbooks typically characterized a stu-dent writer as a person who lacked location in either space or time, who was "newborn, unformed, without social origins and without needs that would spring from his origins. He has no history. Hence the writing he does and the skills he acquires are detached from those parts of himself not encompassed by his new identity as a student" (148). In fact, stu-dents' very studenthood inspired the typically innocuous current-tradi-tional list of potential subjects to write about: the student union, the cafeteria, favorite teachers, roommates, and so on.

Current-traditional composition textbooks also tended to portray stu-dent writers as having been extracted from any community they might have inhabited prior to entering the classroom. As Ohmann observed, the student writer "acts not only outside of time and history, but alone—framing ideas, discovering and expressing himself, trying to persuade others, but never working with others to make a theme that advances a common purpose" (149). That this a-rhetorical nonperson could author a text in the sense of taking responsibility for its shape or of marking it with her voice is difficult to imagine. Indeed, some current-traditional textbooks frankly acknowledged students' nonidentity by insisting that they erase any textual marks of their presence such as first-person pro-nouns.

The rhetorical fiction that governed current-traditional textuality is a grotesque parody of the rhetorical circumstances under which authoritative writing gets done. Richard Whately himself readily acknowledged that the artificiality of the composition exercise was likely to bring about the sort of writing known only too well to composition teachers. "It will often happen," Whately wrote, that "such exercises will have forged a habit of stringing together empty common-places, and vapid declamation,—of multiplying words and spreading out the matter thin,—of composing in a stiff, artificial, and frigid manner." Whately added that students wrote "both better, and with more facility" in *"real occasions"* of life, such as when they answered letters from friends (22). However, he offered a typically modern solution to the problem of disengaged writing by suggesting that students be set to writing about subjects in which they were interested.

Current-traditional composition theorists never examined their attitude toward voice in order to determine whether that might be a potential source of listless student writing. Instead they entered a qualification to their claim to make writing available to everyone. They began to withhold instruction in invention, the wherewithal of having something to write, from their students. As Bain observed, to achieve a "command of language" was a lifetime preoccupation, and in its absence teachers of writing were helpless to instruct pupils who came to them without such preparation. Invention was the secret part of writing, the part that could not be taught but was nevertheless necessary. Either you had it or you didn't.

No current-traditional rhetorician doubted that the "forms and proprieties"—arrangement, style, grammar, good usage—could be quickly and easily imparted to attentive students, however. And this was as it should be. After all, wrote Bain, "the direct bearing of the Rhetorical art is, of course, not Invention, but Correctness; in other words, polish, elegance, or refinement" (*English Composition and Rhetoric* vii). Or in still other words, the purpose of instruction in rhetoric was acculturation to the prevailing etiquette for writing inoffensive discourse. Students were systematically taught that they were not to say anything to anybody but were to write about preselected topics as correctly and (if they got past "correctly") in as elegant a manner as they could muster. Their discourse was forever and always in bondage to someone else's, if not that of a model text, then that of textbook prescriptions or the instructor's enforcement of them. What was left to student writing was to demonstrate progressive mastery of the smaller conventions governing discursive decorum.

The ultimate irony of the history of current-traditional rhetoric, then, is that its initially democratic impetus to invest everyone with discursive authority was subsumed in the appropriation of writers' authority by text, textbook, teacher, and finally, by the academy itself. The current-traditional hedge about invention was so important that, without it, the whole project of composition instruction would have become apparent and hence useless. In its institutionalized form—freshman composition—current-traditional writing instruction served the academy as a useful mud fence, guarding it from the unsupervised and uncontained sprawl of self-initiated analytical or critical student discourse. As Plato complained thousands of years ago, written discourses have the habit of floating all over the place and of getting into the wrong hands unless some means of control is established over who can write and who will be read (*Phaedrus* 275e). Current-traditional rhetoric was the control developed within the academy. When students were instructed in it, all concerned could rest assured that few students would produce writing that demanded to be read and heeded.

Students were not the only persons whose discursive authority was eroded by current-traditional pedagogy. The authority to judge the quality of students' writing rested with professors of rhetoric throughout most of the nineteenth century. However, late in the century, teacherly authority began to be displaced by the authoritative voice of the current-traditional textbook. The reasons for this are not hard to discern: composition was no longer taught by distinguished professors of rhetoric, but by instructors, teaching assistants, and part-timers who often had no training in composition.

The upshot of this situation was that teacherly authority was replaced by the institutional authority represented in composition programs and in textbooks selected by a faculty committee (whose members often did not teach the course). The institution further usurped teachers' authority by imposing on them the standardized expectations about the formal features of discourse derived from current-traditional rhetoric. Some institutions imposed a standardized syllabus and uniform grading standards on their teachers as well.

Since the current-traditional theory of invention posited that the generation of discourse was a natural process, it could be taught by anyone, to anyone. But this initial generosity of spirit has been hampered by a certain professional ambivalence about whether a course that could be taught and taken by "just anyone" was really respectable. Even today, the academy harbors a certain uneasiness about composition teachers. It entrusts them with a function that is loudly proclaimed as crucial to students' education, but it won't give them tenure. Nor does it treat student writing as "real" writing. The composition course socializes young people into the academy. It does not enhance their learning process or help them to become active participants in the ongoing discourse of the academic community—let alone in communities outside the academy. In short, current-traditional rhetoric complies nicely with institutional assumptions about who is allowed to assume discursive authority within the academy and who is not.

9 The Limits of Modern Epistemology for Writing Instruction or Why Current-Traditional Rhetoric Is Not a Rhetoric

Historians of rhetoric have routinely emphasized the decidedly scientific bent of the new rhetoric. But the foremost among them are divided as to its ultimate worth. On the down side, Vincent Bevilacqua has taken issue with the limited view of rhetoric that grew out of modern attitudes toward mind:

> The modern philosophers of the eighteenth century looked too narrowly at their subject. . . . [T]o study rhetoric narrowly as a scientific rather than as an imaginative-poetic concern—to study it in terms of Descartes and Locke rather than in terms of Aesop and Homer—*is to see rhetoric as one sees by a lamp at night*—the object in focus can be seen with clarity but its background is cut off. One sees only what the narrow lamp of science allows one to see. ("Rhetorical Science" 28)

But scholars do not agree about the worth of the new rhetoric.

Wilbur Samuel Howell makes the case that the seventeenth-century discovery of mind, and all that its discovery entailed, required the jettisoning of most of the rhetorical baggage imposed on discourse theory by the dead hand of classical rhetoric. Howell argues that the new rhetoricians "all tended to treat the Ciceronian tradition as something which needed to be measured against the requirements of a new time and to be rejected wherever it failed to meet the standard that the new time would impose" (*Eighteenth-Century British Logic* 447).

While I agree with Howell that the intellectual standards of the "new time" required an overhaul of rhetorical theory, I am not nearly so sanguine as he is about the ultimate worth of the new rhetoric. He credits George Campbell with "freeing rhetoric from its two-thousand-year bondage to the old logic . . . but also in endowing it with a new sense of obligation to truth" (*Eighteenth-Century British Logic* 426). While this observation is accurate enough, Howell's modernist bias prevents him from seeing that to confine the role of rhetoric to a search for ways to communicate "truth" has had unfortunate side effects for rhetorical study and practice.

The Limits of Modern Epistemology

Thanks to its quasi-scientific bias, the new rhetoric persisted in confining the truth it sought to those matters that could be verified either by experience or through introspection. And since current-traditional rhetoric followed suit in positing that the end of rhetoric was the perception and communication of knowledge, its preferred form of discourse represented writers' retrospective reviews of the knowledge they had derived from experience. All such discourses had equal value, no matter who wrote them or how they were received, granted that the writer paid proper attention to the methods by means of which knowledge was created and transferred.

This point of view imposed serious limitations on what could be defined as a serious rhetorical purpose. Bevilacqua is correct: to define rhetoric as an instrument for purveying empirical or introspective truth is to obscure its classical function as the discipline that prepared people to arbitrate ethical, political, aesthetic, and legal questions. Writers may have altogether different reasons for composing than repeating the results of an investigation, reasons such as reaffirming community values or criticizing the decisions made by public officials.

As a result of its emphasis on the communication of knowledge, then, current-traditional pedagogy tended to overlook a panoply of discursive genres. It ignored whole areas of discourse that did not deal in scientific truth: oratory, poetry, epideictic discourse, legal and ethical discussion, and aesthetics, among others.[1] A nineteenth-century commentator on current-traditional rhetoric described the loss this way: "In how many popular texts do we find expositions of the real nature of language power . . . its relation to . . . ultimate aims in life, and of its value to human society? The broader ethical, aesthetic and social imports of the power of verbal expression are generally ignored" (Smyser 141). Even today, to suggest that students in a composition class compose discourse that is immediately related to public events—such as a commemoration of a new city hall or an elegy for some well-known citizen—would be met with puzzled frowns. Ceremonial discourse—what the ancients called epideictic rhetoric—is composed in order to celebrate or reaffirm community values. Much of the writing done in journalism and politics is epideictic in character—from the "person of the week" feature on the nightly news to the president's state of the union address. Nevertheless, the analysis and production of this powerful discursive practice are off limits to current-traditional composition instruction.

The loss of these discursive arenas came about as a result of the privilege awarded to reason in modern epistemology. Of all the categories of mind discriminated by faculty psychology, the workings of reason were assumed to be most stable and uniform. Rational inquiry, which was associated exclusively with scientific and philosophical investigation in early modern thought, simply edged out the claims to knowledge made by other disciplines. Rhetoric, ethics, and aesthetics were identified with the nonrational (or irrational) faculties: the imagination, the will, and the passions.[2] The results of inquiry gained by these means were assumed to be less universally applicable, less predictable, and hence less important, than those made available by science.

Current-traditional rhetoric also associated discourse production with only one faculty—reason. Alexander Bain made its centrality to modern discourse theory explicit when he subsumed appeals to the imagination and the passions under this faculty. His privileging of the understanding ghettoized those genres of discourse—oratory and poetry—which were assumed to appeal to the less uniform and less predictable faculties. More important, it focused on the discursive genre that was intended to eliminate differences of opinion altogether—exposition. The faith of current-traditional rhetoric was that the dissemination of knowledge, if suitably packaged, would eliminate disagreements among informed persons. And for Bain, at least, a welcome consequence of the realization of this ideal would be the death of rhetoric. Bain was skeptical about rhetoric precisely because it acknowledges the importance of irrationality in human decision making. Given his subscription to faculty psychology and modern epistemology, he necessarily defined any appeal to the imagination, the passions, or the will as irrational.

Its emphasis on reason also explains why writers in the textbook tradition were so firmly opposed to students exercising their imaginations. Unfortunately, this position also led them to oppose the exercise of originality or innovation. Artistic method—method that is hardly method at all—was important to the methodical literature as the counterpart of natural method. But it never made the crossing into current-traditional rhetoric, as its companion did, and for one very good reason. Since a writer's use of artistic method depended on the specific rhetorical situations in which she found herself, its movements were not generalizable or predictable. The very reason for the textbooks' subscription to reason as the dominant faculty was its postulated uniform operation in every person; the guarantee for this uniformity was the production of uniformly similar discourses. Deviation from the norm was simply not thinkable, not only because such discourse was imaginative, or impassioned, or willful, but because it was irrational.

The allegiance of the new rhetoric to quasi-scientific models of knowing also led its current-traditional progeny to misconstrue the central role of interpretation in nearly all writing. Strictly speaking, current-traditional rhetoric defined discourse as the disinterested presentation of facts or information. The ideal theme literally represented some bits of information gathered by its author through experience or reading. A relatively minor side effect of the emphasis on facts was that students were denied access to artful or literary means of argument, such as anecdotes, fables, figures, or analogies—all of which were taken seriously in classical rhetoric as means of persuasion. More important, the emphasis on facts ignored the reality that most writing is a tissue of what current-traditional rhetoricians would call opinions. When writers cite facts, they must weave these into a fabric of interpretation; facts simply cannot be used neutrally or nonselectively. Once again, current-traditional strictures against opinions, as well as more rhetorical means of proof, divested students of the right to determine their own discursive choices.

The Limits of the Aims of Discourse

The aim-centeredness of the new rhetoric involved its own host of difficulties. To center a rhetorical theory on writers' aims is to simplify what writers do when they address a rhetorical situation. In other words, the theory of aims is a partial and highly selective description of rhetorical practice. Rhetors must take into full account the given linguistic, cultural, and situational constraints that operate in the composition of each and every discourse. They must know a good deal more than what they intend: they must know which arguments will be well received by an audience and which will not wash, they must know whether linguistic flourishes will be persuasive, they must decide when it is appropriate for them to engage in discourse and when they should remain silent, and so on.

Moreover, Campbell's theory of aims was predictive. Writers and speakers were supposed to know what they intended to accomplish before they began to compose, and thus the actual process of composition was marginalized. Too, the four (or five) aims it discriminated were arbitrarily imposed on rhetors (that they were arbitrary is indicated by the fact that later current-traditional textbooks could discriminate dozens of such aims). And, as I hope I have demonstrated, the aim-centeredness of its inventional theory placed an enormous burden upon the qualities of mind possessed by an individual investigator. As a result, the quality of his discourse could be directly attributed to the quality of his thinking rather than to constraints in the rhetorical situation for which he had composed it. Ironically enough, this is exactly what happened in current-traditional classrooms: the listless quality of student discourse was blamed on their inattentiveness or lack of preparation, rather than on the rhetorical situation for which they were asked to compose it.

Because of its aim-centeredness, current-traditional rhetoricians allotted full privilege to the knowing subject, whose rhetorical tasks amounted to clarifying her purpose and casting it in language in such a way as to transfer her thinking to any docile reader with accuracy and efficiency. Accuracy and efficiency were insured if the progression of the discourse was orderly, that is, if it moved in coherent fashion from an initial generalization that either introduced the writer's subject or expressed her intention, to the details, or facts, which supported the generalization or gave reasons for its being subscribed to by the writer.

Their dependence on method allowed current-traditional rhetoricians to conceive of writing, and of writing instruction, as value-free processes carried on by people who somehow exist outside of ideology and culture. Its theory of invention subscribed to the modern model of the isolated writer, working alone in study or laboratory in order to invent new knowledge that could then be passed along to readers without hitch or distortion. Writing served a distinctly instrumental and secondary function on this model.

The notion of writing as instrument is complicit with the trivialization of composition instruction. Since the search for truth is thought to be somehow distinct both from the practice of discourse and from the community in which it is generated and since writing instruction focuses on what is then necessarily conceived as a simple recording process, teachers of writing have been reluctant to focus their instruction on the quality of their students' arguments, preferring instead to confine their comments to format or method. Theorists of method assumed that application of a properly rigorous method to any area of inquiry would insure the production of the desired results. Method trivialized content simply by ignoring it. Its advocates assumed that any content was equally susceptible to being produced by employment of the proper method.

The modern separation of writing from its content as well as its context denigrated its importance. The best to be hoped for from writing was that it could copy down whatever writers already knew. What writers knew, of course, was the really important stuff—but it was not the province of writing instruction. This is why writing does not enjoy a widespread reputation in the academy as a means of generating knowledge, despite recent developments in composition theory that define it this way.[3]

The centrality of authors' aims to modern theories of invention also diminished the role played by communal exigencies in the invention of discourse. Discourse was initiated primarily by an author's need to know something and only secondarily by the need to communicate this discovery to readers. As a corollary, rhetors no longer needed to take into account the potential reception of a discourse by its readers; in essence, they no longer needed to worry about how specific readers would receive it. Modern rhetoric treated an audience as an undifferentiated group of rational people who would receive any discourse indifferently.

As a result, modern rhetoricians lost interest in ethos and pathos as means of proof. This development has several related sources, primary among them the philosophy of mind that assumed that all rational minds worked alike. But the banishment of ethos and pathos, which both new rhetoricians and current-traditional text writers associated with appeals to the passions and the will, was inevitable in a theory of discourse that appealed only to reason. Appeals to any given human passion such as anger or desire, much less to the will of a given individual, seemed increasingly less necessary as reason became the dominant—indeed the only—faculty to which current-traditional invention appealed.

In turn, current-traditional rhetoric conceptualized an audience as a monolithic abstraction. As one very-current-traditional textbook would have it, writers should visualize readers before they start writing, ask themselves how much background their readers will need, decide on the details that will appeal to them, and "stop occasionally to think about your reader" (Packer and Timpane 14). Audience analysis amounts to determining what readers know, not what they think about the rhetor or her subject. Least of all are readers conceived of as persons who might have passionate commitments of their own.

Beyond concessions such as this, current-traditional textbooks did not acknowledge that writers' messages are not always immediately acceptable to all audiences. To light on some current examples: avowed feminists do not react neutrally to so-called pro-life arguments; environmentalists have difficulty accepting the arguments made by proponents of nuclear energy—some are reluctant even to read such arguments or to respect anyone who would make them.

But current-traditional authors never acknowledged that a writer's ethical relation to her audience was not always immediately acceptable to them. Nevertheless readers' reception of discourse composed, for instance, by members of minority groups—whether they be neo-Marxists or neo-Nazis—is always compromised to some extent by their assessment of the ethical worth of such persons and the importance of their causes to the life of the community. Nor did the text writers speculate on whether this relation was capable of alteration by means of discourse or, if so, to what degree.[4] Can a neo-Nazi mount arguments that are so reasonable that they will be accepted by a liberal audience? Can a liberal mount arguments about social policy—say, socialized medicine—that will convince a reasonable conservative to accept them? Such questions face any potential rhetor, and her answers to them inevitably influence her composing process. And any rhetor who would overcome such obstacles needs much more far-reaching advice than that usually given in current-traditional rhetoric.

Current-traditional pedagogy systematically forgot that readers are people with opinions and attitudes who inhabit a variety of discourse communities. Thus it invented the "general reader"—the neutral, objective teacher or holistic grader who could separate her reactions to a discourse from her relationship to its writer or its subject. According to this article of current-traditional faith, readers always react objectively and fairly to any piece of writing no matter who its author, what thesis she presents, or what subject she chooses. To give a couple of not necessarily hypothetical examples, the reader posited by current-traditional rhetoric could, when reading, stifle or put aside his anger or resentment at a student with whom he had had disciplinary problems; a teacher who adhered to skepticism could put it aside when she read a paper on religion authored by a fundamentalist Christian. In the latter case, current-traditional rhetoric offered her some loopholes. She could reject the paper by denying the validity of the sorts of authoritative appeals to a sacred text that fundamentalists generally make, since such appeals are not "factual"; or, with more finality, she could simply forbid him to write about religious matters, since this sort of discourse was not covered in current-traditional genre theory.

In sum, either the "general reader" is a saint, or the discourses he reads will necessarily be innocuous. Human nature being what it is, students quickly learn to adapt their writing to the rhetorical situation that obtains in current-traditional writing classes.

Knowledge as a Commodity

Perhaps in compensation for its exclusive focus on the originating mind, modern rhetorical thought abstracted authors' thinking out of culture and out of the local circumstances in which they lived and worked. There is a crucial difference between the modern universalization of the thinking process and the theory of communal knowledge advanced in classical rhetoric. In classical epistemology, wise persons were those who had thought long and hard about the cultural assumptions that influenced their lives and those of other persons. In turn, their shared wisdom became part of communal knowledge. Knowledge itself was always changing its shape, depending on who was doing the knowing. Every act of knowing influenced the body of knowledge itself.

In modern thought, however, knowledge was simply there for the taking by anyone who cared to invest the labor. If a thinker were possessed of a normally functioning mind, there was no reason why she could not learn anything she pleased. Nor was the production of knowledge influenced by the perspective brought to her labors by the knower. Since all rational minds worked alike, any idiosyncracies that might exist in the cultural background of an investigator were rendered irrelevant. Read from one point of view, the presumed equality of discourses that adhered to a prescribed method was wonderfully democratic; anyone who could learn to do this could become a purveyor of knowledge. But read from another point of view, this theory of composition was exclusive; if writers' minds took tacks that were innovative, unconventional, digressive, or difficult, they could be suspected of possessing inadequate or unnatural reasoning processes.

In modern rhetorical theory, then, invention became a matter of exerting the powers of mind on some problem whose parameters were relatively unaffected by the fact of its being studied. The modern theory of invention sublimated the classical connection of knowledge with knowers, since its objects were assumed to be relatively stable and indifferent to those who investigated them. Rather, the minds of knowers changed when new knowledge was acquired. A corollary to the assumed stability of the objects of knowledge was that ignorance was the result of human inattentiveness, rather than of any complexity or obscurity in nature that rendered knowledge about it inaccessible. A further corollary was that if investigators became attentive and thorough enough, they could possibly give the world some piece of knowledge it had never before possessed. In short, they could invent "new knowledge," which they then "owned."

This theory of knowledge as a commodity explains some of the features of current-traditional pedagogy: its truncated theory of invention, its insistence that student writing reproduce or repeat some piece or pieces of knowledge acquired by themselves or by someone else (as in the expository theme or the research paper), and its fear of plagiarism. Invention was eventually rendered marginal in current-traditional pedagogy because of its assumption that knowledge could be found or reproduced, but it could never be generated by the composition of discourse or in reaction to a rhetorical situation.

Nor is the dominance of current-traditional composition theory by exposition an anomaly. The expository theme defined writing as a repetition of the reasoning that had gone before the production of discourse—a repetition of the writer's mental processes, a repetition of knowledge already derived, a repetition of method, a representation of reason itself. *Exposition* referred to the "ex-posing" or abstracted assembly of some set of phenomena. Bain, for example, defined exposition as "the mode of handling applicable to knowledge or information in the form of what is called the Sciences," which are "each laid out on the plan of exhausting, in the most systematic array, all the information, respecting one department of nature" (*English Composition: A Manual* 147). Or, in the words of another text writer, expository discourse amounted to a "succinct and orderly setting-forth of some piece of knowledge" (Baldwin, *College Manual of Rhetoric* 40).

The notion persists in current-traditional rhetoric that a piece of writing can hand over knowledge (in its modern guise as "information") from investigator to reader. For example, a very-current-traditional composition textbook acknowledges that an important function of writing is that of "reporting information" (Axelrod and Cooper 128). Of course, the authors of this text are responding to an exigency placed upon them by the modern attitude toward knowledge, which persists both within and without academic institutions.[5] They know that their students will be required to write papers which "organize and report information clearly in order to make a point that readers will find interesting and informative" (129).

So what's wrong with repeatedly asking students to perform this seemingly innocuous task? For one thing, it asks students to put themselves in the position of scientists who have devoted their lives to the achievement of a relatively full knowledge of some area of inquiry. Thus it trivializes the process of knowledge acquisition—any subject whatsoever can be read up on and mastered for the occasion. For another, it pretends that the process of acquiring knowledge about some subject can be completed—which is tantamount to saying that the world's living authority on, say, current-traditional textbooks knows everything there is to know about them and that her book on the subject contains every last word that can be written about them. Their awareness of this subterfuge led current-traditional rhetoricians to advocate that students narrow and limit the subjects under investigation. But when a subject is narrowed and limited so that it can be encapsulated in a five-paragraph theme, its treatment is necessarily trivial.

On a modern model of the mind, knowledge was also a commodity that could be borrowed or stolen. Since investigators could invent "new" knowledge simply by paying sustained attention to some selected object, that knowledge became, in a sense, theirs.[6] As Woodman and Adler told their readers, "you have a responsibility to give credit for facts, theories, and opinions that are as much the property of others as their houses or cars" (428). Among their list of ways to commit plagiarism, Winkler and McCuen include "taking an original idea from someone else and using it in your paper without acknowledging your source" (277). In current-traditional rhetoric, the difference between borrowing knowledge and stealing it had to do with whether writers acknowledged their sources or not.

Ironically enough, the paradigm expository assignment in a current-traditional composition class is the research paper, which could be cynically defined as an elaborate exercise in the art of borrowing knowledge without seeming to steal it. Given the twin current-traditional presumptions that students lack knowledge about the topics they must research and that they lack control over their inventional procedure, this assignment quite literally invites plagiarism. Students find it very difficult to establish dispositional control over the myriad sources they are asked to read ("at least five books and ten articles"); still less are they able to establish an authoritative voice that can be heard over those of the authorities from whose work their own is derivative. Hence the research paper presents students with perhaps the most vicious double bind they encounter in current-traditional composition pedagogy.

Universal Systems and the Teaching of Writing

George Campbell's *Philosophy of Rhetoric* stands at the head of an impressive tradition in which the rules or laws of rhetoric are articulated and integrated into theoretical systems. Systems or sciences of rhetoric dot the intellectual landscape throughout the modern period. Examples include Whately's *Elements of Rhetoric* (1828), Bain's *English Composition: A Manual* (1866), Henry Noble Day's *Art of Discourse* (1867), David J. Hill's *Science of Rhetoric* (1877), I. A. Richards' *Philosophy of Rhetoric* (1936), J. L. Austin's *How to Do Things with Words* (originally published 1955), and Chaim Perelman and L. Olbrecht-Tyteca's *New Rhetoric: A Treatise on Argumentation* (1958). What all these works have in common is their subscription to the notion of commensurability, a term I borrow from Richard Rorty.[7] All of the rhetorics just mentioned assume as a basic premise that a set of rules can be found "which will tell us how rational agreement can be reached on what would settle the issue on every point where statements seem to conflict. These rules tell us how to construct an ideal situation, within which all residual disagreements will be seen to be 'noncognitive' or merely verbal, or else merely temporary—capable of being resolved by doing something further" (316). The hope of "commensurable" rhetorical systems is that disagreement between persons is a product of failure to follow the correct procedure or of simple misunderstanding of the meanings of words. As we have seen, current-traditional rhetoric buys into this program.

For Campbell and his intellectual progeny, the rules insuring that human beings always reached agreement were located in the universal principles of human nature; Austin looked for them in rule-governed uses of language, and Perelman and Olbrechts-Tyteca found them in the potential assent of an imaginary entity called the universal audience. Despite these efforts to ground rhetoric in some epistemological given, however, the fact remains that such a set of rules—which could prescribe how agreement is to be reached among all interested parties to any debate whatever—is probably not to be had. And even if it were, the rules would still not tell us what to do after general agreement is reached. Deciding what to do, after all, is a very different thing than securing agreement among concerned parties. And deciding what to do is the province of rhetoric.

The limitations of current-traditional invention are traceable to its subscription to a philosophy of language use, rather than to a more rhetorical theory of discourse production. My guiding assumption here is that since the necessity for rhetorical theorizing or practice (including the practice of composition) arises from local and special conditions, rhetoric cannot be fruitfully philosophized about. (This generalization holds when *philosophy of rhetoric* is understood to designate some set of universal principles that are thought to govern the production and reception of discourse.) Several formidable difficulties confront any project that would philosophize rhetoric.

First of all, rhetoric pays close attention to the given audience, occasion, and social or political situation that has prompted a rhetor to compose and deliver a discourse. Unless we assume that individual human beings always and everywhere act for the same reasons and respond to the same stimuli regardless of cultural or social context, we must grant that rhetorical force derives from the suitedness of a given discourse to the given social, political, or economic circumstances in which a particular community finds itself.

And unless such a theory includes consideration of the social contexts that always generate rhetorical acts, to generalize about rhetorical principles will necessarily involve reductionism. In the absence of some acceptable theory of specifically rhetorical motivation, philosophical approaches to rhetoric will necessarily assume that the behavior of individuals is ontologically prior to that of communities; they will assume further that there is a causal relation between the forces or effects that motivate individuals and those that move entire communities or societies.[8] This is, in fact, exactly what modern rhetorical theorists did. Eighteenth-century philosophers of rhetoric extrapolated introspective analyses of the workings of their own minds into a general theory of mind. They then devised a set of formal discursive patterns that were to represent the movements of mind, patterns that would hold good for all occasions and audiences. Their rhetorical system did not center on a given rhetorical act located in a given time and place. Rather, it began with an abstracted list of possible rhetorical purposes.

Given its inextricable connection with specific cultural and social contexts, however, rhetorical practice and its effects are not predictable in the ways in which philosophers of rhetoric have assumed them to be. That is to say, rhetorical theory cannot be scientific. This is not to say that rhetoric cannot be theorized about, of course. It is only to point out that any rhetorical theory must be constantly available for revision—sometimes on the spot. Nonphilosophical theories of rhetoric have been developed that allow for the twists and turns of local exigency. For example, the Sophist Gorgias apparently utilized the classical Greek notion of *kairos*—roughly "seizing the moment when it makes itself apparent"—to underscore the importance of a rhetorician's knowing when and where to speak, and what to say, given the immediate circumstances in which she finds herself.

A second difficulty with philosophizing about rhetoric is that rhetoric tends to prefer a more holistic picture of human motivation than has been traditionally congenial to philosophy. To use an eighteenth-century vocabulary, rhetoric attaches as much or more importance to the passions and the will as means of effecting persuasion than it does to logic or to reason. Rhetoricians are not unwilling to make emotional appeals; indeed they recognize that human engagement with language is a very complex phenomenon that may have very little to do with reason. The success of modern advertising and the state of modern political rhetoric are ample testimony to this generalization. For the most part, advertisers and politicians appeal to human fears and desires. While rhetoricians may deplore this state of affairs, they do not hope to correct it, nor do they ignore it, as modern philosophers of mind pretended to do.

Third, rhetoricians tend to view language as something other than a simple medium of representation. Because philosophers are interested in discovering first principles that lie outside language, they have found it necessary to think of language as an instrument, or tool, whose usefulness lies in the accuracy of its representative powers.[9] But language is not always a subservient instrument of thought or reason; indeed, it may shape both. Nevertheless, modern rhetorical theory tried to predict the flow of language and hence to reduce it to a pliant medium that would represent thought accurately.

To put this another way, modern rhetorics are not especially rhetorical. Indeed, if my description of modern attitudes about knowledge production is accurate, I can argue that the modern worldview, at least as this is represented in a rhetorical theory such as Campbell's, is in fact perversely opposed to rhetoric. People need rhetoric precisely because they disagree; people disagree because their circumstances differ. Rhetoric functions where difference is assumed. Differences exist between rhetors and their audiences as well as among members of a given audience. Rhetors and audiences bring different backgrounds, aspirations, and assessments of the current state of affairs to any rhetorical situation. If there were no differences of this kind, after all, rhetoric would not be necessary.

Thus I have serious reservations about the ethics of limiting writing instruction to the current-traditional model. Because it standardizes and forecasts how the writing process should develop, the current-traditional theory of invention elides differences among rhetorical situations, denies the location of any rhetorical act in a given community, and transfers discursive authority away from individual rhetors and onto the academy. Perhaps this presented a less serious ethical problem to Adam Smith, whose audience was relatively homogeneous. But the cultural backgrounds of the young writers who now populate American writing classrooms are far from homogeneous. It is unrealistic, then, to assume that all of these writers bring the same mental equipment to the classroom. It is unethical to force them to pretend that they possess this equipment when they don't.

Finally: The Importance of Invention

Because of its intimate ties with the ethics, politics, and epistemology of the culture it serves, invention is crucial to the maintenance of a complete and effective theory of rhetoric. Invention reminds rhetors of their location within a cultural milieu that determines what can and cannot be said or heard. The only effective arguments are those to which the community is prepared to respond, whether negatively or positively.

If we grant that cultures are held together by the persuasive potential that exists within language (when they are not held together by the overt use of force, that is), we must grant the importance of rhetoric to such a culture. And we must further grant the importance of invention. When rhetoric is taught as a system of rules for arranging words, its students may overlook the fact that language, effectively used, can change the way people think and can move them to act. This denies a central insight of classical rhetoric—that the generation and deployment of discourse is intimately related to the possession of cultural power.[10] Skilled rhetoricians know how to invent culturally effective arguments. Thus they are able to exert noncoercive control over those who don't suspect the power that is resident in language.

Without invention, the practice of rhetoric can degenerate into the disinterested deployment of linguistic techniques—that is, rhetors can use language as though they need not be concerned about its impact on hearers and readers. To teach writing as though the composing process begins with arrangement or style, then, assumes that speakers and writers can deploy discourse in a cultural and ethical vacuum, and hence that what they say or write doesn't matter very much beyond its immediate scene of production. Composition becomes the manipulation of words for its own sake.

Concern with invention has often diminished or disappeared altogether during the long history of rhetoric in the West. This was the case, for example, in the later Roman Empire, where rhetoricians earned their keep by composing and delivering highly ornamented and elaborate display pieces—exercises whose wit and ingenuity were meant only to amuse their rhetorically sophisticated audiences. Here invention was confined to the rhetor's skill in rewriting or reinterpreting a piece of discourse that was already well known. Historians of rhetoric suggest that such rhetorical practices occur in cultures that do not allow for the free exchange of discourse. In such a cultural situation, rhetoric is quite literally cut free from its obligations to be persuasive and is reduced to technique, play, or display.

This is precisely what happens in current-traditional pedagogy. While the current-traditional theory of discourse does have an attenuated theory of invention, its epistemology is out of keeping with current theories of knowledge. Apart from this, however, I worry about the ubiquity of a writing pedagogy that so thoroughly displaces invention. Is the rhetorical environment that obtains in the contemporary college composition class really so similar to that of the late Roman Empire?

Notes
References Cited
Index

Notes

1. Public Knowledge and Private Inspiration

1. Several epistemological systems were in circulation during the fifth and fourth centuries BCE. I refer specifically to those thought to have been espoused by the older Sophists, on the one hand, and by Aristotle in his rhetorical and dialectical treatises, on the other. On the epistemology of the Sophists, see Untersteiner, Kerferd, and W. K. C. Guthrie.

2. Modernism was a dominant discursive practice during the seventeenth, eighteenth, and nineteenth centuries, as well as the early years of the twentieth. Had Weaver compiled his list of ultimate terms in the eighteenth or nineteenth centuries, it would have included the term *reason* as well.

3. I borrow the term *discursive practice* from Michel Foucault. Briefly, a discursive practice is any set of rules that governs what may be said (or not said) in a given social, historical, or cultural arena. For example, classical rhetoricians—bound as they were by their notion of common sense—could not have used, or understood, the currently popular expression "That's just your opinion." This expression depends for its articulation on the discursive practice invented by Lockean empiricism, which defines opinions as the product of individual experience. Following Foucault, I have assumed that the set of texts that propounds the new rhetoric and current-traditional rhetoric, taken together, may be treated as though they articulate one discipline-specific manifestation of one modern discursive practice. In *Order of Things,* Foucault labels the discursive practice that privileges representation rather than resemblance as *classical;* I label it *modern* in order to avoid confusion with the epistemic description I supply for classical—that is, ancient—rhetoric.

Knoblauch and Brannon saddle classical rhetoric with blame for many of the negative practices they find in contemporary writing instruction. My analysis is partly a commentary on their work, a commentary arguing to the contrary that the practice of contemporary writing instruction, warts and all, owes a good deal more to Lockean than to classical epistemology. The differences between our positions result from our different perspectives toward modernism. Knoblauch and Brannon take modern perspectives as fruitful grounds for the development of a theory of composition, while I take a postmodern perspective to be a better alternative from which to understand both rhetorical theory and practice. I read the classical tradition through a postmodern lens, while they attribute to it many of the very features I associate here with modern thought.

4. The revolutionary quality of the intellectual transition from medieval thought to modernism is demonstrated by Reiss and by Foucault in *Order of Things*. The following account is very much indebted to their work. I use the masculine pronoun here to underscore the fact that modern epistemology is permeated with patriarchal assumptions about the way the world works. For an account of the masculine cast of modernism, see Keller and Grontowski.

5. In the chapter entitled "The Masculine Birth of Time," from which this citation is drawn, Reiss brilliantly traces the transfer of authority from the individual speaking subject to the "machinery" that is discourse. Reiss argues that writing is necessary and complicit in the performance of this transfer, since it occults the presence of an enunciating subject. In other words, modern discursive practice is intimately tied to the availability of literacy. Ong made this point, albeit negatively, many years ago.

6. Modern philosophy has, in recent years, foundered on this rock—that is, on its inability to show why the speaking subject should be authorized to speak the world. See Descombes and Rorty for accounts of the philosophical difficulties entailed in according inventional authority to the speaking subject.

7. The representative role of language in modern rhetoric is most obviously manifested in its theories of style and in its dicta about grammar, syntax, and usage. For example, current-traditional rhetoricians taught that grammatical sentences literally represented complete thoughts. Since this study centers on invention, I have not pursued the issue of style here. Interested readers can consult my "Current-Traditional Theory of Style."

8. Howell establishes this point in *Eighteenth-Century British Logic*. I have drawn my account of eighteenth-century inventional theory from the work of five theorists-teachers whose contributions are widely acknowledged to have been central to the development of the new rhetoric: Hugh Blair, George Campbell, Joseph Priestley, Adam Smith, and Richard Whately. My synchronic treatment of the work of these discourse theorists necessarily elides some of the important intellectual differences between them. For example, Priestley was a dissenter, while Whately was an Anglican bishop; Priestley and Smith were somewhat more enamored of empiricism than was Campbell, whose religious convictions required him to tincture his thought with rationalism. Nevertheless, their common interests as middle-class professionals (teachers, clergymen, scientists) lend a certain coherence to their work, a coherence which I exploit here.

Their rhetorical theories have been discussed in detail by Berlin, Bevilacqua, Ehninger, Howell, and others. See the Bibliography.

9. As will become apparent, my account of eighteenth-century invention differs somewhat from the reading made by Bevilacqua, who characterizes eighteenth-century inventional theory as "managerial" ("Philosophical Origins"; "Philosophical Influences" 192). Bevilacqua apparently borrowed this term from Blair. While "managerial" may be an accurate description of eighteenth-century inventional theory when seen as a counterpoint to classical theory, Bevilacqua underestimates the importance of invention to eighteenth-century discourse theory.

10. Scholarly work on nineteenth-century romantic rhetorics has only just begun. Influential British romantics—among them Samuel Taylor Coleridge and Thomas DeQuincey—were interested in rhetoric, even if only to castigate the intellectual poverty of classical thought on the subject. In 1850, American W. G. T. Shedd translated a rhetorical treatise by a German romantic philosopher, Franz Theremin, into English; in this translation, Theremin's work influenced Henry Noble Day, among others. Berlin argues that Ralph Waldo Emerson tried to inaugurate an American romantic rhetorical tradition; see chap. 5 of *Writing Instruction*.

11. See Oravec.

12. Fogarty deserves the credit for coining the term *current-traditional rhetoric* in a treatise written in 1959 to advertise the beginnings of yet another "new" rhetoric. While it is clumsy, the term does capture the fact that a fairly coherent discursive practice dominated institutionalized writing instruction over a remarkable stretch of time—some 150 years at least.

2. How the Outside Gets Inside

1. Scholars are divided about the extent to which Campbell's teleological alteration to rhetoric was a far-reaching change from the goals of classical rhetoric. As is apparent, I am on the side of those who style it a revolutionary move. For the debate, see McDermott; Ehninger, "Campbell, Blair, and Whately: Old Friends in a New Light" and "Campbell, Blair, and Whately Revisited."

The influence of Campbell's *Philosophy of Rhetoric* on subsequent rhetorical theory was enormous. It was cited or quoted in textbook after textbook throughout the nineteenth century; I have found reference to it in texts published as late as 1920. The *Philosophy of Rhetoric* remained in print more or less continuously until 1912. It was edited and reissued by Lloyd Bitzer in 1963.

2. For Bacon's theory of rhetoric and communication, see Karl Wallace, *Francis Bacon;* for his possible influence on George Campbell, see Howell, *Eighteenth-Century British Logic* 582. For an account of faculty psychology, see Wallace, "English Renaissance Mind."

3. For accounts of Locke's influence on rhetorical theory, see Howell, "John Locke" and *Eighteenth-Century British Logic* 269, and Edward P. J. Corbett, "John Locke's Contributions." For an interpretation of the implications of Locke's *Essay Concerning Human Understanding* for composition theory see Knoblauch and Brannon.

4. Bevilacqua gives a detailed account of the indebtedness of eighteenth-century rhetoricians to Kames' work in "Lord Kames's Theory."

5. For a readable history of the very different role played by memory in classical and medieval rhetorical thought, see Yates.

6. For an account of the changing definition of probability during the modern period from its older rhetorical sense to its more current mathematical sense, see Hacking, especially chaps. 4 and 5.

7. Whately's *Elements of Rhetoric* was revised and enlarged through six editions, the last published in 1846. The *Elements of Rhetoric* was issued in an American edition in 1832, and it quickly became a best-seller. Whately was standard reading in American colleges during the middle years of the nineteenth century. *The Elements of Rhetoric* directly influenced the theory of evidence developed by Adams Sherman Hill, and through Hill, hundreds of other current-traditional rhetoricians. A new edition of the *Elements of Rhetoric,* edited by Douglas Ehninger, appeared in 1963.

8. For details, see Leathers.

9. For background on the influence of the principle of sympathy on eighteenth-century discourse theory, see Bator.

3. How Insides Get Outside Again

1. In the following discussion, I ignore the very important role of method in the development of modern science. On scientific, rhetorical, and logical method prior to the eighteenth century, see Crombie; Gilbert; Howell, *Fenelon's Dialogues* and *Logic and Rhetoric;* Lomer; McRae; Ong; Randall, *Career of Philosophy* and "Development of the Scientific Method"; Robinson 88–93; Schouls; and Wallace, "Francis Bacon and Method." For later methodical developments see Alkon. While method was a technical term in seventeenth-century logic, it apparently began to assume something like its contemporary popular use by the late eighteenth century. In his *Lectures on Rhetoric,* for example, Blair used the term both in its technical sense and in its looser sense as any organized approach to some task.

2. See Miller, chap. 11, for the general influence of Ramean method on the pedagogy used at Harvard during the seventeenth century.

3. The historical uses of these terms should not be confused with their contemporary uses.

4. Howell does not comment on the ease with which method found a home among more traditional means of reasoning. He thinks of method as part of the intellectual baggage left over from the old logic, rather than as a conceptual strategy developed to meet the needs of the new philosophy.

5. The influence of Watts' *Logick* on rhetorical and logical pedagogy in the eighteenth and nineteenth centuries cannot be underestimated. Soon after its publication in 1724, it became the standard text on logic in many British and American colleges; it remained so until late in the eighteenth century. The *Logick* had undergone thirty-one editions by 1797. Watts' text may have been one funnel through which the logical process of inquiry I am tracing was passed into nineteenth-century rhetoric texts, where it functioned as a theory of invention.

6. Watts' advice on method as presentation is not original with him. It has a long precedent in methodical history. Compare his list of means for method as presentation to the summary given by Howell of Sanderson's "nine laws of method" from his *Logicke* (1615) (*Logic and Rhetoric* 306–8).

7. Method bears interesting similarities to the qualities Foucault assigns to "discipline" (*Discipline and Punish*). As Foucault makes clear, disciplinarity made possible a new dispersion of knowledge, and hence of discursive power, just as method did.

8. Smith's lectures are available only in a version copied by one or more students who sat in on his course in 1763. Thus any commentary on them, including mine, must be received with caution.

9. Howell attributes the origin of didactic discourse to Ramus (*Logic and Rhetoric* 237). See Connors, "Aristotle to 1850" and "1850 to the Present" for an alternative history of the evolution of this genre.

4. Subjects and Objects

1. For data on the distribution and use of British rhetoric texts in America, see Wozniak and the series of essays by Warren Guthrie.

2. Throughout the nineteenth century and the early years of the twentieth century, many composition textbooks were published that subscribed to an amalgamation of classical and new rhetoric. As a result, they are not mainstream current-traditional rhetorics, although they borrowed some of its features. In general, such works were written by scholars who were acquainted with the history of rhetoric. Examples include a series of textbooks published during the first two decades of the twentieth century by Baldwin, as well as others by Bascom; Boyd, *English Composition* and *Elements of Rhetoric;* Coppee (whom I cite); Henry Noble Day, *Elements of Rhetoric* and *Art of Discourse* (on which I also rely); DeMille; John S. Hart; and James Morgan Hart (whom I cite in the next chapter). Of course there were many rhetorical manuals available in America during the nineteenth century that represented traditions other than the current-traditional version of the new rhetoric, as well as other rhetorical traditions altogether.

3. For example, Parker's *Aids to English Composition* contains a long verbatim passage from Newman's *Practical System of Rhetoric,* borrowed silently (222–23), as well as other passages that do cite Newman.

4. Newman's *Practical System of Rhetoric* enjoyed great popularity through

the 1840s and 1850s, not only at Bowdoin where Newman taught, but in other colleges as well. The text went through an incredible sixty editions in America and was reprinted in England. It was used in many college classrooms after 1828. It was studied by Longfellow and Hawthorne at Bowdoin and was probably read by Dickinson at Amherst Academy. Newman cited Campbell's *Philosophy of Rhetoric* as his "highest authority," calling it "the ingenious, elaborate production of the Quinctilian of English literature" (vii). But Newman was indebted to Blair, as well, as his discussions of taste, style, and genre make clear. For a commentary on Newman, see Kremers.

5. Here Newman drew on an eighteenth-century aesthetic tradition in which the faculty of taste was thought to accrue to those people who worked hard at learning to evaluate the quality of aesthetic productions. Such people are now called critics. For exemplary eighteenth-century discussions of taste, see Gerard; Kames.

6. For background on the pedagogy associated with mental discipline, see Kolesnik. For its employment in nineteenth-century college curricula, see Rudolph; Vesey.

7. Although ostensibly an elementary textbook, Parker's *Aids to English Composition* was listed in the catalog of one Eastern college through the middle years of the century. Parker acknowledged the influence of Blair and Whately, as well as that of Jamieson and Newman. In addition, he quoted or paraphrased a good many other writers on logic and criticism. The book is written in a catechetical style suitable for recitation. Recitation was apparently a staple of instruction in lower schools until late in the nineteenth century, as witnessed by the catechetical arrangement of some very late composition texts. See, for example, David J. Hill, *Elements of Rhetoric;* and Abbott.

8. Woods ascribes the genesis of these lessons to Parker's interest in "inductive teaching" (385).

9. George Payn Quackenbos' *Advanced Course* enjoyed modest popularity in college curricula through the last half of the century. This work was largely derivative of the new rhetoric, although Quackenbos did not always acknowledge his indebtednesses. His *First Lessons in Composition* (1860) was a popular elementary textbook, written in the catechetical style. Wozniak notes that Newman, Day, Shedd, and Parker were presented in college curricula from 1850 to 1870, but that "Quackenbos, Haven, Coppee, Bascom, and Bain were the new crop of authors who were just beginning to compete with the British triumvirate [Campbell, Blair, and Whately] during the Sixties" (41).

10. As we shall see in the next chapter, this scheme for invention was also favored by a couple of midcentury authors who were much more influential than Coppee—Henry Noble Day and Alexander Bain. Coppee's *Elements of Rhetoric* was popular in Eastern colleges during the 1860s, and it was still in use at some schools as late as 1890. The text draws on a mixed rhetorical and logical heritage, displaying some classical influence. Coppee acknowledged his use of an English translation of Aristotle's *Rhetoric*, along with Thomas Hobbes' *Briefe of the Art of Rhetorique* (first published 1637), a redaction of Aristotle. Coppee also cited

the influence of Campbell's *Philosophy of Rhetoric* and Whately's *Elements of Rhetoric* and explained that he had slighted Blair's *Lectures on Rhetoric* because of their excessive emphasis on style. Coppee's allegiance to logic was further demonstrated by his assumption that the amplification was accomplished by the development of a chain of syllogisms.

5. Select, Narrow, and Amplify

1. Kitzhaber uses the phrase "big four" to describe Genung, Hill, Wendell, and Scott and Denney in his 1953 dissertation. Students of the history of current-traditional rhetoric are inevitably indebted to Kitzhaber's pioneering work. Teachers of composition are further indebted to Kitzhaber for his largely unsung and unrewarded efforts to bring scholarly and professional respectability to the profession of teaching writing during the 1960s.

2. Historians of composition studies have tried to account for the ubiquity and longevity of the current-traditional theory of invention, as well as for its theory of style and its horde of grammatical prescriptions. Berlin's rationale for the staying power of current-traditional pedagogy is a tempting one: "The freshman course has been proffered as a concession on the part of the English department to the scientific and meritocratic interests of the university, interests represented by professional schools and many career-minded students" (*Rhetoric and Reality* 27). In other words, the seemingly scientific logic of the expository theme, supported by its supposedly empirical means of investigation, appeals to those members of the academic community who value such ideals. In this view, textbook authors would abandon the traditional scheme of invention at their peril, since most of its audience would simply vanish. Other rationales for its sticking power include the notion that rhetorical theory was pretty much moribund during the early years of the twentieth century, as well as the unpleasant observation that current-traditional textbooks were a lucrative investment of their authors' time, given that their composition did not require a good deal of original thought and that the textbooks sold in huge numbers. I advance yet another series of rationales for the staying power of current-traditional rhetoric in chap. 8.

3. In chap. 6 of *Writing Instruction* Berlin provides a useful guide to the institutional context in which traditional writing theory developed.

4. Day published a number of composition textbooks during the 1850s and 1860s. *Rhetorical Praxis* (originally published 1861) was an exercise book, and *Grammatical Synthesis* (1867) was a sentence rhetoric. The *Art of Discourse* (1867) was an enlarged revision of the *Elements of Rhetoric*. During his productive career, Day also published scholarly works on logic and aesthetics. He acknowledged his indebtedness to Campbell and Whately; he also cited the influence of Franz Theremin's *Eloquence: A Virtue*, along with other German authors. Together, Day's textbooks enjoyed a popularity that momentarily rivaled Bain's; *Rhetorical Praxis* is reported to have been in use as late as 1915. Day's eclectic theory seems to have appealed to other text writers; parts of it

were adopted by Hope, and Gilmore's *Outlines of Rhetoric* (originally published 1877) was an unacknowledged redaction of Day's system. Day was an eclectic rhetorical theorist; if current-traditional authors had adopted his complex but comprehensive system, rather than Bain's more pedantic one, subsequent composition theory and pedagogy might have looked very different. For a sympathetic account of Day's rhetorical theory, see Johnson.

5. According to Jordan, Bain's textbook was in use in schools across the country between 1869 and 1890 (133–34). Bain, who made scholarly contributions to psychology, also published textbooks in grammar, rhetoric, and logic, and was known to his contemporaries as an educational reformer. A Scotsman, he insisted that his work was closely affiliated with the British rhetorical tradition. In the introduction to *English Composition and Rhetoric* he wrote that "the fulfillment of this design has ended in a treatise more closely allied to Campbell's *Philosophy of Rhetoric,* Blair's *Lectures,* and Whately's *Rhetoric,* than to the majority of recent works on English composition" (vi). Bain's little textbook seems to have been influential out of all proportion to its originality or quality.

There is a good deal of scholarship on Bain, and some debate about the sources of his paragraph theory. See Harned; Lunsford; Mulderig; Rodgers; Shearer, "Teaching of Rhetoric," "Psychology as Foundation," and "Genesis of Paragraph Theory." Only Lunsford discusses Bain's two-volume revision of *English Composition and Rhetoric* (294). In this work Bain tied rhetoric more closely to belles lettres than he had previously. For example, he virtually identified rhetoric with criticism: "Criticism has long attained the point where reasons can be given for a very wide range of literary effects; and Rhetoric is but the arranging and methodizing of these reasons" (xiii). Ironically, given his subsequent influence on composition theory, this text makes it pretty clear that Bain didn't have much respect for rhetoric.

6. For background on the modern concept of specialized knowledge and the development of the notion of expertise, see Haskell.

7. Genung's many textbooks, especially the *Practical Elements of Rhetoric* (1886), were enormously popular throughout the late nineteenth and early twentieth centuries. The *Practical Elements of Rhetoric* was kept in print until 1931, and the *Working Principles of Rhetoric* (1900) was in print until 1942. There are a number of scholarly articles devoted to Genung's rhetoric. See especially Allen; Berlin, "John Genung"; Ettlich, "John Franklin Genung"; and Rockas. For a fuller explication of Genung's inventional theory, see my "Invention in Nineteenth-Century Rhetoric."

8. Kitzhaber notices a gradual disappearance of associationism from texts composed during the later years of the nineteenth century. I found remnants of it in texts that appeared throughout the late nineteenth century and well into the twentieth, however. The associational "laws of the mind" form the theoretical basis of David J. Hill's *Science of Rhetoric,* for example, and they were used both by Hill and by Cairns as the basis for a theory of style. Associationism also permeates Espenshade's *Essentials of English Composition and Rhetoric,* which was periodically reissued throughout the first half of the twentieth century.

Scott and Denney's textbooks, especially *Paragraph-Writing*, were enormously influential in twentieth-century current-traditional thought. I saw well-thumbed copies of later editions of *Paragraph-Writing* on the shelves of English department libraries as late as 1970. In a later edition of that work, Scott and Denney cited their indebtedness to Bain, as well as to a host of other eighteenth- and nineteenth-century discourse theorists. Apart from his periodic descents into the current-traditional maelstrom, Scott was an innovative rhetorician and a talented administrator who influenced several prominent rhetoricians, foremost among them Gertrude Buck. For scholarship on his work, see Stewart.

9. For background on Wendell's textbook and teaching, see Douglas.

10. Adams Sherman Hill occupied the Boylston Chair of Rhetoric during the last quarter of the nineteenth century (1876–1904) and taught composition at Harvard for over thirty years. Hill authored a number of influential composition texts during that period, the most popular of which was *Principles of Rhetoric* (1878). Wozniak gives a detailed account of Hill's composition course at Harvard, the notorious "English A," and discusses his subsequent influence (90, 125–27). See Ettlich, "Theories of Invention," for a survey of the inventional strategies adopted by Hill and some of his contemporaries.

11. The organic metaphor also appears in Genung and was widespread in twentieth-century current-traditional thought. It is obviously indebted to a neoromantic theory of discourse. Connors traces the increasing influence of romantic modes of thought on composition theory in "Personal Writing Assignments."

12. Process pedagogy originated as a reaction against current-traditional rhetoric. I locate its beginnings in the publication of Emig's landmark *The Composing Processes of Twelfth Graders*. In that work Emig took issue with "the fifty-star theme." She further made the unprecedented move of watching young writers write in order to learn how they worked through the composing process. The emphasis on process was also stimulated, no doubt, by a revival of interest in classical rhetoric. Weaver's 1957 textbook *Composition: A Course in Rhetoric and Writing* included the classical topics as means of invention. Two textbooks published in 1965, Corbett's *Classical Rhetoric for the Modern Student* and Winterowd's *Writing and Rhetoric*, also borrowed from classical invention. By this time rhetoricians had also begun to take interest in the work done by Kenneth Burke during the 1940s and 1950s. Burke's dramatistic theory of invention was appropriated by William Irmscher for use in the *Holt Guide to English*. Young and Becker appropriated a theory of invention from the tagmemic linguistics of Pike; all three authored *Rhetoric: Discovery and Change*, which devoted over half of its pages to invention, something that hadn't been done since the publication of Genung's *Practical Elements of Rhetoric* some eighty-five years earlier.

13. For a developmental history of McCrimmon's text, see Connors, "Thirty Years of *Writing with a Purpose*." Connors needs to issue a new edition of his article every so often if his history is to keep up with new editions of McCrimmon's text. For example, recent editions (8 and 9), authored in part by other writers, adopt techniques from process pedagogy. But as McCleary demonstrates, the approach and organization of *Writing with a Purpose* hasn't changed

radically since 1950. According to McCleary, McCrimmon himself still subscribes to the current-traditional inventional process, which predicts writing
before it happens. He quotes McCrimmon as saying, "Don't sit down to write
until you have some idea of what you want to do" (3).

6. EDNA Takes Over

1. If any issue in the historiography of nineteenth-century composition theory
can be said to be hotly debated, it is the origin of the "modes of discourse,"
which is variously attributed to Newman, Quackenbos, Bain, or Day. In "Rise
and Fall of the Modes of Discourse," Connors notes both Newman's and Bain's
adoption of EDNA, but shies away from ascribing its genesis to Campbell's
Philosophy of Rhetoric, preferring Kitzhaber's rationale that points to the sterility
of rhetorical theory during the nineteenth century (453–54). However, D'Angelo
firmly grounds the modes in Campbell's faculty and association psychology and
traces this indebtedness through the late nineteenth century (36–38). Harned
presents an overview of Bain's indebtedness to the new learning in general
and to association psychology in particular, from whence he drew the modes.
Kitzhaber's account is much like mine, spreading the blame among several
folks. Berlin, on the other hand, attributes the authoritative formulation of the
modes to Henry Day (*Writing Instruction* 39). Rockas finds the first appearance
of the modes in George Payn Quackenbos' *Advanced Course* (65). Miller and
Joliffe review the history of the modes of discourse, and offer a critique, in order
to make room for a more rhetorical theory of genre.

2. Connors traces the nineteenth-century evolution of expository discourse
in "1850 to the Present." He places the heyday of exposition in the 1920s and
1930s and says that by 1950 composition was virtually identified with exposition.

3. Harned argues that Bain's interest in narration and description derives
from his subscription to associationist principles. While I do not disagree with
Harned's reading, I think that nineteenth-century interest in these two forms of
discourse owes something to eighteenth-century methodical analyses of their
structural possibilities.

4. See Mill's discussion of these processes. I cite Mill because Bain imported
his treatment of induction into traditional composition theory. Bain's successors
made even less use of Mill's subtle distinctions than he had.

5. According to Ong, Ramean method also tended to picture induction and
deduction as simple reciprocal movements and "not as radically different kinds
of psychological performances" (258).

6. See Berlin for a discussion of EDNA's fortunes during the late nineteenth
century (*Writing Instruction* 66–68). Kitzhaber discusses the demise of the
modes in chap. 6.

7. The Methodical Memory on Display

1. The *Grammar of Rhetoric* went through at least twenty-four editions in
this country prior to 1844, something over one edition a year. Jamieson was

read in many American colleges during the 1820s and 1830s and was used at some schools in conjunction with Blair and Campbell. Jamieson cited Campbell as his authority on style and mentioned Blair and Kames as the mentors of his discussion of taste. Despite these demurrers, Jamieson's text is so thoroughly indebted to Blair that it might fairly be called a summary or redaction of the *Lectures on Rhetoric*—which explains its late appearance in this book, since Blair's rhetorical theory was oriented toward style and arrangement rather than invention.

2. I seem to be alone in connecting Bain's paragraph principles with method. Rodgers argues that Bain deduced these principles by making an analogy between paragraphs and sentences. Shearer disputes this interpretation in "Genesis of Paragraph Theory," arguing Bain's possible indebtedness to Murray's *English Grammar*, as well as other contemporary sources. Kitzhaber discusses Bain's possible indebtedness to Angus' *Handbook of the English Tongue* (245). Lunsford rejects Rodgers' argument that Bain derived his principles deductively.

3. Ong notices a parallel movement in the confluence of printing with Ramus' popularization of method. Ong writes that "the diagrammatic tidiness which printing was imparting to the realm of ideas was part of a large-scale operation freeing the book from the world of discourse and making it over into an object, a box with surface and 'content' " (311). Ong sees this movement as taking the logical concept of "place" literally; that is, a seat or locus of argument became, in the farthest extension of method, a structure on the page.

4. Kitzhaber attributes unity, coherence, and emphasis to eighteenth-century principles of style (183–84). Indeed, the notion that sentences were to represent a complete thought can be traced via associationism to eighteenth-century discussions of style. See, for example, Campbell's discussion of perspicuity in book 2 of the *Philosophy of Rhetoric*. Cautions about the necessity for sentences to display unity appear in current-traditional textbooks written throughout the nineteenth century. But it was only in mature current-traditional theory that all three principles were marshaled into service on all levels of discourse. For another discussion of current-traditional treatments of unity, coherence, and emphasis, see Connors, "Static Abstractions."

5. Some institutions allow some students to exempt themselves from the composition requirement—but this possibility makes the requirement itself nonetheless universal. The universal requirement was suspended in many institutions during the late 1960s and early 1970s, thanks to students' assertion of its irrelevance to their education. However, it was firmly back in place in many institutions by 1975 or so. The benefits of the composition requirement to the academy are enormous. Because the composition course is institutionalized as freshman English, faculty across the university can ignore their responsibility to inculcate literate skills in their students. If their students' level of literacy is unacceptable, faculty can blame the composition course, which is in place precisely so that they do not have to bother with this supposedly elementary work. Faculty in English departments reap the added benefits of its huge enrollments and cheap labor.

6. Stegner's essay, which was an overt plea for the institutionalization of what is now called creative writing, was a covert diatribe against the structure of English departments and the teaching of writing done in composition classes.

7. I am not arguing that no discursive conventions should be made available to students, nor is Wright. Rather, we are objecting to the current-traditional habit of smuggling middle-class social values into composition instruction by disguising them as inflexible rules for discursive behavior.

8. So What's Wrong with Current-Traditional Rhetoric, Anyway?

1. According to a recent survey of 375 departments of English, reported by Larson, about half of all departments surveyed organize their composition courses around the modes of discourse and employ the current-traditional paradigm in their syllabi. I am indebted to my friendly textbook salesperson for the figure about composition teachers. At his suggestion, I examined the lists of institutions given in publishers' advertisements in order to get a sense of the extent to which current-traditional textbooks are still used. I resorted to this means of estimating numbers because publishers are reluctant to disclose the numbers of copies they sell.

2. I except Adams Sherman Hill's *Principles of Rhetoric* and Genung's *Practical Elements of Rhetoric* from this generalization. I hope it has become clear that even though they repeat the current-traditional litany, some textbooks are superior to others. Some manifest a distinctive voice; others attempt to resolve the inherent contradictions in the paradigm; others try, on occasion, to incorporate new developments in rhetoric or logic into their conceptual structure. On the other hand, many current-traditional textbooks are simply inane. I've tried to draw my commentary from the first class of books, for the most part, but I have had to concentrate on members of the second class in some cases, such as Wendell's, because of their subsequent influence on the tradition.

3. Adams Sherman Hill's own style was charming and occasionally clever. Some samples from the *Foundations of Rhetoric:* "It is wiser to write with fury and correct with phlegm than to write with phlegm and correct with fury"; "A good figure springs naturally out of the subject in hand; it is not dragged into the text by the head and shoulders" (202, 196). I cannot be sure that Hill would have approved of his students' writing such sentences, since they do not display unity.

4. According to his biographer, Kittredge—a famous scholar and teacher of English literature—wrote composition textbooks in order to supplement his income (Hyder 85).

5. Charles Sears Baldwin, a historian of rhetoric, published a series of composition texts between 1902 and 1917 that were unusual for their conflation of traditional prescription with a few classical rhetorical principles. But not even Baldwin, with his enormous learning in rhetorical history, could buck the

current-traditional tide altogether. Certainly he tried nothing so daring as reintroducing the topics—his textbooks employ the current-traditional model of invention. In 1919, John Manly and Edith Rickert, who were Chaucer scholars, collaborated with Martin Freeman to produce a humane textbook that was to see four editions within ten years. The *Writing of English* grew out of a series of pedagogical experiments undertaken with "below-standard" students at the University of Chicago, most of whom were not native speakers of English. Only in the 1960s and 1970s, when current-traditional rhetoric and freshman composition were under attack from scholars and students alike, were rhetoricians able to reintroduce classical systems of invention into otherwise conventional textbooks. Weaver's classy *Composition: A Course in Rhetoric and Writing* (1957) anticipated this development.

9. The Limits of Modern Epistemology for Writing Instruction

1. An attenuated faculty psychology seems to be at work, still, in the organization of English departments. There, discourse is implicitly carved up into "rational" and "imaginative." Thanks to their continuing subscription to neoromantic ideals, many professors of English privilege imaginative discourse—which is more "difficult" to write and somehow more "special"—over its rational counterpart. The association of rational discourse with introductory composition exacerbates this tendency. Creative writing engages students in the composition of "imaginative" discourse—poetry and fiction. Indeed, one could argue that the establishment of creative writing programs was a reaction to the rigorous exclusion of imaginative composition from current-traditional writing instruction. Until very recently, literary study also focused on imaginative discourse, relegating what is now called the literature of fact to marginal status. By centering their instruction on the production and consumption of imaginative discourse, creative writers and literary scholars managed to express both their distinction from, and their disdain for, the grubby discursive work that is the province of freshman composition. Aside from the occasional course in argumentation, English departments relegate the study of persuasive discourse to speech departments.

2. For accounts of how nonscientific investigation came to be identified with the passions or the imagination during the eighteenth century, see Bevilacqua, "Rhetorical Science" and IJsseling, especially chap. 12, which describes Immanual Kant's influence on ways of thinking about reason.

3. Writing is still defined in the academy as a docile medium of communication. For example, Rose reports that this position was taken by the academic senate at UCLA, which used it to recommend that basic writing courses be eliminated at that institution.

4. During holistic readings, such as those conducted of Advanced Placement exams by the Educational Testing Service, authors' names are expunged from their texts. This is testimony to the fact that even an author's name provides readers with cues that influence their evaluation of texts.

5. As I suggested in the introduction, modern attitudes toward knowledge, which are encapsulated in the expository theme, are currently under fire. Pirsig's *Zen and the Art of Motorcycle Maintenance* (1974) is a readable attack on what Pirsig calls the "Church of Reason." Another sort of attack has come from persons influenced by "postmodern" epistemological assumptions. See, for example, Derrida, and Ryan, especially chap. 7 on modern pedagogy. A separate attack has been launched by thinkers influenced by Rorty's notion of "anti-foundationalism." See the essays by Fish and Bizzell.

6. This overlooks the assumption crucial to postmodern critiques of modernism that no one can "invent" knowledge in a complete or original way; one must always stand on the shoulders of one's predecessors even to find out where to look for stuff to know. Brookes acknowledges the influence of cultural attitudes on students' notions about plagiarism and argues that it might be avoided by a more positive approach that concentrates on teaching students to acknowledge their sources.

7. I am indebted to Rorty, chap. 7, for the following discussion. I think that Rorty's "hermeneutics," which he would substitute for modern epistemology, has certain affinities with what I think of as rhetoric. At the very least, rhetoric and hermeneutics generate the same responses from philosophers, who characterize both as relativist and chaotic.

8. While I am willing to grant the remote possibility that a comprehensive theory of human motivation will someday be developed, no such theory currently exists, despite efforts made in this direction by Burke. See his *Grammar of Motives* and *Rhetoric of Motives*.

9. Rhetoricians, on the other hand, think of language as a medium that presents infinite resources for human learning, exploitation, and delight. During much of its history, the study of rhetoric was dominated by interest in style, where rhetoricians attempted to catalog some of the generative potential of language. It is safe to say that a viable rhetorical theory must take its starting point from language (or from linguistic communities), as did the rhetoric of the older Sophists and as do postmodern theories of rhetoric, such as those of Foucault or Derrida.

10. Foucault is the chief theorist of the connection between discourse and power. See, for example, *Archeology of Knowledge* or *Discipline and Punish*. Anyone who doubts the potency of this relation should reflect upon the powerful inventions produced every day by skilled media rhetoricians, inventions designed to convince us to buy this or that product. Herman and Chomsky advance the thesis that media rhetoricians collude with a corporate elite. If this is so, advertising constitutes a fine contemporary example of the collusion of discourse with power.

References Cited

Primary Sources

Abbott, Edwin A. *How to Write Clearly: Rules and Exercises on English Composition.* Boston: Roberts, 1896.

Angus, Joseph. *Handbook of the English Tongue, for the Use of Students and Others.* London: Religious Tract Society, 1862.

Aristotle. *The Rhetoric and Poetics of Aristotle.* Trans. W. Rhys Roberts. Ed. E. P. J. Corbett. New York: Random, 1984.

Arnauld, Antoine. *The Art of Thinking; or, The Port-Royal Logic.* Trans. James Dickoff and Patricia James. Indianapolis: Bobbs, 1964.

Axelrod, Rise B., and Charles R. Cooper. *The St. Martin's Guide to Writing.* 2nd ed. New York: St. Martin's, 1988.

Bacon, Francis. *The Works of Francis Bacon.* Ed. James Spedding, Robert Leslie Ellis, and Douglas Heath. 14 vols. Boston: Tarrard, 1860–64.

Bain, Alexander. *English Composition and Rhetoric.* Enl. ed. 2 vols. New York: American Book, 1887. Appleton, 1888.

———. *English Composition and Rhetoric: A Manual.* 4th ed. London: Longmans, 1877.

Baker, Sheridan. *The Complete Stylist and Handbook.* 3rd ed. New York: Crowell, 1984.

———. *The Practical Stylist.* 4th ed. New York: Crowell, 1977.

Baldwin, Charles Sears. *A College Manual of Rhetoric.* 2nd ed. New York: Longmans, 1909.

Ball, Margaret. *The Principles of Outlining.* Boston: Sanborn, 1910.

Bascom, John. *The Philosophy of Rhetoric.* New York: Woolworth, 1872.

Blair, Hugh. *Lectures on Rhetoric and Belles Lettres.* Ed. Harold F. Harding. 2 vols. New York: Garland, 1970.

187

Boyd, James R. *Elements of English Composition, Grammatical, Rhetorical, Logical, and Practical.* New York: Barnes, 1860.

————. *Elements of Rhetoric and Literary Criticism.* New York: Harper, 1844.

Brooks, Cleanth, and Robert Penn Warren. *Modern Rhetoric.* 3rd ed. New York: Harcourt, 1970.

Burke, Kenneth. *A Grammar of Motives.* Berkeley: U of California P, 1945.

————. *A Rhetoric of Motives.* Berkeley: U of California P, 1950.

Cairns, William B. *The Forms of Discourse.* 2nd ed. Boston: Ginn, 1909.

Campbell, George. *The Philosophy of Rhetoric.* Ed. Lloyd F. Bitzer. Carbondale: Southern Illinois UP, 1963.

Cicero, Marcus Tullius. *On Invention.* Trans. H. M. Hubbell. Cambridge: Harvard UP, 1949.

————. *Topics.* Trans. H. M. Hubbell. Cambridge: Harvard UP, 1949.

Clark, John Scott. *A Practical Rhetoric, for Instruction in English Composition and Revision in Colleges and Intermediate Schools.* New York: Holt, 1891.

Coleridge, Samuel Taylor. *The Friend. The Collected Works of Samuel Taylor Coleridge.* Gen. ed. Kathleen Coburn. London: Routledge, 1969.

Coppee, Henry. *The Elements of Rhetoric.* New ed. rev. Philadelphia: Butler, 1860.

Corbett, Edward P. J. *Classical Rhetoric for the Modern Student.* New York: Oxford UP, 1965.

Crews, Frederick. *The Random House Handbook.* 4th ed. New York: Random, 1984.

Cunningham, Robert N., and Frank W. Cushwa. *Reading, Writing, and Thinking.* New York: Scribner's, 1943.

Curl, Mervin James. *Expository Writing.* Rev. ed. Boston: Houghton, 1931.

Day, Henry Noble. *The Art of Discourse.* New York: Scribner's, 1867.

————. *Elements of the Art of Rhetoric.* Hudson, OH: Skinner, 1850.

————. *Grammatical Synthesis, The Art of English Composition.* New York: Scribner's, 1867.

————. *Rhetorical Praxis.* Cincinnati: Moore, 1876.

DeMille, James. *The Elements of Rhetoric.* New York: Harper, 1878.

Descartes, René. *The Philosophical Writings of Descartes.* Trans. John Cottingham, Robert Stoothoff, and Dugald Murdoch. Cambridge: Cambridge UP, 1985.

Espenshade, A. Howry. *The Essentials of English Composition and Rhetoric.* Boston: Heath, 1904.

Espenshade, A. Howry, T. J. Gates, and R. D. Mallery. *The Essentials of English Composition.* Boston: Heath, 1945.

Fernald, James. *Expressive English.* New York: Funk, 1918.

Flesch, Rudolf, and A. H. Lass. *The Way to Write.* Rev. ed. New York: Harper, 1949.

Fletcher, J. B., and G. R. Carpenter. *Introduction to Theme-Writing.* Boston: Allyn, 1893.

Foerster, Norman, and J. M. Steadman, Jr. *Writing and Thinking*. Boston: Houghton, 1931.

Gardiner, John Hays, George Lyman Kittredge, and Sarah Louise Arnold. *A Manual of English Composition*. Boston: Ginn, 1907.

Genung, John Franklin. *The Practical Elements of Rhetoric, with Illustrative Examples*. Boston: Ginn, 1885.

————. *The Working Principles of Rhetoric*. Boston: Ginn, 1900.

Gerard, Alexander. *An Essay on Taste*. New York: Garland, 1970.

Gilmore, Joseph Henry. *The Outlines of Rhetoric*. Boston: Leach, 1891.

Hart, James Morgan. *A Manual of Composition and Rhetoric*. Rev. ed. Philadelphia: Eldredge, 1897.

Hart, John S. *A Manual of Composition and Rhetoric: A Text-Book for Schools and Colleges*. Philadelphia: Eldredge, 1877.

Haven, Erastus Otis. *Rhetoric: A Text-Book Designed for Use in Schools and Colleges and for Private Study*. New York: Harper, 1873.

Hefferman, John, and James Lincoln. *Writing: A College Handbook*. New York: Norton, 1982.

Hegel, G. W. F. *The Philosophy of History*. Trans. J. Sibree. Rev. ed. New York: Collier, 1900.

Hill, Adams Sherman. *The Foundations of Rhetoric*. New York: American Book, 1892.

————. *The Principles of Rhetoric and Their Application*. Rev. enl. ed. New York: American Book, 1878.

Hill, David J. *The Elements of Rhetoric and Composition: A Textbook for Schools and Colleges*. New ed. New York: Sheldon, 1884.

————. *The Science of Rhetoric*. New York: Sheldon, 1877.

Hirsch, E. D., et al. *The Dictionary of Cultural Literacy*. Boston: Houghton, 1989.

Hobbes, Thomas. *Briefe of The Art of Rhetorique*. *The Rhetorics of Thomas Hobbes and Bernard Lamy*. Ed. John T. Harwood. Carbondale: Southern Illinois UP, 1986.

Hope, Matthew. *The Princeton Text-Book in Rhetoric*. Princeton: Robinson, 1859.

Irmscher, William. *The Holt Guide to English*. New York: Holt, 1972.

Jamieson, Alexander. *A Grammar of Rhetoric and Polite Literature, Comprehending the Principles of Language and Style, the Elements of Taste and Criticism, with Rules for the Study of Composition and Eloquence, Illustrated by Appropriate Examples Selected Chiefly from the British Classics, for the Use of Schools or Private Instruction*. 24th ed. New Haven: Maltby, 1844.

Jeliffe, R. A. *A Handbook of Exposition*. New York: Macmillan, 1927.

Kames, Lord [Henry Home]. *The Elements of Criticism*. 2 vols. New York: Garland, 1972.

Kirszner, Laurie G., and Stephen R. Mandell. *Writing: A College Rhetoric*. 2nd ed. New York: Holt, 1988.

Knox, Samuel. *A Compendious System of Rhetoric, Arranged in a Catechetical Format and Abstracted from Blair, Holmes, Stirling, Etc. and the Best Authors on that Art.* Baltimore: Swain, 1809.

Locke, John. *An Essay Concerning Human Understanding.* Ed. Peter H. Nidditch. Oxford: Clarendon Press, 1975.

McCrimmon, James. *Writing with a Purpose: A First Course in College Composition.* Boston: Houghton, 1950; 5th ed., 1972; 8th ed., 1982; 9th ed., 1988.

Manly, John, Edith Rickert, and Martin Freeman. *The Writing of English.* New York: Holt, 1929.

Mill, John Stuart. *A System of Logic.* 8th ed. London: Longmans, 1967.

Murray, Lindley. *An English Grammar.* Boston: Manning, 1800.

Newman, Samuel. *A Practical System of Rhetoric or the Principles and Rule of Style Inferred from Examples of Writing, to Which is Added a Historical Dissertation on English Style.* 7th ed. Boston: Newman, 1838.

Ogilvie, John. *Philosophical and Critical Observations on the Nature, Characters, and Various Species of Composition.* New York: Garland, 1970.

Packer, Nancy Huddleston, and John Timpane. *Writing Worth Reading: A Practical Guide with Handbook.* 2nd ed. New York: St. Martin's, 1989.

Parker, Richard Green. *Aids to English Composition, Prepared for Students of all Grades.* New ed. New York: Harper, 1845.

Pearson, Henry G. *The Principles of Composition.* Boston: Heath, 1908.

Pence, Raymond Woodbury. *College Composition.* New York: Macmillan, 1929.

Perelman, Chaim, and L. Olbrechts-Tyteca. *The New Rhetoric: A Treatise on Argumentation.* Notre Dame: Notre Dame UP, 1958.

Plato. "Phaedrus." *Plato: The Collected Dialogues.* Ed. Edith Hamilton and Huntington Cairns. Princeton: Princeton UP, 1961.

Priestley, Joseph. *A Course of Lectures on Oratory and Criticism.* Ed. Vincent Bevilacqua and Richard Murphy. Carbondale: Southern Illinois UP, 1965.

Quackenbos, George Payn. *Advanced Course of Composition and Rhetoric.* New York: Appleton, 1864.

———. *First Lessons in Composition.* New York: Appleton, 1860.

Quackenbos, John Duncan. *Practical Rhetoric.* New York: American Book, 1896.

Quintilian, Marcus Fabricius. *The Institutes of Oratory.* Trans. H. E. Butler. 4 vols. Cambridge: Harvard UP, 1920.

Richards, I. A. *The Philosophy of Rhetoric.* New York: Oxford UP, 1936.

Rippingham, John. *Rules for English Composition and Particularly for Themes: Designed for the Use of Schools and in the Aid of Self-Instruction.* 1st Am. ed. Poughkeepsie: Potter, 1816.

Scott, Fred Newton, and Joseph Villiers Denney. *Composition-Literature.* Boston: Allyn, 1902.

———. *Composition-Rhetoric, Designed for Use in Secondary Schools.* Boston: Allyn, 1897.

———. *The New Composition-Rhetoric.* Boston: Allyn, 1911.

————. *Paragraph-Writing: A Rhetoric for Colleges*. Ann Arbor, MI: Register Publishing, 1891; 3rd ed. Boston: Allyn, 1893.

Smith, Adam. *Lectures on Rhetoric and Belles Lettres*. Ed. John M. Lothian. Carbondale: Southern Illinois UP, 1971.

Smyser, Selden F. "The Lack of Scientific Work in Rhetoric." *The Dial* 23 (1897): 141.

Stegner, Wallace. "Writing as Graduate Study." *College English* 11 (1950): 429–32.

Stewart, Dugald. *Elements of the Philosophy of the Human Mind*. 2 vols. Boston: Munroe, 1842.

Theremin, Franz. *Eloquence: A Virtue*. Trans. W. G. T. Shedd. New York: Wiley, 1850.

Thomas, Joseph M., Frederick A. Manchester, and Franklin W. Scott. *Composition for College Students*. 4th ed. New York: Macmillan, 1937.

Thorndike, Ashley. *The Elements of Rhetoric and Composition*. New York: Century, 1905.

Watts, Isaac. *Logick or the Use of Right Reason in the Inquiry after Truth*. London: Buckland, 1790.

Weaver, Richard. *Composition: A Course in Rhetoric and Writing*. New York: Holt, 1957.

Wendell, Barrett. *English Composition*. New York: Ungar, 1963.

Whately, Richard. *The Elements of Rhetoric*. Ed. Douglas Ehninger. Carbondale: Southern Illinois UP, 1963.

Winkler, Anthony, and Jo Ray McCuen. *Rhetoric Made Plain*. 5th ed. San Diego: Harcourt, 1988.

Winterowd, W. Ross. *Writing and Rhetoric*. Boston: Allyn, 1965.

Woodman, Leonora, and Thomas P. Adler. *The Writer's Choices with Handbook*. 2nd ed. Glenview, IL: Scott, 1988.

Young, Richard, Alton Becker, and Kenneth Pike. *Rhetoric: Discovery and Change*. New York: Harcourt, 1970.

Secondary Sources

Aarsleff, Hans. *From Locke to Saussure: Essays on the Study of Language and Intellectual History*. Minneapolis: Minnesota UP, 1982.

Alkon, Paul. "Critical and Logical Concepts of Method from Addison to Coleridge." *Eighteenth-Century Studies* 5 (1971): 97–121.

Allen, R. R. "The Rhetoric of John Franklin Genung." *Speech Teacher* 12 (1963): 238–41.

Bator, Paul G. "The 'Principle of Sympathy' in Campbell's *Philosophy of Rhetoric*." *Quarterly Journal of Speech* 68 (1982): 418–24.

Berlin, James A. "John Genung and Contemporary Composition Theory: The Triumph of the Eighteenth-Century." *Rhetoric Society Quarterly* 11 (1981): 74–84.

————. *Rhetoric and Reality: Writing Instruction in American Colleges, 1900–1985*. Carbondale: Southern Illinois UP, 1987.

————. *Writing Instruction in Nineteenth-Century American Colleges*. Carbondale: Southern Illinois UP, 1984.

Bevilacqua, Vincent. "Campbell, Vico, and the Rhetorical Science of Human Nature." *Philosophy and Rhetoric* 18 (1985): 23–30.

————. "Lord Kames's Theory of Rhetoric." *Speech Monographs* 30 (1963): 309–27.

————. "Philosophical Influences in the Development of English Rhetorical Theory: 1748 to 1783." *Proceedings of the Leeds Philosophical and Literary Society*. Vol. 12, pt. 4: 191–215. Leeds: Maney, 1968.

————. "Philosophical Origins of George Campbell's *Philosophy of Rhetoric*." *Speech Monographs* 32 (1965): 1–12.

Bizzell, Patricia. "Foundationalism and Anti-Foundationalism in Composition Studies." *Pre/Text* 7 (1986): 37–56.

Brookes, Gerry H. "Exploring Plagiarism in the Composition Classroom." *Freshman English News* 17 (1989): 31–35.

Bruns, Gerald L. *Inventions: Writing, Textuality, and Understanding in Literary History*. New Haven: Yale UP, 1982.

Connors, Robert J. "Mechanical Correctness as a Focus in Composition Instruction." *College Composition and Communication* 36 (1985): 61–72.

————. "Personal Writing Assignments." *College Composition and Communication* 38 (1987): 166–83.

————. "The Rhetoric of Explanation: Explanatory Rhetoric from Aristotle to 1850." *Written Communication* 1 (1984): 189–210.

————. "The Rhetoric of Explanation: Explanatory Rhetoric from 1850 to the Present." *Written Communication* 2 (1985): 49–72.

————. "Rhetorical History as a Component of Composition Studies." *Rhetoric Review* 7 (1989): 230–40.

————. "The Rise and Fall of the Modes of Discourse." *College Composition and Communication* 32 (1981): 444–55.

————. "Static Abstractions and Composition." *Freshman English News* 12 (1983): 1–4, 9–11.

————. "Thirty Years of *Writing with a Purpose*." *Rhetoric Society Quarterly* 11 (1981): 208–21.

Corbett, Edward P. J. "John Locke's Contributions to Rhetoric." *College Composition and Communication* 32 (1981): 423–33.

Crombie, A. C. *Robert Grosseteste and the Origins of Experimental Science: 1100–1700*. Oxford: Clarendon, 1953.

Crowley, Sharon. "The Current-Traditional Theory of Style: An Informal History." *Rhetoric Society Quarterly* 16 (1986): 233–50.

————. "Invention in Nineteenth-Century Rhetoric." *College Composition and Communication* 35 (1985): 51–60.

D'Angelo, Frank. "Nineteenth-Century Forms/Modes of Discourse: A Critical Inquiry." *College Composition and Communication* 35 (1984): 31–42.

Davidson, Hugh. *Art, Audience, Word: Studies in Seventeenth-Century French Rhetoric.* Columbus: Ohio State UP, 1965.

Derrida, Jacques. *Of Grammatology.* Trans. Gayatri Chakravorty Spivak. Baltimore: Johns Hopkins UP, 1976.

Descombes, Vincent. *Modern French Philosophy.* Cambridge: Cambridge UP, 1980.

Douglas, Wallace. "Barrett Wendell." *Traditions of Inquiry.* Ed. John Brereton. Oxford UP, 1985.

———. "Barrett Wendell and the Contradictions of Composition." *Arizona English Bulletin* 16 (1974): 182–90.

Edney, Clarence W. "George Campbell's Theory of Logical Truth." *Speech Monographs* 21 (1948): 19–32.

Ehninger, Douglas. "Campbell, Blair and Whately: Old Friends in a New Light." *Western Speech* 19 (1955): 263–69.

———. "Campbell, Blair and Whately Revisited." *Southern Speech Journal* 28 (1963): 169–82.

Emig, Janet. *The Composing Processes of Twelfth Graders.* Urbana: NCTE, 1971.

Ettlich, Ernest E. "John Franklin Genung and the Nineteenth-Century Definition of Rhetoric." *Central States Speech Journal* 17 (1966): 283–88.

———. "Theories of Invention in Late Nineteenth-Century American Rhetorics." *Western Speech* 30 (1966): 233–41.

Fish, Stanley. "Consequences." *Critical Inquiry* 11 (1985): 433–58.

Fogarty, Daniel. *Roots for a New Rhetoric.* New York: Columbia Teachers' College P, 1959.

Foucault, Michel. *The Archeology of Knowledge and the Discourse on Language.* Trans. A. M. Sheridan Smith. New York: Harper, 1972.

———. *Discipline and Punish: The Birth of the Prison.* Trans. Alan Sheridan. New York: Random, 1979.

———. *The Order of Things: An Archeology of the Human Sciences.* New York: Random, 1973.

Gilbert, Neal. *Renaissance Concepts of Method.* New York: Columbia UP, 1960.

Guthrie, Warren. "The Development of Rhetorical Theory in America, 1635–1850. *Speech Monographs* 13 (1946): 14–22; 14 (1947): 38–54; 15 (1948): 61–71; 16 (1949): 98–113; 18 (1951): 17–30.

Guthrie, W. K. C. *The Fifth-Century Enlightenment.* Cambridge: Cambridge UP, 1969. Vol. 3 of *A History of Greek Philosophy.* 5 vols. 1969–78.

Habermas, Jurgen. "Modernity—An Incomplete Project." *The Anti-Aesthetic: Essays on Postmodern Culture.* Ed. Hal Foster. Port Townsend, WA: Bay Press, 1983.

Hacking, Ian. *The Emergence of Probability.* Cambridge: Cambridge UP, 1975.

Harned, Jon. "The Intellectual Background of Alexander Bain's 'Modes of Discourse.'" *College Composition and Communication* 86 (1985): 45–50.

Haskell, Thomas L., ed. *The Authority of Experts: History and Theory*. Bloomington: Indiana UP, 1984.

Hauser, Gerard A. "Empiricism, Description, and the New Rhetoric." *Philosophy and Rhetoric* 5 (1972): 24–45.

Herman, Edward S., and Noam Chomsky. *Manufacturing Consent: The Political Economy of the Mass Media*. New York: Random, 1988.

Howell, Wilbur Samuel. *Eighteenth-Century British Logic and Rhetoric*. Princeton: Princeton UP, 1971.

———. *Fenelon's Dialogues on Eloquence: A Translation with an Introduction and Notes*. Princeton: Princeton UP, 1951.

———. "John Locke and the New Rhetoric." *Quarterly Journal of Speech* 53 (1967): 319–33.

———. *Logic and Rhetoric in England, 1500–1700*. Princeton: Princeton UP, 1956.

Hyder, Clyde K. *George Lyman Kittredge: Teacher and Scholar*. Lawrence: Kansas UP, 1962.

IJsseling, Samuel. *Rhetoric and Philosophy in Conflict: An Historical Survey*. The Hague: Martinus Nijhoff, 1976.

Johnson, Nan. "Three Nineteenth-Century Rhetorics: The Humanist Alternative to Rhetoric as Skills Management." *The Rhetorical Tradition and Modern Writing*. Ed. James J. Murphy. New York: MLA, 1982.

Jordan, Harold M. "Rhetorical Education in American Colleges and Universities, 1850–1915." Diss. Pennsylvania State U, 1952.

Keller, Evelyn Fox, and Christine R. Grontkowski. "The Mind's Eye." *Discovering Reality: Feminist Perspectives on Epistemology, Metaphysics, Methodology, and Philosophy of Science*. Ed. Sandra Harding and Merrill B. Hintikka. Dordrecht, Holland: Reidel, 1983.

Kerferd, George Briscoe. *The Sophistic Movement*. Cambridge: Cambridge UP, 1981.

Kitzhaber, Albert. "Rhetoric in American Colleges, 1850–1900." Diss. Washington U, 1953.

Knoblauch, C. H., and Lil Brannon. *Rhetorical Traditions and the Teaching of Writing*. Montclair, NJ: Boynton/Cook, 1984.

Kolesnik, Walter B. *Mental Discipline in Modern Education*. Madison: Wisconsin UP, 1958.

Kremers, Marshall. "Samuel Newman and the Reduction of Rhetoric in the Early Nineteenth-Century American College." *Rhetoric Society Quarterly* 13 (1983): 185–92.

Larson, Richard. "The Ford Foundation Study of the Writing Curriculum: Implications." NCTE Convention. St. Louis, Nov. 1988.

Leathers, Dale. "Whately's Logically Derived 'Rhetoric': A Stranger in its Time." *Western Speech* 33 (1969): 48–58.

Lomer, Gerhard R. *The Concept of Method*. New York: Teachers' College P, 1910.

Lunsford, Andrea. "Alexander Bain's Contributions to Discourse Theory." *College English* 44 (1982): 290–300.

McCleary, Bill. "Ninth Edition of Popular Text Thrives by Combining the Old and the New." *Composition Chronicle* 2 (1989): 1–3.

McDermott, Douglas. "George Campbell and the Classical Tradition." *Quarterly Journal of Speech* 49 (1963): 403–8.

McKerrow, Ray. "Campbell and Whately on the Utility of Scholastic Logic." *Western Speech Communication* 40 (1976): 3–13.

McRae, Robert. *The Problem of the Unity of the Sciences: Bacon to Kant*. Toronto: Toronto UP, 1961.

Miller, Carolyn, and David Joliffe. "Discourse Classifications in Nineteenth-Century Rhetorical Pedagogy." *Southern Speech Communication Journal* 51 (1986): 371–84.

Miller, Perry. *The New England Mind: The Seventeenth Century*. New York: Macmillan, 1939.

Mulderig, Gerald. "Nineteenth-Century Psychology and the Shaping of Alexander Bain's *English Composition and Rhetoric*." *Rhetorical Traditions and the Teaching of Writing*. Ed. James J. Murphy. New York: MLA, 1982.

Neel, Jasper. *Plato, Derrida, and Writing*. Carbondale: Southern Illinois UP, 1987.

Ohmann, Richard. *English in America*. New York: Oxford UP, 1976.

Ong, Walter. *Ramus, Method, and the Decay of Dialogue*. Cambridge: Harvard UP, 1958.

Oravec, Christine. "The Democratic Critics: An Alternative American Rhetorical Tradition in the Nineteenth-Century." *Rhetorica* 4 (1986): 395–421.

Pirsig, Robert. *Zen and the Art of Motorcycle Maintenance*. New York: Morrow, 1974.

Randall, John Herman, Jr. *The Career of Philosophy from the Middle Ages to the Enlightenment*. New York: Columbia UP, 1962.

———. "The Development of the Scientific Method in the School of Padua." *Journal of the History of Ideas* 1 (1940): 177–206.

Reiss, Timothy. *The Discourse of Modernism*. Ithaca: Cornell UP, 1982.

Robinson, Forrest G. *The Shape of Things Known*. Cambridge: Harvard UP, 1972.

Rockas, Leo. "The Quintilian of Amherst: John Franklin Genung." *The New England Quarterly* 54 (1981): 54–73.

Rodgers, Paul C. "Alexander Bain and the Rise of the Organic Paragraph." *Quarterly Journal of Speech* 51 (1965): 399–408.

Rorty, Richard. *Philosophy and the Mirror of Nature*. Princeton: Princeton UP, 1979.

Rose, Mike. "The Language of Exclusion: Writing Instruction at the University." *College English* 47 (1985): 341–59.

Rudolph, Frederick. *Curriculum: A History of the American Undergraduate Curriculum Since 1936*. San Francisco: Jossey-Bass Publishers, 1977.

Ryan, Michael. *Marxism and Deconstruction: A Critical Articulation*. Baltimore: John Hopkins UP, 1982.

Schouls, Peter. *The Imposition of Method: A Study of Locke and Descartes*. Oxford: Clarendon, 1980.

Shearer, Ned. "Alexander Bain and the Genesis of Paragraph Theory." *Quarterly Journal of Speech* 58 (1972): 408–17.

———. "Alexander Bain and the Teaching of Rhetoric." *Central States Speech Journal* 23 (1973): 36–43.

———. "Psychology as Foundation to Rhetoric: Alexander Bain and Association Psychology's Relation to Rhetorical Theory." *Western Speech* 35 (1971): 162–68.

Stegner, Wallace. "Writing as Graduate Study." *College English* 11 (1950): 429–32.

Stewart, Donald C. "The Barnyard Goose, History, and Fred Newton Scott." *English Journal* 67 (1978): 14–17.

———. "Introduction to Nineteenth-Century Rhetoric." *Historical Rhetoric: An Annotated Bibliography of Selected Sources in English*. Ed. Winifred Bryan Horner. Boston: Hall, 1980.

———. "Rediscovering Fred Newton Scott." *College English* 40 (1979): 539–47.

Untersteiner, Mario. *The Sophists*. Trans. Kathleen Freeman. New York: Philosophical Library, 1954.

Vesey, Lawrence. *The Emergence of the American University*. Chicago: Chicago UP: 1965.

Wallace, Karl R. "The English Renaissance Mind and English Renaissance Theory." *Western Speech* 28 (1964): 70–83.

———. "Francis Bacon and Method: Theory and Practice." *Speech Monographs* 40 (1973): 243–72.

———. *Francis Bacon on Communication and Rhetoric*. Chapel Hill: North Carolina UP, 1943.

Warren, Howard. *A History of the Association Psychology*. New York: Scribner's, 1921.

Weaver, Richard. "Ultimate Terms in Contemporary Rhetoric." *The Ethics of Rhetoric*. South Bend, IN: Regnery/Gateway, 1953.

Woods, William F. "The Reform Tradition in Nineteenth-Century Composition Teaching." *Written Communication* 2 (1985): 377–90.

Wozniak, John Michael. *English Composition in Eastern Colleges, 1850–1940*. Washington, DC: UP of America, 1978.

Wright, Evelyn. "School English and Public Policy." *College English* 42 (1980): 328–34.

Yates, Frances. *The Art of Memory*. Chicago: Chicago UP, 1966.

Young, Richard. "Paradigms and Problems: Needed Research in Rhetorical Invention." In *Research on Composing: Points of Departure*. Ed. Charles R. Cooper and Lee Odell. Urbana: NCTE, 1978.

Index

197

Sharon Crowley is professor of English at Northern Arizona University, where she teaches rhetoric and writing. She has authored articles on the history of rhetoric and composition studies and on postmodernism and the teaching of writing. Her recent monograph is *A Teacher's Introduction to Deconstruction*. She is completing a textbook that adapts classical rhetoric to contemporary writing instruction.